e-commerce
essentials

with Microsoft®
FrontPage®
version 2002

GREG HOLDEN

PUBLISHED BY
Microsoft Press
A Division of Microsoft Corporation
One Microsoft Way
Redmond, Washington 98052-6399

Library of Congress Cataloging-in-Publication Data
Holden, Greg.
    E-Commerce Essentials with Microsoft FrontPage Version 2002 / Greg Holden.
      p. cm.
    Includes index.
    ISBN 0-7356-1371-0
    1. Microsoft FrontPage.   2. Electronic commerce--Computer network resources.   3.
Business enterprises--Computer networks.   4. Web sites--Design.   I. Title.

HF5548.32 .H65   2001
658.8'4--dc21   2001034514

Printed and bound in the United States of America.

1 2 3 4 5 6 7 8 9   QWT   6 5 4 3 2 1

Distributed in Canada by Penguin Books Canada Limited.

A CIP catalogue record for this book is available from the British Library.

Microsoft Press books are available through booksellers and distributors worldwide. For further information about international editions, contact your local Microsoft Corporation office or contact Microsoft Press International directly at fax (425) 936-7329. Visit our Web site at mspress.microsoft.com. Send comments to *mspinput@microsoft.com*.

Acquisitions Editor: Alex Blanton
Project Editor: Mary Deaton

Body Part No. X08-04493

Contents

Part 1

Taking It to the Web!

Chapter 1

Getting Your Business Online   1

Chapter 2

Getting to Know Your Online Customers   21

Chapter 3
Keeping Your Customers' Information Private   37

Chapter 4
Assembling What You Need to Do   49
Business Online

Chapter 5
Building an E-commerce Tool Kit   65

Part 2

Making It All Happen

Chapter 6
Blueprinting Your Online Store   77

Chapter 7
Adding Search and Navigation Links   107

Chapter 8
Streamlining Web Sales with an Online Catalog   127

Chapter 9
Accepting Online Payments   155

Chapter 10
Managing Sales and Customer Contacts   161

Part 3
Open the Doors to Your Online Store

Dedication

To my daughters Zosia and Lucy, who are my own essentials in life.

Acknowledgements

I took time out from finishing this book to accompany my young daughters on an Easter Treasure Hunt sponsored by my neighborhood's Merchant Association. As I watched their delight in collecting plastic eggs filled with candy and toys, I noticed how differently merchants had chosen to present their goods or services. Each store or restaurant had the basics, of course; their survival depended on their sales. Yet, without exception, there was something special that the proprietor wanted to share with customers just for fun. In my own business of writing, I sometimes experience a conflict between what I want to do creatively and what I must do to earn a living. This book, however, allowed me to get paid for having fun. Rather than mechanically writing a solely straightforward, step-by-step guide, I was encouraged to create personas and then play with them. People who were extraordinarily competent professionals, but who also had that zest for life that repeatedly revealed how much they enjoyed their own work, guided me. Smart and sassy as always, Lucinda Scharbach provided able assistance gathering permissions. Neil Salkind, Kristen Pickens, and David and Sherry Rogelberg of Studio B never failed to brighten my day with an exciting new project or good news on the success of our former collaborations. On this book, Mary Deaton, the editor, taught me a lot about customer-centric e-commerce, and Alex Blanton at Microsoft got the project going and was helpful all the way through. The FrontPage and bCentral teams were extremely generous with their time and support — in particular, I wish to thank Nancy Buchanan, Kelly Weadock, Marcus Schmidt, and Shravan Goli.

Of course it is my family, friends, and neighbors who provide me with frequent happiness bubbles and remind me to get out of my head and into the moment so I can enjoy them. My parents, as well as my brother and my sister and their families, continue to amaze me with their capacity for caring. Ann Lindner and Betty Contorer are my constant guides and support system. My spiritual community, Jewel Heart (a Tibetan Buddhist meditation and study group based in Ann Arbor, Michigan), gives me useful teachings and many friends to help me put them in perspective. I feel very fortunate to be living the life I always wanted.

Introduction

Like an artist with a new canvas or a poet with a blank piece of paper, everyone who creates an e-commerce Web site starts out with the same standard tools. You have a computer and an Internet connection. Your challenge is to use the standard equipment to make your business site uniquely your own. Each storefront and owner needs to distinguish himself or herself so that each interaction with an individual customer is special. The first step on your road to success is choosing the right vehicle — Microsoft FrontPage 2002.

The new version of FrontPage, which is available in a stand-alone version or integrated with Microsoft Office XP, presents you with a number of advantages over competing Web page programs. In fact, FrontPage isn't a Web page editor *per se*. To use FrontPage to create a few personal Web pages is fine, but it's like using a bazooka to kill a fly. FrontPage gives you a powerful solution for creating e-commerce Web sites, such as interactive catalogs with shopping carts, usage reports, and database connections, plus it offers a very important connection to the Microsoft bCentral business hosting site.

Who You Are and What You'll Learn from this Book

This book is for you if you are a small business owner who wants to expand to the Web. You are probably already somewhat familiar with the online world and have an e-mail account, but now you are ready to use FrontPage to conduct business-to-consumer e-commerce. You are likely to find yourself somewhere among the following descriptions:

- Existing FrontPage users who want to set up an e-commerce site for a home-based or small businesses.

- Experienced small business owners who are new to the Internet and need an all-in-one Web design/e-commerce solution.

- Technical novices who need a user-friendly yet powerful application for designing and managing fully functional Web sites.

Although this book is written for the entrepreneur, the focus is actually on the customer. It doesn't do any good to create a Web site if you don't address your customers' needs. This *customer-centric* approach will help you develop your Web site with FrontPage by always keeping in mind what your ideal customer wants to get from you.

How This Book is Organized

E-commerce Essentials with Microsoft FrontPage leads you from the basics to the advanced aspects of starting up an e-commerce site. You start with the most important part — identifying your customers — and then move to organizing your site, setting up an interactive catalog and accepting online payments, and marketing and improving your site.

Part I: Taking It to the Web!

The first part of *E-Commerce Essentials* begins with a general introduction to e-commerce and e-business that explains different ways of doing business online, as well as the essential components of a successful e-commerce site. In Chapter 2, you learn how to identify the customers you want to reach online by creating personas that describe typical shoppers.

Chapter 3 examines the thief that steals many prospective sales: security. Chapters 4 and 5 provide overviews of the types of hardware and software a home-office or small business user will need to set up an e-commerce Web site.

Part II: Making It All Happen

The second part of the book tackles the basic bread-and-butter activities that play an essential role in e-commerce. Chapter 6 discusses Web design issues that are specific to e-commerce sites, with an emphasis on a site's cosmetic appearance and how looks can attract visitors and keep them on your site. Chapter 7 explores how to make your site easy to use: how effective organization can help shoppers find what they're looking for and make purchases, too. Chapter 8 shows how to use the bCentral Commerce Manager Add-in for Microsoft FrontPage to create a catalog of sales items. Chapter 9 examines ways to accept credit card and other payments online, and Chapter 10 emphasizes the importance of managing customer contacts and following through on fulfilling sales. In Chapter 11, you learn about the importance of testing your site to make sure everything works before it goes online.

Part III: Open the Doors to Your Online Store

In Part III, you learn about all the activities that go into maintaining and improving business for your Web site after it goes online. Chapter 12 discusses marketing and advertising strategies to attract customers, while Chapter 13 shows how to gather data about your shoppers and do research to make your e-business more successful. Chapters 14 and 15 show how providing effective customer service and building a sense of community can turn casual browsers into purchasers and even more importantly, into *return* customers.

Chapters 16 through 18 help you look down the road by telling you how to keep your site fresh and functional as your business grows. You get a roundup of tips for making your content current and managing your site's performance. Plus you'll find software solutions that can help make a small home-based or other business into a large and thriving business. A glossary at the end of the book is a handy reference of definitions of terms used throughout the book plus others that shed light on the technical aspects of setting up an e-commerce Web site.

What's New in FrontPage 2002

The newest version of FrontPage builds on earlier versions' features while enhancing the ability to create both business and personal Web sites. These features now include a Photo Gallery, Usage Analysis Reports that let you track how your Web site is used, and integration with the Microsoft bCentral Web site through the bCentral Commerce Manager Add-in for Microsoft FrontPage.

The Add-in allows you to quickly create catalog listings on bCentral with a shopping cart and Buy button, and then sell your products through online marketplaces. It is the kind of catalog construction and database integration that would cost you thousands of dollars if you paid to have a consultant set it up.

Like any good Web site, bCentral is constantly changing and evolving to make its contents easier to find and use. In the course of writing this book, bCentral's organization changed. Some of the links and page titles you see in this book might not match what you see on the Web today. But the basic e-commerce catalog and marketing features are the same.

Part 1

Taking It to the Web!

Chapter 1
Getting Your Business Online

E-commerce is all about choices. Your customers make the choice to visit your Web site. Every mouse click represents a decision to learn more about you. Whether or not they make the ultimate choice you are hoping for — making a purchase from you — depends a great deal on choices that you have made. If you are an online merchant, the decisions you make when you first get started in e-commerce determine how successfully you will reach the customers with whom you want to do business.

Chances are that you already have some experience in business. You are probably looking for a way to expand existing sales or to branch out into new commercial ventures. You know from experience that a "cookie-cutter" approach to creating a business venture doesn't work. You want to put your heart and soul into your venture and place your personal stamp on it. You want a tool that streamlines the technical aspects of creating Web sites while giving you the freedom to be creative and present your content just the way you want. In other words, you're a "technology-savvy businessperson."

You might, in turn, love computers and be new to the business world. You've been browsing the Web for a long time. You're comfortable with the Internet and related technologies, and you have a passionate interest in a particular field of expertise. You want to share that knowledge by marketing the goods and services you've developed. You're comfortable with technology and the Internet. Although you've never created a business Web site before, you're ready to take advantage of the tools you possess to create your first commercial endeavor. You're a "business-savvy technologist." By the way, the terms *technology-savvy businessperson* and *business-savvy technologist* are taken from the introduction to *The Inmates are Running the Asylum* by Alan Cooper (Indianapolis: Sams, 1999).

Today's Web-savvy customers are sophisticated about shopping online. They demand well-designed content that appears quickly in their Web browser and is easy to navigate. Any software solution that leverages your existing abilities — one that streamlines the process of developing an e-commerce site and making it successful — gives you an advantage. You've already taken an important step toward successful e-commerce: You've chosen Microsoft FrontPage 2002 as your software for creating a professional-quality commercial Web site.

FrontPage offers you plenty of choices for creating your Web site. You can use FrontPage all by itself or with a set of affiliated resources — Microsoft Office XP and Microsoft's bCentral Web hosting site — that give you a wider range of e-commerce solutions than any other Web page editor. Because FrontPage is part of the Office XP software suite, you can create catalogs or other sales information using Microsoft Word and Microsoft Excel, then open the files in FrontPage and edit them for use on the Web. FrontPage works seamlessly with Microsoft's bCentral, a site designed to help small business succeed on the Web. From that site, you can download a new e-commerce add-on for FrontPage which lets you create sales catalogs that are connected to a database — highly technical functions that are normally the province of experienced Webmasters.

By now, you're probably anxious to start spinning a Web site full of linked pages into a well-coordinated e-commerce presentation. First, take a moment to step back and get an overview of the goals and strategies that are critical to making an e-commerce effort successful. FrontPage makes the mechanics of setting up a basic e-commerce site relatively easy: The hard part is deciding what you want to do. This means focusing on your target market and coming up with an effective business plan as described later in this chapter and throughout the book.

Microsoft
bCentral

Learn More

Throughout this book, we will frequently mention an online resource that's geared to work with Microsoft FrontPage. Microsoft bCentral (www.bCentral.com) gives you an integrated set of services that can help you create, promote, and market your Web site. It's designed to help growing businesses find the resources they need to compete effectively in e-commerce. You'll learn more about bCentral and how to use it with FrontPage in later chapters.

What Do You Want Your Site To Do?

Just a few years ago, e-commerce was a simple concept. If you were to ask me then to define *e-commerce,* I would have said, "E-commerce is the process of conducting transactions on the Internet, usually between a Web site that has product or service to sell, and an individual or business that wants to buy it." That's only a part of what you can do with FrontPage, however. You can also create a site that functions as an online resource and attracts enough visitors that other businesses pay to advertise with you. Or you can exchange supplies with other businesses.

You may have a perfectly clear view of what your current business does or what you want it to do on the Web. But even if you are already in business, the online part of your operation needs unique features and qualities in order to succeed. You'll find a complete checklist in Chapter 4.

Don't go into e-commerce without first setting goals. Know exactly what you want to do and — most importantly — get a clear picture of the individuals you want to reach online. The following sections describe common sales goals. We'll talk about how to pinpoint your target market in Chapter 2.

Learn More

Despite a tight market in the new century, most analysts believe the Business-to-Consumer (B2C) e-commerce market is still growing, and in fact, the true opportunities are only now being revealed. According to Forrester Research, total spending for online sales hit $6.1 billion in December 2000. Sales dropped to $3 billion in January 2001, but this is still more than the $2.8 billion Forrester reported for January 2000.

Selling Products

This is the obvious way to make money on the Internet. Most people plan to conduct sales of products when they think about setting up a profitable online business. Products can be sold through an online catalog such as Amazon.com's, which sells an extensive line of books, CDs, and other goods, or through a manufacturer's online store, such as Microsoft's store of Microsoft products as shown in Figure 1.1.

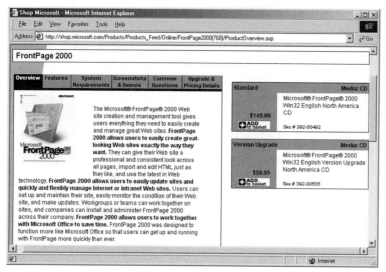

Figure 1-1.

You can create an online catalog like this with the help of FrontPage and a Web hosting service like Microsoft's bCentral.

Selling Subscriptions

Online businesses, including the Web-based versions of newspapers like the Wall Street Journal (http://www.wsj.com) and research services like International Data Corp (http://www.idc.com), make money by charging for subscriptions or "premium content," such as news articles, white papers about market research topics, or research into financial issues. Business users to whom such information is critical subscribe to these services and let their employer pick up the tab. But the public has been slow to decide whether they should pay to receive information on the Web when so much free information exists.

Selling Advertising

If you have a strong customer base and consistently attract visitors to your site, you may be able to offer advertising to other businesses that want to reach your customers. You can also make money as an affiliate — a Web site owner who receives a fee when visitors go from the your site to another online business's site and then make a purchase on that other site. FrontPage lets you create, edit, and manage banner ads — the Web's version of display advertisements — to help you boost your revenue.

Learn More

Find out more about online advertising by visiting the Internet Advertising Board's Web site (http://www.iab.net). ClickZ Today (http://www.clickz.com) contains columns on marketing to women, affiliate marketing, brand marketing, cross media strategies, online public relations and much more.

Why Do You Want To Sell Online?

One of the worst reasons you can have for going into e-commerce is the notion that everyone else is doing it. What are *your* individual goals are for going online? Look at the possible goals we list below. Choose those that work for you. Add your own. Write them all down on a sticky note and attach the note to your monitor. These goals are now your e-commerce mantra.

You Want to Find More Buyers

You're probably thinking of starting up, or you are already operating, a service-oriented or sales-oriented business. You want to sell your goods or services to individual consumers on the Internet. Business-to-Consumer (B2C) e-commerce of the sort conducted by the site FoodNouveau.com, shown below in Figure 1-2, works well with specialty products for a niche audience. These consumers put a premium on making speedy and convenient purchases in the comfort of their homes.

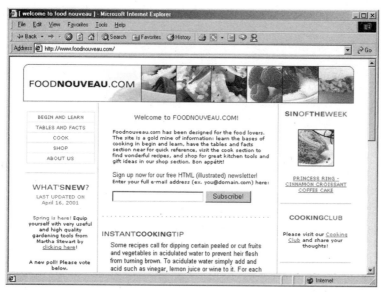

Figure 1-2.

This B2C sales site, FoodNouveau.com, was created with FrontPage and uses many sophisticated Web page features, including a searchable database.

You Want to Promote Your Offline Store

As explained in the section "Supplementing Your Bricks-and-Mortar Business" later in this chapter, you can create a Web site that will supplement your company's existing presence in the "bricks-and-mortar" business world. Such an informational Web site adds considerable value to a company's products and services. On the Web, you can put customer service data online, provide your address and hours of business, give contact information, or spell out your policies on returns and exchanges. If your Web site generates sales, so much the better. Rather than generating revenue, it generates customer loyalty, which leads directly to sales.

You Want to Reach Other Businesses

A growing and increasingly lucrative segment of e-commerce is trade that occurs between businesses. Business-to-Business (B2B) e-commerce works because one business needs to obtain specific commodities from other businesses in order to stay in business. A company that regularly needs cleaning supplies establishes an account with an online cleaning supply house so authorized employees can buy cleanser by clicking a button. A company that needs new employees can search the resume database of a personnel agency and avoid the hassle of placing newspaper ads.

The Jordan Machine Company's Web site, for example, was created by the owner of a machine tool manufacturing and assembly company. Its products aren't intended to reach individual consumers, but to reach businesses that need precision parts and design services.

Figure 1-3.
Many e-commerce sites sell products and services to other businesses. Most consumers don't need machined parts, but many businesses do.

Business Tip

You don't have to choose between doing B2C or B2B e-commerce. Many sites address both audiences successfully if both consumers and businesses need the product. A recent survey of e-commerce executives by the research firm IDC (International Data Corporation) indicated that businesses that sell to *both* businesses and consumers are more likely to turn a profit.

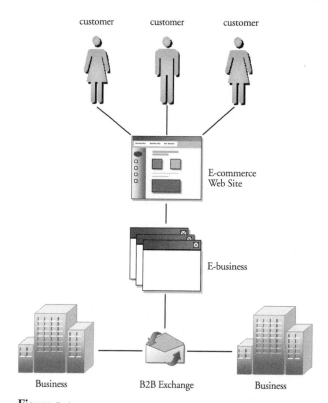

Figure 1-4.

By setting up a functional Web site, you can reach consumers or business customers — or both.

What Do You Want To Sell?

Chances are you already know what you want to sell online. It still pays to take a few moments to ponder the two special needs for selling online: Products need to be easy to ship and easy to photograph and to describe.

The things you sell online should be easily shipped. People aren't going to pay high shipping charges (for example, $10 for an item that costs $20) when, in many cases, the only reason they're shopping online is to find something at a lower price than they could by shopping at a bricks-and-mortar store.

You also have to be able to photograph or describe your products in a way that creates interest in them, and that makes up for the inability to physically touch and experience the product.

Tom Cox, President and CEO of Golfballs.com (http://www.golfballs.com), thinks his company's product is the "perfect" online commodity. "You can tell a golf ball by its cover," says Cox. "You don't have to try them out. One size fits all. The products we sell are the same as at pro shops or at a department store plus, they're compact and easy to ship."

Figure 1-5.
You can tell a good Web sales product by its cover — not to mention its physical dimensions and shipping weight.

The perfect product for your e-business doesn't have to be a physical object such as a book, CD, or golf ball. It can take other forms:

- Your employees' experience and expertise
- Your employees' talent for organization
- Your level of customer service and personal attention
- Your ability to customize solutions to each client's needs

Whatever you sell, be aware that shoppers need encouragement. They may be wary of goods and services that promise much but don't arrive on time or don't meet their expectations. Unless your products are well known and your company is well established, you need to distinguish your virtual products — and yourself — from other e-commerce offerings and sites. Third-party recommendations — testimonials from satisfied customers — can go a long way toward making your products more desirable to the online shopper.

Decide How to Reach Your Customers

One way to focus your goals for your online store is to determine the form your e-business is going to take. You've already determined you're going to do business on the Internet. But are you *only* going to sell online, or are you going to combine your e-commerce site with a traditional bricks-and-mortar store? It's important to understand the difference between the two approaches in order to understand exactly what you have to accomplish when building a customer base, accepting online payments, and providing customer service.

Making an Internet Pure Play

A "pure play" is a company that exists only online. If you're going to operate a Web-only business, one of your first questions to yourself ought to be whether you're going to do all the work yourself. If not, you'll need to find people to help you. Unless you're lucky enough to have some competent family or friends at hand, you'll have to hire someone.

Now that you've resolved who's going to do the work on your site, the next step is to determine how you're going to attract customers. Unless you're already selling your goods and services, you'll need to develop your customer base from scratch. A pure play site has to build a reputation and attract visitors through the quality of its product and presentation because it doesn't have a history to draw upon. Every customer contact is a new one and you need to learn how to manage these customer contacts. Besides the challenge of attracting visitors to a new online business, there are the physical challenges of setting up an office, buying furniture, registering with state and local authorities, not to mention filling out income tax forms you may never have seen before. Anything you can do to automate the "cyber" part of your operation can help — which includes using FrontPage to set up the site without having to learn HTML or JavaScript.

Definition

HTML Hypertext Markup Language, the set of markup instructions used to create Web pages.

JavaScript A scripting language designed to add functionality to Web pages.

Supplementing Your Bricks-and-Mortar Business

Many owners of traditional stores — ones with real street addresses and front doors that customers can actually walk through — turn to FrontPage to give their businesses a new doorway for visitors, a virtual doorway on the Web. Operating a Web site in tandem with a real physical facility gives you a number of advantages:

- **You're not starting from ground zero.** You can build on distribution, fulfillment, sales, and marketing techniques that are already working in your physical location.

- **You can share the wealth — and the problems.** You can distribute profits and losses over more than one channel to even out your financial situation.

- **You can do cross-channel selling.** You can use your Web site to point people to deals and promotions available at your physical location. Put your Web site name on your receipts and on signage at your store, and create promotions that point visitors to your online offerings.

The ideal situation, and a goal you should shoot for, is to have your Web site and physical store work together as a team. Both together provide a higher level of customer service than either one can do alone. If you are a printer, use your Web site to track each job online or to let customers download proofs. If you sell cosmetics, shoes, or other items, your electronic catalog can attract customers from around the country or around the world.

Business Tip

It's perfectly OK to use your Web site as a front-end advertisement for your bricks-and-mortar operation rather than a location where sales are conducted. Use the Web site as a customer service resource to help people learn about you and your products; publish your store hours, your postal and email addresses, and data sheets about your products or white papers about your services. Let the Web publicize your business round the clock, but leave the selling to your physical store. You can encourage customers to phone or fax in their orders. When you're ready, you can add an electronic shopping cart (see Chapter 8) or credit card transactions (see Chapter 9) so customers can make purchases online as well.

Let Your Customer Drive Your Content

Now you know what type of e-commerce you will conduct, you should focus next on the audience you want to visit your Web site. Let their needs and habits drive the process of developing compelling sales content.

Your instinct is probably telling you to talk about what you do and why your products and services are desirable from *your* point of view. You are the expert, after all. But keeping your audience and what *they* want in the forefront of your thoughts increases the chances your site becomes a truly useful resource for your customers — a place on the Web that they'll visit not just once, but on a regular basis. We'll spend some time later in this chapter talking about how you identify your specific customers and find out what they want from your online store.

Luckily, you don't have to worry about how to best sell your products *and* how to organize the products into a Web site. The Microsoft folks who create FrontPage have already developed a site framework that draws on research and experience about the basic requirements for selling on the Web. When you use one of FrontPage's complete Web site templates, you get a set of pages in minutes into which you put your words and images.

Definition

Template A Web page designed by a professional that contains "dummy" content you replace with your own headings, words, and images. FrontPage comes with templates both for individual Web pages and for complete Web sites of multiple linked pages.

Let's browse through some of the FrontPage templates for ideas on the types of pages and content you may need.

To open the templates, follow these steps:

1. Start FrontPage.

2. From the **File** menu, point to **New,** and then click **Page or Web.**
   The Task Pane opens on the right-hand side of the FrontPage window.

3. To open the **Page Templates** dialog box, click **Page Templates.**
   These pages are a selection of individual Web pages with headings and sections that you can customize, including a Feedback Form and a Frequently Asked Questions page.

4. To close the **Page Templates** dialog box, click **Cancel.**

5. To open the **Web Site Templates** dialog box, in the Task Pane, click **Web Site Templates.**
   The **Web Site Templates** dialog box opens.

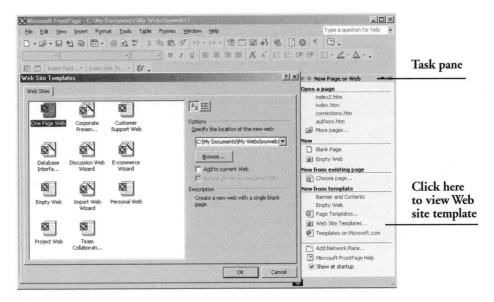

Figure 1-6.

*All of the available templates and Web site wizards are displayed in the **Web Site Templates** dialog box.*

6. Click the icon for one of the templates to see a description of its contents, which appears under **Description**.

Opening an entire Web site is as easy as clicking a template icon. FrontPage automatically creates a set of Web pages, each of which is a template you can edit to add your own content. We will use one in Chapter 6 when we begin building your Web site.

Customer service is a must-have for any e-commerce site. FrontPage's Customer Support Web, shown in Figure 1-7, contains the options that you need to add customer service to your site.

Click on tabs to toggle
between currently open pages

Title bar

Menu bar

Standard toolbar

Views bar

Minimize/Maximize/
Close boxes

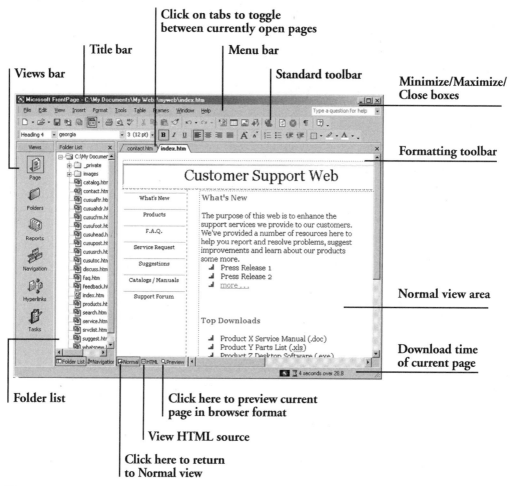

Formatting toolbar

Normal view area

Download time
of current page

Folder list

Click here to preview current
page in browser format

View HTML source

Click here to return
to Normal view

Figure 1-7.

When you open a template, such as the customer service template above, FrontPage gives you all of the tools you need to work with the template. You can modify the look of FrontPage by closing elements you don't need or moving items like toolbars to a location that makes it easier for you to access the commands you want to use.

Technical Note

Some Web templates are called "wizards." Wizards help you customize pages as FrontPage creates them by asking you for answers to simple questions about how you want the site to be configured. Your answers determine what FrontPage creates. The E-commerce Wizard, shown in Figure 1-6, requires that you register to use bCentral's Commerce Manager feature. We will work with this wizard in Chapter 8.

Creating a List of Features for Your Site

How do you decide the type of content your customers want to see in your online store? Ask them. Even if you think you know your customers well and think they have a clear idea of what you do, write up a list of the features they'll want in your store and then find out if your customers agree with that list. You may be surprised!

Here are some ideas for features and pages to get you started:

- **Welcome page.** Every customer wants to enter a store feeling welcome, feeling that it's a place they want to spend some time. Bricks-and-mortar stores sometimes do this by placing a receptionist or greeter near the front of the store. You can do it with a welcoming first page.

- **Photos.** In a real store, you can see and touch what you're shopping for. You can't do that when you're shopping online. Photos are essential to help people get acquainted with the products they're thinking of buying.

- **Sales catalog.** A Web catalog is far less expensive to produce than a printed catalog. You can update an online catalog any time, and if you're doing the work yourself, the only cost is the time involved in capturing images, writing product descriptions, and publishing the information to your site.

- **Customer service area.** Customer service, which helps any business retain a loyal base of satisfied customers, plays an even more important role in e-commerce than it does in the traditional business world. Even if you already have loyal customers in the bricks-and-mortar world, you have to win their confidence all over again on your e-commerce site. In Chapter 14, we will spend more time on this subject.

- **Check-out area.** You want to close the deal. You want your customer to mail in that check, phone in that order, or fill out that online form and click the Submit button. You can't force shoppers to do this. Instead, you can provide a comforting environment for shoppers by addressing safety concerns, providing safe payment options, and making the check out process as friendly as possible. (See Chapter 9 for more about encouraging customers to pay you online.)

- **Navigational aids.** In a physical store, aisles are positioned to guide the shopper around the store in a particular way. You do something akin to this online by providing links and featuring items that you want shoppers to see first. Suggest pages for them to visit in your online store. We will focus more on creating a good experience for your shoppers in Chapters 7 and 8.

Business Tip

Learn from what other FrontPage users do, and don't be afraid to ask for advice. The Web designers and businesspeople that contribute to Thomas Brunt's OutFront discussion forums (http:// www.frontpagewebmaster.com) are very helpful. OutFront has a forum called Site Critiques that is intended for inexperienced Web designers to get advice and suggestions from more experienced users. It's also a good place to find examples of sites that have been created with FrontPage.

How Two Successful Online Businesses Use FrontPage

To help you plan your own e-commerce endeavor, let's look at two Web sites created by individuals with little or no experience in Web design or programming. Maria Kinsey runs an existing company with her husband and wants to diversify by selling new products online. Mark Craig is starting a Web site that reflects a personal interest; he is creating a site that is an informational resource he hopes will attract advertisers.

Striking Out on a New Path

Maria Kinsey is an experienced businessperson in the bricks-and-mortar (or more accurately, tool and die) world. She and her husband own and operate, with three other employees, a machine shop in Bridgeport, Texas. According to Maria, the shop "has had its difficulties of late," so she's decided to create a Web-based business called The Meandering Path (http://www.themeanderingpath.com) as a way to diversify and bring in added business. The site sells garden tools and accessories.

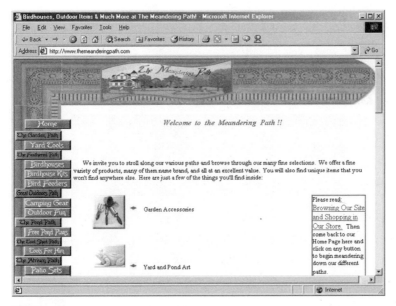

Figure 1-8.
Maria knew nothing about designing a Web site. She used FrontPage to create this e-commerce site's pages while importing graphics she created herself.

Maria is a beginner to Web design and knows nothing about HTML. She chose FrontPage to create The Meandering Path's Web site after trying other Web page editors that offered only "cookie cutter templates." She wanted a product that makes creating personalized Web pages simple and gives her the flexibility to create Web sites her way. She says she wants to "reflect a bit of myself in the creation process."

Maria also found a community of FrontPage users at www.Outfront.net who gave her advice and encouragement and urged her to try the program. Although she is a new-comer to Web design, she created all her site's graphics using Microsoft PhotoDraw. "It is very easy to import and include graphics in FrontPage — to optimize their size, to create forms, and copy and paste content," she says. "For a beginner who knows zilch about Web building, and very little about computers, FrontPage has been fairly easy to use, and I am positive I could not have accomplished this much without it."

Maria describes her customers as "Homeowners who want to explore their own cre-ativity and beautify their patios and yards. One thing can lead to another, they can make their backyard into whatever they dream about, and can find the satisfaction and stress-relieving time spent outdoors in the yard to be an added benefit in their lives." Knowing this helps her provide the right mix of products.

Exploring New Horizons in Health and Spirituality

Mark Craig says his experience with Web design was "virtually nil" when he got the idea to develop Metta (http://www.metta.org.uk), a Web site devoted to his interest in alternative health, spirituality, and healing. He had previously created a simple home page for himself. "I discussed it with a number of people who all said it was a great idea but asked how was I going to raise the £500,000+ to get it off the ground!" he remembers. "I took a view that it could be done with time and dedication for substantially less."

Mark, who left his full-time job to take graduate courses in psychotherapy in England, obtained the domain name metta.org.uk and used FrontPage to set up his first version of Metta in March 2000.

Since then, he has written press releases and added content to the site. He wanted the site to be content-rich and fully functional before visitors started using it. He also thoroughly tested his pages before Metta (shown below in Figure 1-9) finally went live in March 2001. We'll talk more about in Chapter 11 about making sure everything works before you open your virtual "doors" to the public.

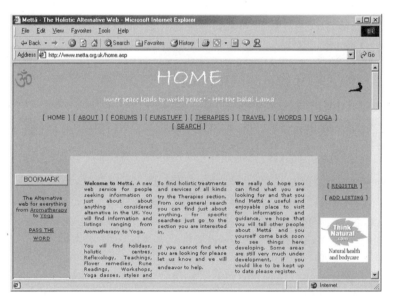

Figure 1-9.

Metta is strictly informational, but its creator plans to attract advertisers by attracting a large community of readers.

"FrontPage offered a fairly simple way of creating a professional looking site with all the necessary facilities, such as database search, forms, and a choice of preset layouts," says Mark. "FrontPage did not require me to have a detailed understanding of HTML, ASP, or JavaScript, etc., so it was the obvious choice for me as a totally inexperienced Web designer and creator."

Definition

ASP (**Active Server Pages**) A Microsoft technology that adds small scripts to HTML Web pages; the scripts are processed on the Web server that hosts the pages.

Mark operates Metta as a nonprofit organization and hopes to cover his development costs through advertising. He has a good idea of the kinds of customers that he wants to reach with Metta: "The customer base is varied: The Yoga section mainly appeals to middle-class, fairly affluent people; the alternative therapies and remaining sections appeal to those who have a different lifestyle from the mainstream population. Their income varies from low to the middle/high income population who are looking for a more meaningful way of life. The age range is generally 30-50 and the target audience is UK-based."

FrontPage's templates helped him get started with the organization for his site. "Once I had played around with FrontPage a little, I found a standard template that loosely fitted my needs and worked from there. Looking at the structure now it seems very different, yet I can still see some elements of that template, so FrontPage did provide a fantastic starting block for the site."

Technical Tip

Mark's original Web hosting service did not support the FrontPage Server Extensions. He switched to a new host so he could publish a fully functional site with FrontPage. The FrontPage Server Extensions are a set of applications that reside on servers that host your Web site. When the FrontPage Server Extensions are present, they let you achieve some highly interactive and technical effects using Web sites that created with FrontPage. If the Extensions are present, you can set up pages to be searchable, to permit discussion Webs, and many other things. Some Web hosts charge extra fees for use of the Extensions, however. Microsoft's own bCentral does not. In Chapter 4, we go into detail about finding a Web hosting service.

Chapter 2

Getting to Know Your Online Customers

Give yourself a pat on the back: The groundwork for your e-commerce Web site is in place. OK, so you haven't started using Microsoft FrontPage yet, but in Chapter 1, you answered questions about your online business and the goals of your Web store that many e-business owners never bother to consider. There's still one question that remains to be answered, however; and it's such an important one, we will address it in its own chapter: *Who are the individuals that you want to reach, and what needs and desires do they hope to fulfill by coming to your Web site?*

In this chapter, you'll learn about the importance of developing a clear description of the customers that you want to attract. You'll learn to locate likely prospects by doing online research and to develop customer profiles that define what these customers want from your site. You'll then use the profiles to guide the creation of your site and to strike up a relationship with customers resulting in loyalty and repeat business.

Understanding Those Fickle, Hurried, Skeptical Online Shoppers

You've heard talk about "The New Economy" and "The Internet Economy." But who, exactly, are the average consumers that drive this new economy? You can't buttonhole online shoppers and ask them to talk about themselves the way you can with mall shoppers. The geographic location of each shopper is impossible to pin down unless they volunteer their contact information or you have tracking software to figure it out. These are some of the fundamental characteristics of online shoppers, in fact. Online shoppers are:

- **Highly mobile.** Consumers and business people aren't necessarily tied to a computer network to shop the Web. You have to keep your information simple and straight-forward because it's increasingly likely that your shoppers are using handheld devices or Web-enabled phones in addition to "traditional" Web browsers.

- **Hurried and harried.** Web surfers can and do shop at any time — in the office during "coffee breaks," in the airport waiting for their flight, or in the brief interval between dinner and the children's bedtime. They want to find things fast, and they want Web sites to be available whenever they're ready to visit. Your content must display quickly. Service outages and technical glitches turn visitors away to more reliable sites and are the kiss of death for online companies struggling to build a customer base.

- **Comfortable with predictability.** Innovation is important when it comes to software, but it isn't the most important thing to individual consumers. Convenience and strong content rank higher than technical gimmicks and frills like animations or video clips.

Research Likely Customers Online

You can consider your e-commerce site successful when your first customers spend money there. But if you don't know who your customers are, you may never entice them to open their pocketbooks. Do your own market research by scouring the Internet to find your customers online and get acquainted with their needs and shopping habits. Use this information to determine who is most likely to purchase your goods and services by doing some market research. Talk to existing customers of similar products or services, other purveyors of these products or services, or experts in the field. Read the Guerilla Marketing series of books and newsletters (http://gmarketing.com). Then ask your existing customers what they would like to see on your site.

Who Are Your Online Competitors?

Does anyone else already do what you plan to do? Don't be discouraged if you discover an existing business has gone online before you — you need to find ways to do the job better. And the existence of similar businesses can indicate that there is a market for your product. Go online to find the Web sites of your prospective competitors. Customer guest books and message boards are both good starting points for your research. Take note of other features, such as:

- **Navigation.** How easy is it to find specific items for sale or other product information?

- **Ease of use.** How quickly do the page's entire contents appear in your browser window? Do any pages fail to appear?

- **Depth.** How far can you click into the site and keep finding more information? The more information you offer, the "stickier" your site becomes, and the longer customers will stay on your site.

- **Selling.** Does the site do cross-selling, with one part of the site promoting another part? Does it do up-selling, making suggestions about related items that a customer might like in addition to their current choices? Does the site convince shoppers that they are making a wise choice when they pick an item? Do product recommendations or ratings support product descriptions?

If any of these features are lacking or missing, you can do them better and make your e-commerce store a better place to shop.

Definition

Guest book A feature that enables visitors to a Web site to enter comments in a Web page form and then submit them to the site, where they are posted on a page so everyone can read them. Guest books are intended for visitors to make comments about the Web site that they have just visited.

Message board A Web page on which messages are posted, so that visitors can read them and respond with their own comments, thus creating a virtual discussion. Similar to a guest book but with a different purpose, message boards are usually organized around specific topics.

Learning About Your Customers by Eavesdropping

Psst...did you hear what your potential customers are saying? A little virtual snooping can come in handy when you're looking to understand your potential market base. What's that you say? You don't know where to find your customers? Don your private eye hat and head over to Usenet. Usenet is a part of the Internet that's separate from the Web but that predates it by many years and is just as popular in its own way. Usenet (short for the Users' Network) is a set of 30,000 different forums called newsgroups. Usenet's newsgroups give individuals with similar interests the chance to "converse" by typing messages to one another. Users can post message topics, respond to questions, and carry on virtual conversations called threads. A *thread* is a series of responses and counter-responses organized by topic. You "eavesdrop" on newsgroup discussions by finding groups that fit your own area of business and then *lurking* — reading the messages without responding to them. Once you get a feel for the group's concerns, you can post your own newsgroup messages with the help of newsgroup software like Microsoft Outlook Express.

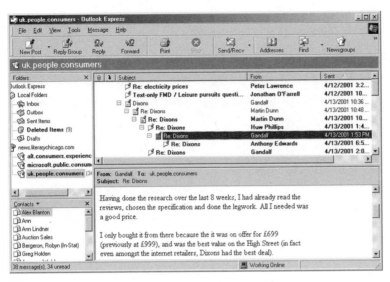

Figure 2-1.

Listen to customer conversations by following threads like this one, and then approach individual participants to determine whether they might need your products or services.

Many of Usenet's forums can act as ready-made focus groups. They've been broken down into specific areas of interest, covering everything from **alt.aardvark** to **rec.windsurfing**. Find a group that covers your own area of interest. If you sell mountain bike equipment, for instance, go to **alt.mountain-bike** or **rec.bicycles.off-road**. Read the messages and take note of people's likes and dislikes. Better yet, participate by answering questions and providing helpful information so that your prospective customers can get to know you. (Including the URL of your new Web site in the signature file you append to your newsgroup postings or mailing list messages doesn't hurt, either.)

Business Tip

If you encounter consumers who fit your customer profiles (see "Creating a Customer Profile" later in this chapter) ask them some questions about how they might use your site or what they might want to see on it. You can even ask them to take a free survey — you can post one online at Zoomerang (http://www.zoomerang.com).

What Do Your Customers Need?

If you understand what your customers need, you will be able to design your site from their perspective and they will be more likely to purchase what you have to offer. Because the notion of shopping online is still new to many people, online consumers tend to be a needy bunch. They need a higher level of guidance than their counterparts in bricks-and-mortar retailing do.

In the sections that follow, I'm going to be the average online shopper — a statistical creature telling you what the researchers say are concerns of the average online shoppers. Just remember, your customers are not average; don't assume that they hold the same opinions as some fictional "average" person. Use my "average" opinions as a place to start when finding out what your customers want.

"Make me feel welcome."

"I'm skeptical about this whole online shopping thing. The instant I see your home page, I want to feel this is a place I'm going to enjoy visiting."

"I hate it when you make me enter a username and a password or any other information about myself until I've found what I'm looking for and I'm certain I'm going to make a purchase here. What are you doing with all of this information, anyway?"

Keeping Up With an Ever-Changing Market

Online shoppers are changing all the time. They're becoming more sophisticated and technically adept. How do you keep up with them? By visiting some Web sites that do research on the subject of online consumers' needs and tastes.

AllNetResearch (http://allnetresearch.internet.com/) charges for its retail reports, but some of the files aren't expensive and they cover e-commerce demographics and market analysis. International Data Corp. (IDC) is one of the biggest Web research firms around, and it makes some of its reports available free, including some that cover e-commerce demographics. Go to IDC's Research Store (http://www.idc.com/Store/default.htm), and then click on the **Free Research** heading.

CyberAtlas (http://www.cyberatlas.com), on the other hand, collects survey results and articles about Web usage and e-commerce trends from many different sources. You can read their articles free of charge. Click the **Demographics** link in the **Big Picture** set of links on the left side of the site's home page to find articles about online consumers and what they're looking for.

"I'm in a hurry; I don't want to wait to watch Flash animations before I start using your site. I just want to shop — now!"

"I have no idea who you are. Do real, live human beings run this site? Can I call you on the phone? Can I send you mail? (That's snail mail, not just e-mail). Are you in the United States or another country?"

"I am not going to wade through clutter on your home page. Fill it with useful links and with simple graphics and colors that I like."

"Make purchasing a no-brainer."

"Did I say I'm in a hurry? I haven't come to your site randomly — I'm looking for some specialty items that are hard to find through other channels. I'm hoping you can get them to me more quickly and/or more cheaply than other stores."

"I want to start looking for some particular items right away. I want to use a Search box so I can enter a keyword that describes what I'm looking for."

"I want to see a row of buttons or other links near the top of the page or along the left-hand side of the page that will let me instantly access your product catalog."

"I also want to get to any part of your sales catalog from any other part. Don't make me look for anything for more than a few seconds!"

"I have a preconceived notion of how a Web site should look, and it's more important to me that you have what I'm looking for and it's easy for me to find it than it is that you look unique or exceptional in some way."

"Once I find what I'm looking for, I want to purchase it with just a few mouse clicks. Yeah, I know I have to fill out some forms so you can get my shipping and billing information. That's to be expected. I want you to get me to those forms immediately."

"Make me feel safe about shopping here."

"Did I mention that I'm a skeptical person? I'm skeptical about whether you're going to protect my identity from hackers who (I think) are all over the Web, looking for credit card numbers to steal."

"No matter — I want to know if you have enough security to protect me, and that you won't send me unsolicited e-mail or abuse my personal information in any way."

"What will you do if some hacker or thief uses my credit card to buy stuff from you without my permission?"

"There are plenty of other merchants out there on the Web who have been doing this longer than you and who have reputations for consumer safety. You've got to convince me that you care about my safety, too."

Business Tip

Although many consumers voice concerns about the danger of credit card fraud on the Web, that isn't the most common type of crime to hit online consumers. A report on Internet fraud by the Internet Fraud Complaint Center, released in early 2001 and covering a six-month period in the year 2000, reported that nearly 66 percent of all the consumer complaints received in that time period had to do with fraudulent online auction sales. In contrast, 22 percent of complaints concerned merchandise that was purchased online but never delivered. Only 5 percent of that amount resulted from credit card or debit card fraud. (See Chapter 3 for a detailed discussion about Web site security.)

"Give me a reason to buy from you."

"Hey buddy. I can buy things from my TV, from the local shopping mall, and from catalogs that I receive in the mail whether I ask for them or not. Why should I buy from you, the e-commerce merchant?"

"Can I get some sort of advantage by shopping online? Can I get something from your site that I can't find anywhere else because you made it yourself or it's a hard-to-find item?"

"Can I get my stuff quicker from you than I can from a catalog?"

"I'm very eager to hear about discounts you offer on the Web or special promotions for return customers. Those are the kinds of things that'll keep me returning to your site in the future."

Reviewing What You've Learned

Now you know what your online shopper needs from you. Can you apply what you've learned to creating content on your site so that your site will get a positive reaction? Let's have a little test to review what you have just learned. First, consider the column of Web site links, shown in Figure 2-2, which were created using one of FrontPage's themes.

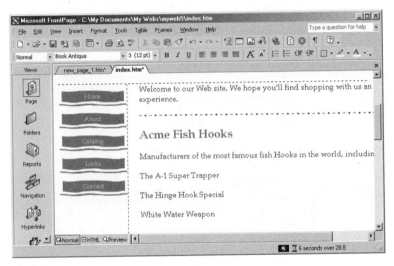

Figure 2-2.

Many e-commerce sites give minimal, generic information without taking into account what customers need to know.

Your customer has already told you that speed is of the essence. Your fickle, harried customer will glance at these links, do some head-scratching, and move somewhere else — maybe to a different site altogether.

You have to guide the visitors so they'll quickly find what they want in a flash. What kinds of links will do the trick? Take a look at the links shown in Figure 2-3. They take up more space because they are separated into several subcategories, but they are also more specific and customer-oriented.

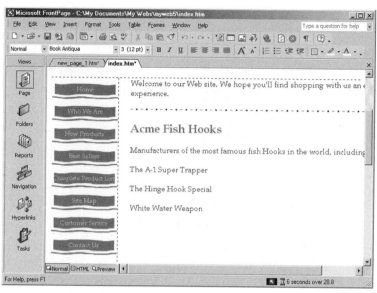

Figure 2-3.

Try to guide customers through your site by providing specific information and explaining the benefits of clicking different links.

Creating a Customer Profile

OK, so you've done some research. What did you learn? Can you distill this new knowledge into a description of a potential customer? Sure, this customer is fictional, but he or she is based on fact. How do you create this customer? This shopper can become your muse, someone to ask questions of (not out loud, please, or your staff will think you are losing it!) while you work on the design of your site. "Hey, Jane Doe, do you like blinking ads?"

- Be as specific as possible. Don't describe a generic "type" shopper, but describe one, two, or three individuals that you want to reach.

- Give each customer a name, age, and hometown.

- Describe what each person wears. Say what he or she does for a living and for fun and recreation.

    You can even base your fictional customers on real ones, if the real individuals have characteristics that represent a large number of your customers.

Let's say you manage a rural radio station. You might create this customer:

Roy Nelson, 54, owns a small family farm located 20 miles west of Omaha, Nebraska. The farm has been in Roy's family for more than 85 years. Roy is married and has four children. Every morning, Roy gets up at 4:30 a.m. and turns on the radio so he can get the news and weather. He also listens to the radio while eating lunch. In the evening, he likes to get the sports scores, especially those of his children's high school teams. He drives a GMC pickup around the farm and a Buick Regal on evenings and weekends. Roy is clean-shaven, and he usually wears a flannel shirt and blue jeans.

Also consider what your customer's current relationship to your products or your store might be:

- Do your customers already know about products like yours? Do they know how to use them, or will it be part of your job to educate and instruct them?
- Do they currently buy the products from someone else?
- Are your products unique on the market?
- Will you need to educate people about the benefits of your product?
- Are they beginners or advanced users — or do you want to reach both? Are they going to need help using the product?

Answering such questions helps to determine how much introductory or "instructional" material you need to include on your site. They also help to determine the level of product support that you can expect to provide.

How Do You Meet Your Customers' Needs?

In a customer-driven field like e-commerce, the job of the merchant (that's you, of course) is to create an environment that invites interaction and makes it easy to purchase goods and services.

Once you have defined the customers that you want to reach and determined what those customers need from you, your job is to meet those needs through the words, images, links, and interactive features you put on your e-commerce site. The sections that follow describe some common features of e-commerce sites. Keep these in mind as you continue designing your online store. Ask your fictional customer what he or she thinks.

Making Your Customers Feel Welcome

In most traditional retail stores, someone greets you the moment you come through the door. The "greeter" asks if you need help and directs you to the items that you're looking for. You feel, at the very least, that the store's employees are paying attention to you and that they'll be available should you need help.

Get Personal

You can't personally greet each customer on a Web site, so how do you make the customer feel welcome? You have to create a "look and feel" for your site through graphics and personalized content; that's how.

Include a short, personal greeting on your home page to welcome your customers and to invite them to shop with you. Create an "About Us" or "About Our Company" page that describes who you are, why you started your online business, and what your goals are for helping your shoppers. Any content that creates a one-to-one relationship with your visitors and makes them feel catered to will set you apart from your competition and encourage customers to further explore your store.

The Web site for radio station KWPN in West Point, Nebraska includes an "About Us" page (http://www.kwpnfm.com/goto/about_us.htm) created in FrontPage. It provides a short history of the station and explains its alliance with a local farmers' association, as well as its commitment to local news and sports. Another page, shown in Figure 2-4, provides photos of the station's staff.

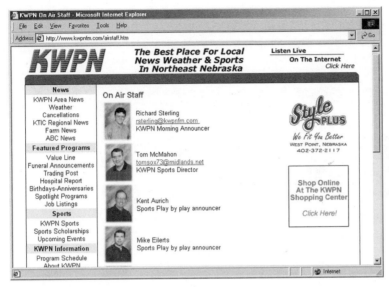

Figure 2-4.

When you talk about yourself or your company, you begin a personal relationship with your customers.

Let Color Talk

Select colors and typefaces that your customers respond to in a positive way. If your customers are conservative, choose muted colors and use simple and easy-to-read typefaces, such as Helvetica. If, on the other hand, your customers are mainly teenagers, select bright primary colors for your Web page backgrounds, headings, and graphics. The key is making the contents consistent with the characteristics and needs of the customers whose profiles you've already created.

Learn More

The best color choices for Web graphics will not shift dramatically from browser to browser or platform to platform. The best palette for use on the Web is a set of 216 colors that is common to all browsers. Designer Lynda Weinman's Lynda.com (http://www.lynda.com) talks about this "browser-safe palette" in detail. CNET's Builder.com site has a good page on color (http://www.builder.com/Graphics/CTips/ss01.html). Adobe Systems has created some technical guides that contain introductory information about typography (http://www.adobe.com/support/techguides/main.html). Also, visit Planet Typography (http://www.planet-typography.com/) for more information.

Your site's colors can highlight your own product line. The Gold Claw Lobsters site (http://www.goldclaw.com), which was created with FrontPage, uses black and gold to create a classy, expensive feel.

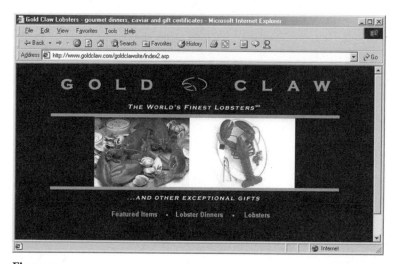

Figure 2-5.

The dark, rich colors of the Gold Claw Lobsters site make the bright red of the lobsters jump out at the viewer.

Use reds and fiery orange shades if you sell spicy chili sauces like the HotHotHot (http://www.hothothot.com) site. Then choose typefaces that themselves look lively and "spicy."

Figure 2-6.

The HotHotHot site has a look and feel that reflects its product line and that will attract its spice-loving customers.

Buying the Easy Way

Your customers' need for speed and convenience demands that you streamline the process of selecting products and purchasing them. Selecting and paying for online goods are two different steps: creating a list of products and then paying for the selected products. The list of goods is often called a "shopping cart."

Placing a "Buy" button on every page with a product on it helps the shopper add to their "cart." The items that the customer selects remain in the cart until they choose to check out or leave the site. You, the merchant, collect payment and shipping information with a check out system. You'll learn how to set up a cart-and-check-out system in Chapter 8.

Arrange your site so that customers can complete purchases in the fewest clicks possible. Every page on your site should let people view their shopping cart, move to another part of your catalog, or get more information about the buying process. I will discuss site navigation in detail in Chapter 7.

The Extra Touch that Means So Much

Online shoppers need incentives to make purchases. If you already have a bricks-and-mortar store, why would customers shop on your Web site rather than knocking on your door? Sales that exist only on the Web encourage people to look online, as do contests and giveaways.

Web surfers who are new to shopping online need reassurance that they are doing the right thing. They want you to provide evidence that your products are of good quality and that they're getting a good buy. Reassure them by including testimonials from satisfied customers, and even providing excerpts of product reviews if they're available. Free shipping and money-back, no-hassle returns policies help, too.

The ultimate goal of all these customer-oriented communications is to strike up a relationship with the people who visit your site and, hopefully, purchase your goods and services. On the Web, your customers learn about you before you learn about them. If your shoppers feel that you understand where they're coming from, then you'll have real communication — a two-way street. You'll learn more ways to make your site interactive and get feedback from your visitors in Chapters 13 through 15.

Chapter 3
Keeping Your Customers' Information Private

Instant gratification is one of the big attractions of online shopping. The Web not only enables shoppers to locate what they want at competitive prices, but to pay for it quickly and receive it in a matter of days. One of the best ways to let your shoppers get immediate results when they shop on your e-commerce site is to let them pay by credit card. They don't have to wait for you to receive a check, wait for the check to clear, and *then* wait for the item to be shipped. And you don't have to wait to have the money in the bank!

With credit cards, shoppers receive their items in a matter of days, or even hours. And it's easy to use Microsoft FrontPage to design interactive forms that customers fill out to give you their names, addresses, and credit card numbers. But in order to successfully conduct credit card transactions on a Web site that you create with FrontPage and publish on Microsoft bCentral or on a Web server equipped with the FrontPage Server Extensions, you have to overcome three obstacles:

- **Security for your customers.** The barrier to e-commerce for many prospective shoppers is security. The idea of transmitting credit card or other sensitive information over a worldwide network still keeps many folks from shopping online. A recent Forrester Research survey of online consumers found that 67 percent were concerned about data privacy. The survey concluded that those fears resulted in $2.8 billion in lost sales for Internet retailers in 1999.

- **Security to protect your business.** Without encryption to protect the personal data that your customers send you, your reputation can be ruined if their information is stolen. Your business's own customer lists and financial records can be compromised, too.

- **A merchant account for credit cards.** The traditional way to become a credit card merchant is complex and time-consuming. You assemble business records, go to a bank or other financial institution, and apply for a merchant account. Your application goes before a board that has to approve it. Then you need to obtain hardware and/or software to process the credit card information.

Tools that enable you to analyze the information gathered from your customers and send targeted advertising to those customers are proliferating and becoming more sophisticated. Finding out who your clients are and what they want is an important marketing strategy. But don't abuse your growing ability to find out about the people who use your site, lest you destroy consumer trust — which, in turn, can incur the wrath of your investors.

This chapter discusses what you need to know about Web security before you start accepting credit card numbers from your customers. You will also learn about ways to keep your e-commerce site secure so that your own data is protected. See Chapter 9 for a user-friendly way to avoid the third obstacle — the merchant account application process — by using bCentral's Order Manager.

Mitigating the Risks of E-commerce

No matter how secure e-commerce vendors try to make their sites, hackers occasionally find a way to break in and steal consumer information. A few days before Christmas 2000, Egghead.com's computer system was compromised, potentially exposing the company's 3.7 million customer accounts. Although it was not immediately clear how many customers' accounts were actually compromised, the negative publicity caused Egghead.com plenty of public relations headaches, and potentially lost the company some of its customers as well.

To get an introduction to the risks of privacy and security breaches on the Internet, visit the Web sites of organizations that have established themselves as leaders in the field of Internet security. VeriSign, Inc. (http://www.verisign.com) makes free guides, like "Securing Your Web Site for Business," available on its site for budding online business owners like you. TRUSTe, a non-profit group dedicated to improving Internet security, maintains a Consumer Education area on its Web site (http://www.truste.org). Microsoft's own Safe Internet: Privacy and Security Fundamentals Web site (http://www.microsoft.com/privacy/safeinternet) also provides good introductory information.

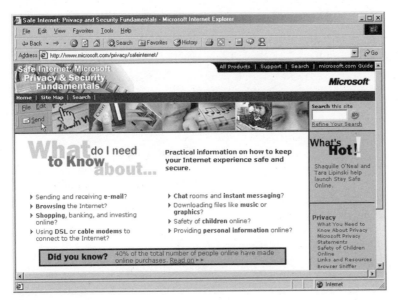

Figure 3-1.
This page includes links to Microsoft's own privacy statement as well as a list of "best practices" that you can follow to make your own business site more secure.

Protecting Data

Secure Sockets Layer (SSL) is the *de facto* standard for Web security and is built into major Web servers and browsers. When a Web page or site is "secure," that usually means that it has implemented SSL on its Web server. SSL gives you:

- Positive ID of your server as yours.

- Message privacy.

- Message integrity. You can often tell a secure page from an unsecured page by looking in the browser status bar for a small lock icon.

So, what behavior or threats does SSL protect against?

- SSL prevents hacking of transmissions of sensitive data, such as credit card numbers.
- SSL helps limit hacking of your site to alter data or gain access to files.

The SSL protocol (a widely agreed-upon set of instructions) for data transmission uses a security method called "public-private key encryption." *Encryption* is the process of encoding information as it is transferred from one computer to another over the Internet. The sending computer encodes the message and the receiving computer then decodes it.

Business Tip

Your credit card vendor may require you to use SSL. MasterCard requires merchants to encrypt cardholder information, including card numbers, so that theft cannot occur. MasterCard's "Best Practices" for e-commerce merchants who want to participate in its "Shop Smart!" program are described online at http://www.mastercard.com/shoponline/set/safeshopping.html.

An SSL-protected transaction involves the exchange of public and private *keys*. Like house keys, these "keys" lock and unlock data that moves across the Web.

The Details about Keys

A *key* is a long series of encoded numerals and letters. Keys vary in size depending on the strength of the security used: the longer the key, the more secure the data. Some keys consist of 40 bits of data (a data bit is an individual unit of digital information). A more powerful variety contains 128 bits of data.

In a form of online security called *public-key encryption*, you purchase a license to use a security formula called an algorithm. The algorithm generates a private key. The private key is then used to generate a public key. When visitors gain access to a secure area of your Web site, the public key is "issued" to them through their Web browsers. The browsers can then encode personal information when it leaves the browser. Only the server that generates the private key can decode the information.

The steps involved in processing an Internet transaction secured with SSL technology are illustrated in a diagram on the Web site of the hosting service XO Communications, which includes secure hosting and merchant account services for businesses.

(continued)

A company wanting to conduct secure transactions over the Web must first obtain their key and the right to generate public keys from a certification authority (CA), a company in the business of issuing keys. VeriSign is one well-known certification authority. The CA issues a digital certificate to the company.

Learn More

In the offline world, people like you and me have our identities certified by the government, which issues us passports and driver's licenses. On the Web, a CA does much the same thing. A CA issues a certificate, which is also sometimes called a digital ID. The CA assumes responsibility for stating that the person who owns the certificate is actually the individual identified on the certificate. When someone accepts your certificate, that recipient has to put a level of trust in the CA. The Internet Law & Policy Forum has issued a report that describes the role of CAs in electronic transactions (http://www.ilpf.org/work/ca/draft.htm).

When a Web shopper connects to a site secured by SSL, the Web server for that site sends the digital certificate to the shopper's browser. The certificate may also include the server's public key. The shopper's browser can check to see if a valid CA issued the key

The Details about Keys *(continued)*

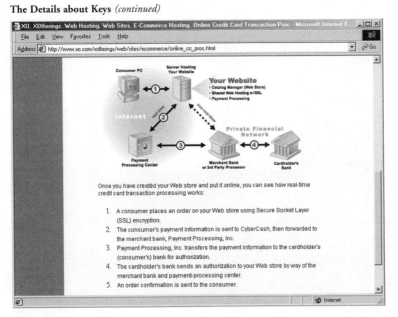

Figure 3-2.

Web security schemes that use public and private keys to encrypt information protect customer data.

and if it is still valid. Checking certificates is typically an option that users can select for their browser. If everything is fine, the shopper's browser generates a private key and sends it back to the Web server. This sets up a secure transaction in which all information passing back and forth between the server and the browser is encrypted. Once the shopper leaves the secure server, the private key is deleted and the secure transaction is ended.

Learn More

You may have heard about "digital signatures." A digital signature is not something used in securing credit card transactions, but is instead a means of authenticating an individual's identity as a signer of e-mail or documents. A digital signature is the equivalent of signing a form with a pen: It is unique to one individual. Some states have set policies determining how to use digital signatures to replace "wet" or hand-written signatures and allow digital documents to carry the same legal weight as paper documents. You can learn more about digital signatures at http://www.softwareindustry.org/issues/1digsig.html.

Reassuring your Customer with a Privacy Policy

It might sound obvious, but the need for a privacy policy is still news to some companies doing e-commerce. A privacy statement is a document that you publish online to explain your company's privacy policy to customers. When you publish a privacy statement, your customers can be reassured about how you use, or don't use, their personal information. Display a link to the statement prominently on your site, and adhere to it strictly.

Show Customers That They Can TRUSTe You

TRUSTe is a nonprofit organization formed in 1996 with the goal of raising consumer trust and confidence in the Web. It puts its logo (or "trustmark") on Web sites that observe its Fair Information practices — and that pay a one-year renewable license fee of $299 to $4,999 for the use of the seal (the exact fee depends on the company's annual revenues).

Simply having the logo on a Web site doesn't guarantee that customers won't have their credit card numbers or other personal information stolen. TRUSTe licensees must meet a number of requirements to obtain a license, however. They must have a privacy statement and give consumers the option to not submit personal information to the site. The tourneau.com Web site (which was created with FrontPage) includes an excellent privacy statement (http://www.tourneau.com/privacy/index.htm).

Writing a Privacy Statement

Developing a privacy policy isn't necessarily a simple operation because it may involve several departments in your company, including sales, marketing, and customer service. Assemble the key players and discuss customer privacy. You may also need to consult your attorney. Your goal is to develop a policy that clearly states your company's policy on customer privacy.

Business Tip

Privacy statements aren't written in stone. Once you create one, you can update it to make it even more comprehensive and reassuring to your customers. If, for instance, your company decides that it needs to collect more information from customers, revise your policy statement before the data-collection changes kick in. That way, customers can make informed choices and still retain their trust in your company. Also, be responsive to any inquiries that customers make about your policies. bCentral provides its customers with a wizard (sponsored by TRUSTe) that they can use to generate a privacy statement (http://privacy.bcentral.com).

Encouraging Customers to Share Information

Responsible e-commerce Web site owners who are concerned about customer privacy offer to let each customer who registers on the site "opt out" of (choose not to participate in) any of the ways the company might want to use the information. This typically means that the registration form ends with boxes you can clear or select in order to give permission for your name to be sent to others, for e-mail to be sent to you, or for other programs. But more and more companies are letting visitors choose to register and share information without making it a prerequisite for browsing the Web site. The courtesy of asking first gives your visitors more confidence that you will respect their privacy.

A good approach to voluntary registration is to offer it on your home page or on other pages where you have high traffic. Give the user some value for giving you their information, however. Registration might give them access to pages that non-registered users can't see. Perhaps the registration is for an e-mail newsletter, a notice of sales, or other special offers. An online coupon is also a good incentive when asking people to share information with you.

A very good reason to ask people to register is to get their permission to give them a "cookie." No, not the chocolate chip kind. *Cookies* are bits of electronic data left behind on a computer after the browser on that computer has opened a Web site. The cookie typically enables the Web server that owns the cookie to identify the client browser if subsequent visits are made to the same site. The advantage of cookies is that they can speed login procedures. But many shoppers fear that businesses use secret cookies to track their activity on a site or gather data from their computer. Since some disreputable companies have used cookies for these reasons, you need to make sure your customers know exactly when and why your site would put a cookie on their machine, either temporarily or more permanently.

Decide before you start creating your Web site if you need to use cookies, what you will use them for, and how you are going to ask your customer's permission. Be sure that your policy on cookies is included in your general privacy statement.

Technical Tip

The most recent versions of Web browsers can notify the user when a site wants to leave a cookie on their computer. Users can also block cookies altogether. If you decide to use cookies to track your customer activity, have a backup method in place for those users who decline to accept cookies. See Chapter 13 for more information.

Knowing your Responsibilities as a Credit Card Merchant

If you decide to accept credit cards on your site, you need to observe some "best practices" in order to protect both you and your clients' information and to provide those clients with a good level of customer service. You need to encrypt any data that is transmitted over the Internet between your customers and your site. You need to store any customer data that you receive in a secure place. You should also be prepared to face disputes that leave you liable for fraudulent purchases.

A credit card processing service like Cardservice International (http://www.cardsvc.com) checks the data submitted to you by shoppers to verify that the person submitting the information is actually the cardholder, rather than a criminal using a stolen card number. Such services also give you real-time reporting via your Web browser. Both Cardservice International and bCentral's Commerce Manager store transaction data on their secure servers so that you can refer to records of past sales if you need to prepare reports or do some number crunching.

Whether or not you use a credit card payment service, there are some things that you need to know about before you decide to accept payments online.

Preventing Trouble by Knowing What Can Go Wrong

Shoppers have less at stake than merchants do when it comes to online fraud. Consumers enjoy protection in the form of limited liability thanks to the Fair Credit Billing Act. They are only liable for $50 worth of unauthorized credit card charges. In addition, Visa International, MasterCard International, and American Express have all introduced zero-liability programs, which mean that consumers who are the victims of online fraud aren't liable at all.

The actual act of transmitting credit card information from one computer to another is safer than many consumers realize. The Internet Fraud Watch arm of the National Consumers League (http://www.natlconsumersleague.org) reported that in 1999, only 5 percent of fraud incidents reported had to do with credit card transactions. Many more problems occurred when businesses stored customer data on computers hackers could gain access to from the Internet.

In September 2000, the e-commerce transaction service CyberSource polled 100 e-businesses, including Nike, Beyond.com, and Starbucks, and found that 83 percent cited online fraud as a problem (http://www.cybersource.com/fraud_survey). Other studies report the opposite — most businesses say that they have not encountered online fraud. Some merchants are reluctant to report problems for fear that weakened consumer confidence will result in lost sales.

Business Tip

Merchants who sell items that can be easily transferred into cash, such as jewelry or electronics, tend to be hit by credit card thieves more often than others are.

Watch Out for Chargebacks

One of the biggest and best-known fraud problems facing merchants involves *chargebacks.* If the consumer disputes a transaction and it's discovered that proper bankcard acceptance and authorization procedures were not followed at the point of sale, the merchant takes the hit in the form of a chargeback: The credit card company debits the amount of a disputed charge from the merchant's account.

In the bricks-and-mortar world, the customer or a clerk swipes a credit card through an electronic reader. The credit card network verifies the information and produces a receipt for the customer to sign. The physical signature is the important element. If the transaction is later disputed and the signature is present, the bank that issued the credit card is liable for the fraudulent charge. But physical signatures don't exist on Internet transactions. Either you, the merchant, or a credit card processing service has to take steps to reduce fraud.

Developing Best Practices for Credit Card Payment

It's difficult to offer lower prices for your online goods and services when you are forced to absorb the cost of chargebacks. Consider paying outside services for credit card verification. Companies such as bCentral's affiliate Cardservice International, CyberSource (http://www.cybersource.com), or Digital Courier Technologies, Inc. (http://www.dcti.com) verify that the credit card data you receive is accurate. Such services might add as much as 22 cents to every transaction. But the short-term expense pays off in the long run if you are able to avoid being defrauded by credit card thieves.

A verification service checks dozens of variables to make sure the purchaser is indeed the owner of the credit card whose number is being submitted. For extra large orders, these companies might even contact individual customers, asking them to call the credit card verification company to verify their identity for their own protection.

As a first line of defense against credit card fraud, either you or your credit card service should verify that the shipping address you receive with an order matches the billing address that is associated with the card number. If the billing address is in Ohio and the shipping address is in Ecuador, for instance, you have reason to be suspicious.

Warning

Checking to see that the shipping address and the address that the bank has on file are the same is a good way to prevent fraud. Studies by ActivMedia indicate that such checks result in as many as one in 10 transactions being thrown out. The danger, of course, is that you might throw out legitimate payments along with the fraudulent ones. Often, purchasers are buying a gift that would go to an address other than their own. One solution is to actually phone credit card holders to confirm that such purchases are legitimate.

Here are some other simple but effective fraud protection strategies:

- In your payment forms, ask the customer to submit the four-digit number above the credit card number as well as the number and expiration date. Only a legitimate customer with the actual card on hand is likely to have the four-digit number.

- You can also request the three-digit card verification value (CVV) above the signature panel on the back of the card. If you check the CVV, you can substantially reduce fraud.

- One of the best ways to prevent online fraud by consumers is to hold shipment of goods until the payment has been received.

- Store your customer information on a computer that is not connected to the Internet so that hackers can't get it. Remove credit card numbers or other customer information you receive from any of your computers that are connected to the Net.

Larger businesses that can't depend on simple address verification can install transaction-risk scoring software that checks a customer's shopping patterns and makes note of any dramatic deviations from the usual purchases. Look into systems from CrediView (http://www.crediview.com) or Mindwave Software (http://www.mindwavesoftware.com).

If you are hacked, take action immediately. Quickly contact customers — don't try to keep the problem a secret. Shut down your site and isolate consumer information on a computer that is not connected to the Internet. Thereafter, be reassuring and matter-of-fact when you're up and running again.

Learn More

Register for free to gain access to useful information for online merchants on the Worldwide E-Commerce Fraud Prevention Network site (http://www.merchantfraudsquad.com). This organization seeks to reduce merchants' exposure to online fraud and promote the growth of e-commerce. You can take the organization's quick eight-question test to determine if you're at risk for fraud.

Keeping Directories Secure

When you think about security, don't just focus on your Web site. Security experts say that the real security problems are in the computer systems that store customer and company information. In September 2000, "human error" reportedly enabled a hacker to gain access to and copy more than 15,000 credit card numbers from the Web site of the well-known financial services company, Western Union Holdings Inc. (http://www.westernunion.com). The company reported that "performance management files" were left open on the site during routine maintenance, allowing the hacker to get to them.

Your company may be small compared to Western Union, but the servers that hold data about your customers and your business still need to be secured from unauthorized access. Some of the steps you can take are:

- Locate your Web server at a hosting company that has sophisticated security in place. This provides a "moat" around your company network because there is no permanent link between the two. We will talk about choosing a Web host in Chapter 4.

- Never store credit card numbers on your Web server. Use bCentral's Order Manager or a service like CyberCash (http://www.cybercash.com) to handle all credit transactions. For details on Commerce Manager, see Chapter 9.

- Store any customer data that you download from your Web host behind a firewall to prevent any unauthorized access to anyone hacking through your connection to the Internet into your private network. You can learn more about network security at About.com's Internet/Network Security page, http://netsecurity.about.com/compute/netsecurity, or by reading an article called "Windows 95 / NT Server Security Issues" at http://mdwin.com/win-faq/win95_12.4/95security.html. The article contains general information that should be useful for other versions of Microsoft Windows as well.

- Set up a Virtual Private Network (VPN) if you need to allow large customers or vendors to gain access to your internal network. You can learn more about VPNs at http://www.alliancedatacom.com/vpn-tutorial.htm or ask your Internet Service Provider (ISP) or Web hosting vendor.

Being Careful with Service Providers

Even if you secure your own e-commerce site, you can still run into trouble if the companies with whom you contract to set up your e-business haven't implemented the same security procedures. Make sure that your ISP has a solid plan for handling security issues. If it is not doing e-commerce now, you want to seriously consider the implications of being its first e-commerce customer. If your ISP is already supporting e-commerce (and most ISPs are, in one form or another), ask for a list of existing clients so that you can find out how the company has performed.

Chapter 4

Assembling What You Need to Do Business Online

When you go shopping, you need a list. When the time comes to create a welcoming and full-featured environment in which others can go shopping, a list comes in handy, too. In this chapter, we start with an itemized rundown of the essential functions that you'll need to follow when you set up your e-commerce site.

Microsoft FrontPage can do many things, but it can't perform every task needed to set up an online business. Before you can publish your pages and throw open your store's virtual doors to the public, you need a reliable Internet connection, a place to host your pages, a Web address, and a development computer for creating your content.

This chapter provides a roadmap to getting a fully functional e-business up and running. First, we'll look at a project task list. Then, we'll talk about connecting your site to the Internet itself. Finally, we'll talk about what you, the Web designer and developer, need in your office to create and maintain your Web site.

Your Site Planning Checklist

When you're in business for yourself, time is money. You need to know exactly what you need to do in order to cover all the essentials and not skip any important steps by mistake. You don't want to get halfway through the process and then have to redo a step or even the whole project, which is not only time-consuming but also expensive. Whether you are paying someone to help you create your Web site or doing all the work yourself, a checklist gets you to think before you act.

The checklist below gives brief descriptions of what each step involves. Subsequent chapters in the book will guide you through the process with more in-depth procedures. You don't need to follow every step in the order shown — you can plan your site before you get a domain name, for instance. If you already have a Web site, skip to the tasks you haven't covered yet, such as creating the product catalog or creating a shopping cart.

Table 4-1

Task	Chapter	Comments
Obtain a domain name.	4	A domain name gives a Web site an alias for its computer addresses that customers can easily remember.
Plan your site and the pages within it.	6	You need to have an overview of your site's organization so that you can make it easy to use. Draw out a visual map of the pages you want to create and how you want to link them to one another.
Create the core pages of your site.	7	You need to create your site's most important pages so you can organize links to other pages. Starting with a few essential pages is less overwhelming than trying to do everything at once.
Create the product catalog.	8	Every e-commerce site needs to make it easy for customers to browse the goods or services for sale. Presenting goods in catalog form helps shoppers find what they want, make selections quickly, or look for more products.
Create a shopping cart and check out system.	9	Make selecting and paying for your merchandise a no-brainer. If customers get confused at check out time, they won't finalize their purchases.
Process and deliver orders.	10	You need to handle delivery in an efficient manner to seal deals and satisfy your customers. Be sure to develop procedures for adding sales tax as well as policies on handling returns.
Test your site online.	11	Make your planning pay off by ensuring that your pages load quickly and everything works right. Try out your site and road test it to guarantee a good experience for your customers.

(continued)

Table 4-1 *(continued)*

Task	Chapter	Comments
Spread the word about your site.	12	Take advantage of resources provided by FrontPage and bCentral to help customers find your site more easily.
Track your customer activity.	13	Know who your visitors are and how they use your site so you can provide them with more of what they need — and remove features that aren't working.
Provide customer service.	14	Turn casual shoppers into paying customers by providing good service. Use FrontPage's Customer Service Wizard to organize your resources.
Create a community.	15	Real success comes from loyal customers. Build loyalty by providing shoppers with ways to share their thoughts and interact so that they have more reasons to return to your site.
Update your site.	16	Retain customers by keeping your content updated on a regular basis. "Tune up" your site periodically to make sure links work and all your content appears the way you want.
Evaluate usage level and online performance.	17	You need to keep your site up and running smoothly so customers can find you whenever they want. Any time your site is offline due to problems with your hosting service can cost you money and hurt your reputation.
Add features to your site.	18	After your site has been online for a while, upgrade it to serve a larger number of customers more efficiently.

Learn More

When you make the commitment to create and maintain a commercial Web site, you need to take on a new set of responsibilities. Visit sites that help Webmasters keep up with development issues, such as Web Developer's Journal (http://www.WebDevelopersJournal.com), Webtools (http://www.webtools.com), or WebTomorrow (http://www.webtomorrow.com).

Setting up Your Infrastructure

You need to have two critical things in place before you have even an empty Web site. These are a domain name and a Web server. Once you have those, you can worry about what you need to do to create pages for the Web site.

Technical Note

How does the post office get mail to you? It uses your street address and a zip code. Each one will guide the mail carrier to your location, but the address is easier to remember. In the same way, a Web site has a couple of addresses associated with it, too. The familiar ones are addresses like http://www.yahoo.com or http://www.internet.com. The yahoo.com or internet.com part of such addresses is called a *domain name.* They're part of the *domain name system,* which is the way information is distributed worldwide across the Internet. Domain names are actually easy-to-remember addresses that stand for something called an IP address.

Definition

IP Address A series of four numbers separated by dots, such as 206.211.117.12, which is what a computer actually uses to find another computer on the Internet.

Web server A computer that stores images, text files, and other files available on the Internet and allows them to be downloaded by individual web surfers.

Getting a Good Domain Name

Where does a business likes yours get the easy-to-remember addresses that will make your Web site easy to find? You purchase a domain name from a company that is authorized to register such names, like Network Solutions, Inc. (http://www.networksolutions.com), Register.com (http://www.register.com), and DomainRegistry.com (http://www.domainregistry.com). You'll find a complete list of registrars at http://www.internic.net/alpha.html.

Finding a Domain Name Suffix that Suffices

Online businesses are staking out claims to names faster than sodbusters in the Oklahoma land rush. The good news is that you've got a better chance of getting what you want — a domain name that's as close as possible to the name of your company — thanks to a new set of domain name suffixes. The suffix at the end of the domain name (such as .com for "commercial") reflects the purpose of the organization that owns the domain. Since the 1980s, there have been only a few such suffixes:

- .com for commercial organizations
- .mil for the U.S. military
- .gov for the U.S. government
- .edu for educational institutions
- .org for non-profit organizations
- .net for network providers

With the exploding popularity of the Internet, catchy domain names (especially those with the .com suffix) are becoming scarce. As a way to get around the logjam, some companies have used the country codes for their addresses, and some use .net and .org when they find that another business is using the .com name they really want.

The Internet Corporation for Assigned Names (ICANN, http://www.icann.org) has made a new set of domain name suffixes available. The new suffixes include the long-awaited .biz for businesses. Other more specific ones include:

- .aero for the air transport industry
- .coop for cooperative businesses
- .info for general use
- .museum for museums
- .name for individuals
- .pro for accountants, lawyers, and physicians

The important thing is to pick a domain name for your business that customers can remember immediately without having to write it down and that fits your organization's identity. Also, keep it short (ideally, no more than 6-8 letters) and easy to spell. In addition, be sure the name is clearly different from those of your competitors. If the only domain name that fits all of these criteria is in the .biz category, purchase it — as well as similar, alternate spellings that visitors might mistakenly enter. Also consider buying domain names with alternate suffixes so that competitors can't purchase [yourname].biz, [yourname].pro, or [yourname].aero and thus infringe on your identity.

To find the domain name that's right for your online business, take a page from the world of psychology and do some free association. Ask customers and colleagues: What's the first thing you think about when you think of our company? Write down the answers and try to get domain names that correspond. Then make sure that no one else already has the name you want — it's as easy as typing www. [thenameyouwant].com into Microsoft Internet Explorer's address box. If the name is not taken, a registrar's site will appear. The domain name registrars make it easy for you to search for available names.

Warning

You need to be cautious when choosing domain names lest you infringe on someone else's trademark or cause confusion by choosing a name that's too close to someone else's name. Do a thorough search with the domain name registrar of your choice to make sure that other names that are close to the one you want don't already exist. It's also a good idea to discuss trade name registration and trademark issues with a knowledgeable attorney, too, so that you don't end up losing your domain name because it is taken.

Once you find the right name, purchase a license from a registrar to use that name for at least two years. Domain names have a tremendous effect on e-commerce. Treat yours like a treasure. After you select it, you need to protect it by purchasing a two-year license or even a five- or ten-year one. Then, keep track of the expiration date and don't let the license lapse.

When a Santa Monica, Calif. company paid a whopping $7.5 million for the domain name Business.com, observers scoffed. The easy-to-remember name probably helped the company endure criticism and survive tough economic times. In September 2000, Business.com raised $61 million from a respectable roster that includes the *Financial Times,* Cahners, McGraw-Hill, Primedia, Mo Zuckerman (the owner of *U.S. News & World Report),* Fast Company, and the *New York Daily News.*

Finding a Home for Your Web Site

Every e-commerce site needs a "host" that makes it available on the Web. Think of a Web host as a landlord from whom you rent office space. The "space" isn't a physical room with four walls and a door, but space on a Web server, a computer connected directly to the Internet. It's the Web server's job to make Web pages and other files available to any Web browser that asks for them. The "host" is the company that runs this server, keeps it online reliably, and makes sure your pages appear quickly. If you don't have a Web server, no one will be able to find you on the Internet.

Definition

Web host A company that rents out space on a Web server so that companies like yours can post your files there for everyone to see. The Web host is responsible for making sure that the server is up and running around the clock and that users can quickly gain access to files. A Web host functions much like a landlord that rents out business space in the bricks-and-mortar world.

You have several choices for the kinds of companies that want to rent you Web space:

- Renting Web space on the servers of an Internet Service Provider (ISP) that also sells connections from your computer to the Internet

- Renting shared space on a Web server through a specialized Web hosting company

- Renting a dedicated computer and Web server on which yours is the only Web site

- Subscribing to a free Web hosting service that posts ads in return for the use of their servers

When comparing all these alternatives, you need to consider the overall cost, reliability of the vendor, and availability of technical support.

Should You Host Your Own Web Site?

If you're a do-it-yourselfer who likes overhauling automobiles or rehabbing living quarters, you might be tempted to go it alone and host your own Web site. Technically, you can do this by getting a direct connection to the Internet, such as DSL or cable modem technology, and then installing and configuring your own Web server. To do this, you can use the popular (and free) program Apache (http://www.apache.org).

But before you start downloading, wait: When you host your own site, the responsibility for setup, maintenance, and quality of performance falls to you and you alone. If your kids unplug the computer or you blow a fuse, your business becomes unavailable. If your computer lacks sufficient memory or processing power, or if someone's using the machine to download a video clip from another Web site, customers might find your pages load slowly — or not at all. For this reason, it's best to leave the hosting to the professionals. Full-time Web hosts have lots of hardware running at top speed in controlled environments, not to mention technicians who are available to solve problems around the clock. Let them do their work, so you can concentrate on important things like making sales and serving your customers' needs.

What Do You Need From a Web Host?

No matter where you host your Web content, in order to run an e-commerce site, you need a host that provides reliable service, good technical support, and the features listed below:

- **Room to do business.** How much room do you need to build an e-commerce site? The minimum of 10 to 20 MB of Web space that hosts typically provide should be more than enough for even a medium-sized business. You should be able to find this much capacity for $19.95 to $39.95 per month. Some hosts, however, give you much more. The popular hosting service/ISP EarthLink (http://www.earthlink.net) has several business packages ranging from $34.95 per month for 200MB of space to $129.95 per month for 500MB of space, for instance. Each package includes a $50 setup fee; e-commerce capability — the ability to conduct credit card transactions online — costs an additional $45 to $90 per month.

- **Business e-mail addresses.** If you surf the Web, make purchases, and register for Web site use and other services, chances are that you already get plenty of e-mail, both solicited and unsolicited. Keeping your business e-mail separate from your personal accounts makes your inbox more organized, and enables customers to get better service. Most Web hosts give you more than one e-mail mailbox. You can configure different e-mail addresses for different parts of your businesses. An address like info@mycompany.com can automatically return a text message to anyone who sends you an inquiry, for instance. EarthLink gives businesses 30 mailboxes or more. Verio (http://www.verio.com) has a $24.95 per month Bronze package that gives users 10 e-mail address plus 40MB of storage space.

- **FrontPage Server Extensions.** No matter where your Web site is located, FrontPage makes it easy to publish your Web site — that is, to move the files from the local computer where you create and edit them to the Web server where they will reside online and where your visitors can find them. Many ISPs support FrontPage Server Extensions, making it easy for you to operate discussion groups, interactive forms, and other elements that enable your customers to get involved and "talk back" to you and to other customers online. The more involved you get, the more repeat business your Web site will attract, and loyal return customers are key to making an e-commerce effort a success. Many hosts charge their customers an extra monthly fee to use the extensions, however. To use the extensions, your site must be hosted on a computer that runs Microsoft Windows NT — make sure you specify this with your host. If you plan to use FrontPage's "one-step" publishing and other features that make use of the extensions, shop for a site (such as Microsoft's own bCentral) that includes the extensions as part of their basic business hosting services.

- **Technical support.** You'll almost certainly encounter some questions that you just can't answer or problems like service outages when you're creating a Web site. Be sure to pick a host that will give you good technical support around the clock and that seems receptive to your questions. Don't pick one that puts you on hold for ten to fifteen minutes only to provide you with a harried, tired-sounding tech person who seems impatient with you.

- **Marketing services.** Some Web hosts include services that help spread the word about your online business. The free hosting service Hypermart (http://www.hypermart.net) lets its customers submit their site to 12 search engines for free. For a $9.99 fee, users can submit listings to 100 search services.

- **File transfer capability.** File transfer fees represent one of the hidden "gotchas" of hosting a Web site. The host may charge you a monthly fee for a certain amount of data being transferred to or from your site — each time a page is viewed, data goes from the server to the viewer's browser. Watch out for hosts that put a limit on the number of MB or KB of information that your site can transfer each month before they charge an additional fee. Successful e-commerce sites can easily pile up thousands of page views a month, and if you go over your hosting limit, the extra cost could be an unwelcome surprise.

- **Reliability.** A personal Web site for you or your family can go down and most people won't notice. But if you're in business, your site must be available twenty-four hours a day, seven days a week. If your site goes offline for hours or even days at a time, the impact is in your pocketbook. How do you judge the reliability of a Web host? Ask questions! Ask the host for a report of any recent service outages, and ask for customer references, then send e-mail inquiring about the customers' level of satisfaction.

You can tell a lot about a Web host by the businesses that are located on its servers. Most hosting services have a page with a list of the companies they support. Check these customers' own Web sites and judge the level of their presentation. Complex sites that seem to attract lots of attention, operate correctly, and appear on the screen smoothly are encouraging signs that the host is a good one.

Hosting with an ISP

Most ISPs give you both a connection to the Internet and a place to publish your Web pages. They may also offer a full range of other Web services including:

- Domain registration
- E-mail mailboxes
- Web design templates or services
- Search engine submissions
- Vanity domain names

ISPs range from small, local firms to national and international service providers. The big companies, like Microsoft MSN (http://www.msn.com) or EarthLink, are big and reliable — you can be sure that they'll be around despite economic ups and downs. They can offer goodies like toll-free access numbers or business-marketing features — sign up with MSN, for instance, and you can promote your business in MSN's online marketplace. On the other hand, a local ISP like my own InterAccess (http://www.interaccess.com) can provide you with better support than the bigger companies. A few ISPs like NetZero (http://www.netzero.com) even offer free access — in exchange, you have to view ads in your browser window.

The access packages offered by all of these ISPs vary widely. If you're on a tight budget, look for packages like EarthLink's SmartSite, which gives you 75MB of disk space, five e-mail boxes, and a traffic allowance of 5GB for less than $20 per month. If you can spend a few more dollars, you'll be better off in the long run with a package like EarthLink's BizSite — for just over $20 per month, you get 175MB of disk space, 10 e-mail boxes, and a traffic allowance of 10GB. To find out more about ISPs, browse through CNET's Internet Access section (http://webservices.cnet.com/html/aisles/Internet_Access.asp).

Using a Web Hosting Service

You may find that you want to have the additional services and expertise offered by a company that only hosts Web sites. You may pay less than you would if you used an ISP, and you may get better service.

A Web host can provide 20 to 50 MB of space (or more) for your text, images, and other Web business files. You'll also get multiple e-mail addresses and possibly even *auto responders*, e-mail addresses that you can set up to automatically respond to e-mail inquiries by sending a text message or a file. (You can respond to such inquiries in person by e-mail after the auto responder sends an immediate message.) The host should streamline the process of obtaining a virtual domain name and give you access to FrontPage Server

Extensions so that you can use Web page forms. You might also get an electronic shopping cart, automatic backups, and site statistics that record the number of visitors to your site, as well as other information.

Definition

Auto responder A utility that e-mails an automatic reply to a request for information about a product or service that you offer. The auto responder can be set up to respond to a message sent to a designated e-mail address, such as info@mycompany.com.

The cost of a Web host varies widely, but can range from free to hundreds per month. If you opt for a free Web host, such as http://www.Freemerchant.com, you may get limited server space and have to include ads on your site. Most services that charge base their rates on the amount of server space that you use, the number of e-mail mailboxes, and the type of other services you want to use. For example, sophisticated features, such as streaming audio and video files and regular backups of your site to another server, can boost the monthly fee.

Finding a FrontPage-Friendly Host

In order to take advantage of FrontPage's many business-related features, such as interactive forms and discussion groups, you can't sign up with just any Web hosting service. You need to find one that supports FrontPage Server Extensions. This means the provider runs software on its site (the Server Extensions) that enables you to run forms, set up discussion groups, and perform one-step publishing.

The obvious FrontPage-friendly host is Microsoft bCentral (http://www.bcentral.com). However, if you want to shop around, you can find a host that supports the FrontPage Server Extensions on Microsoft's own site (http://www.microsoftwpp.com/wppsearch/).

Microsoft bCentral

If you don't already have a "home" for your FrontPage Web site, Microsoft's bCentral is an obvious service to consider. Through bCentral, you gain access to the FrontPage Server Extensions. You'll also find helpful advice for marketing your site on the Web.

Through bCentral, you can download and install the FrontPage Commerce Manager Add-in, which enables you to create catalog listings and manage sales from within FrontPage. See Chapter 8 for more information. bCentral also offers a variety of services that can help you market and manage your site, including Traffic Builder, which helps you list your site with search engines; ListBot, which enables you to create your own mailing list; and Customer Manager, which helps you manage customer contacts.

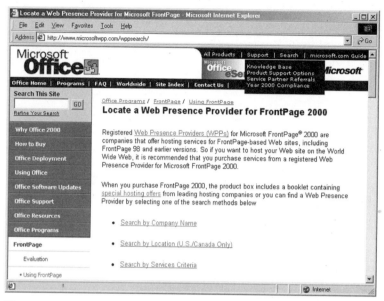

Figure 4-1.

Use this page to determine whether the host that you're interested in supports FrontPage or to find a FrontPage-friendly Web host in your area. Even though this page is for hosts of FrontPage 2000, you can use the same hosting services for FrontPage 2002.

Finding an E-commerce Host

The place where your Web site resides might be different from the place where you actually do e-commerce. Most Web hosts don't offer their customers the ability to create a shopping cart (software that "holds" selected sales items until the customer is ready to check out) or the ability to accept credit card payments online.

Often, FrontPage users publish their informational Web pages with a Web host with which they're familiar, but sign up to use another service's e-commerce features. It makes sense to offload your e-commerce and credit card services to a service that runs it on the Web for you because setting up the software and/or hardware from scratch can be time-consuming and complex. Some options for e-commerce hosting are mentioned below.

Connecting Your Office to the Internet

If your office does not have an Internet connection, you can head to the local library, sign up for time on one of their machines, work feverishly on your Web site, and then quit when you have to give up the computer to someone else. I wouldn't recommend this, however.

If you are creating the content of your Web site with FrontPage, you need an Internet connection at your office in order to publish the pages that you create to the Web server at your hosting service. You also need an Internet connection to visit your own or anyone else's Web site! In addition, you need to use the Web so you know what your customers experience when they shop online at sites like yours.

Business Tip

If you have a reliable hookup and you are satisfied with it, you can skip ahead to Chapter 5 to read about the hardware and software that you might need.

Finding the Right Connection for Your Needs

There are many ways to connect to the Internet, but the primary options fall into two general categories: dialup connections and direct connections. You can use a computing device equipped with a modem to connect to the Internet for the length of a phone call, which is called a dialup connection. On the other hand, you can use wiring and a service that keeps your computer connected to the Internet all the time, referred to as a direct connection.

The option that you choose depends on your budget and the amount of time that you expect to be online. A constant, high-speed connection via a cable modem or DSL is becoming more widely available and their prices are becoming closer to those of telephone service or television cable service. It's probably worth paying more each month for high-speed Internet access and the convenience of an "always-on" connection.

Technical Tip

Dial-up, DSL, and cable are cheaper and more accessible to a small business than other forms of Internet connections that use ISDN or T1, T2, or T3 connections. Some ISPs sell shared T1-T3 connections. If you can afford it, such a connection will be faster than most cable or DSL connections.

The nuts and bolts of the three options look like this:

- **Dialup.** Dialup connections work fine for many businesses that don't need to be online 24 hours a day. You need a modem, a second phone line, and the connection itself. Get the fastest modem you can buy, usually 56.6 Kbps.
- **DSL.** DSL stands for Digital Subscriber Line, a technology that uses part of a conventional phone line to connect to the Internet around the clock.
- **Cable:** Cable provides a high-bandwidth, always-on connection to the Internet over the same line that gives you cable TV. Speeds are comparable to DSL, but may become faster.

You can obtain these connections from a number of different types of Internet Service Providers (ISPs). Your local cable company might provide a high-speed Internet connection along with its television service. Many local phone companies provide dialup or direct connections, too. Finally, you've got ISPs that provide Internet access as their only business.

Business Tip

What constitutes a "good" Internet connection? You want a connection that gives you sufficient bandwidth for conducting business transactions; one that is reliable and won't break down frequently; and one that provides customer support when you need it.

Learn More

If you click on the **Tutorial** button on the first Internet Connection Wizard page, Microsoft Internet Explorer launches and leads you through a series of pages that teach you how to use the Internet.

Finding an ISP

You won't have problems finding ISPs as long as you're able to get online from someone else's computer and surf the Web a little bit. If you prefer to do the searching on your own, go to a site that collects links to ISPs in one location. Visitors can search by geographic region or the type of Internet connection you want (dialup or direct). To search for an ISP, visit CNET's Internet Access section or The List (http://www.thelist.com), which gathers links to nearly 10,000 ISPs in one location — as well as Web hosts and designers, too. Also, visit sites that review ISPs, such as ISP News (http://www.internetnews.com/isp-news/) or dslreports.com (http://www.dslreports.com).

You also have a tool on your own computer that can help you find an ISP. It's called the Internet Connection Wizard and it's an accessory that comes with Microsoft Windows. Whether you are getting a new connection or upgrading an existing connection for your home office, you can get started by clicking the **Start** button on the taskbar, pointing to **Programs**, pointing to **Accessories**, pointing to **Communications**, and finally clicking **Internet Connection Wizard**. When the first page of the Internet Connection Wizard appears, you need to identify your current connection status and tell the wizard how you want it to help you get a connection.

Figure 4-2.
The Internet Connection Wizard, built into Windows operating systems, can help you make a new connection or connect to an existing account.

Chapter 5

Building an E-commerce Tool Kit

Once you have a reliable Internet connection, adequate hardware, and a place to host your Web site, what's next? Gather and install the software tools you'll need to build your e-commerce site. You know you need to purchase and install Microsoft FrontPage for Web site creation, and you need to have a Web browser. This chapter provides you with more information about these essential programs, plus information about other software and hardware you may need, including programs to create graphics, facilitate communication, and test your Web site to make sure everything on your pages looks and functions correctly.

Pushing the Web Envelope with FrontPage

FrontPage supports Hypertext Markup Language (HTML) 4.0, the programming language Java, and graphics formats GIF, JPEG, and PNG. But it also supports major standards that enable you to present dynamic, consistent content on your e-commerce site. If you are a technology-savvy businessperson, you may be familiar with these Web standards.

Groups such as the World Wide Web Consortium (W3C) (http://www.w3.org) and the Internet Engineering Task Force (IETF) (http://www.ietf.org) develop the standards that enable computers on the Web to speak the same language. You can find out more about how such languages and formats are developed and implemented by visiting these groups' Web sites and reading the notes of their regular meetings. The Web standards that FrontPage supports include:

- **Cascading Style Sheets (CSS):** A set of markup instructions that let you precisely position content and achieve a consistent presentation from page to page across a Web site. You don't need to learn how to create or edit a CSS unless you want to because FrontPage automatically adds the style sheet instructions for you.

- **eXtensible Markup Language (XML):** A language that describes the content of Web pages and other documents in such a way that their contents can be easily transported from one application to another. Unlike HTML, XML describes content in terms of what data is being described. An XML file can be processed purely as data by a program, be stored with similar data on another computer, or, like an HTML file, be displayed on the Web. Whenever you save a Microsoft Office document as a Web page, XML does the translation from one format to another.

- **Active Server Pages (ASP):** A technology that enables Web servers to process small embedded programs called scripts before they send a Web page to a visitor. The script responds to the user's request for a page by gathering information from a database. The Web page is constructed "on the fly" and sent to the user with up-to-date information.

- **Database Connectivity:** FrontPage's Database Wizard lets you access and manage Microsoft Access databases and other databases from the Web. See Chapter 18 for more about databases.

- **Web Components:** FrontPage includes Web components that allow you to easily add functionality to your site without doing complex programming, such as hit counters, marquees, and search forms. Some components, like hit counters, require you to find a Web host that supports FrontPage Server Extensions. See "Finding a FrontPage-Friendly Host" in Chapter 4.

Technical Tip

One of the nice things about FrontPage's level of support for all of these languages and protocols is that you can choose when to implement support for a particular standard. You can remove some elements if you don't want to use them because a certain version of a Web browser might not support them. You can limit use of some technologies by selecting **Options** from the **Tools** menu, selecting the **Compatibility** tab, and then clearing those options you don't want to use. You can also choose to target specific browsers or Web server programs, which will restrict functionality in FrontPage to your targeted platforms — FrontPage only uses commands that are specific to selected browsers or servers.

Gathering Web Site Development Tools

When you're talking about running graphics, database, and Web page software all at the same time, you've got to ask yourself whether you need any additional equipment to create your Web site. The answer? Oh yeah, a computer! You've also got to think about purchasing peripheral equipment to help give your e-commerce site some graphic impact, such as a digital camera, a scanner, and some graphics software.

Choosing the Right Computer

You are about to become a Web developer. The computer you have been using for business may not be up to the task. Even if you are not hosting your Web site on your own computer, you are going to be running several pieces of software. Your equipment must be reliable and have enough disk storage space and memory (random access memory or RAM) to run your Web site-related applications. To operate FrontPage, Microsoft Internet Explorer, and Microsoft Word, as well as graphics programs, you need:

- A minimum of 64 MB of RAM, but 128 MB or more is better.
- At least 2 gigabytes (GB) of hard disk space.
- A color monitor. Get one 17 inches in diameter or larger.

Using FrontPage with Microsoft Office XP

FrontPage includes a full range of features, but its basic bread-and-butter function is formatting Web pages. FrontPage is the only Web editing program you need. Other components of Microsoft Office XP also produce formats you can use online, and you can use FrontPage with Word, Microsoft PhotoDraw, Microsoft Excel, and other Office programs. For instance, you can:

- Write and edit text in Word, use Word to spell check your files, and then convert the Word file to a Web page (HTML) so you can put it online, as the contents of a printed catalog or press release, for example.
- Create interactive spreadsheets, charts, and graphs for your Web sites.
- Set up databases with Access and link them to FrontPage.
- Browse the 25,000 pieces of clip art on the CD that comes with FrontPage.
- Use PhotoDraw to edit graphics files to insert on Web pages using FrontPage.

- A color printer. An inkjet one is fine.
- A video graphics card with at least 2 MB of memory.
- A sound card, microphone, and speakers if you intend to use audio.
- A video adapter if you need to transfer video from tape or a video camera.
- Adequate ports to handle a printer, scanner, and camera.
- A power protector.
- A CD-ROM or CD-RW.
- A file backup system.

Making and Managing Graphics

In order to attract customers to your Web site, you've got to have compelling graphics. Not only that, but the quality of the images you put online also needs to be professional so as to build credibility in your operation — and to stand out from your competitors' as well.

Whether you're simply trying to publish clear photos of catalog items for sale or attempting to create a complete visual identity, you've got to have some graphics tools at your disposal. You can use Office XP applications directly with your scanner or digital camera to capture digital images.

Get Your Phone Lines Up to Speed

If you run your business from your home, put in an order for a second, third, or fourth phone line right now. You need lines for your business voice connection and your family voice connection, a line for your modem if you are using a dialup connection, and possibly a fax line.

If you have a DSL or cable connection to the Internet, you can use a second phone line for your fax machine. You can bypass the need for that line, though, by subscribing to a Web-based fax service, such as j2.com (http://www.j2.com/), that lets you handle all of your faxing using your Internet connection and your computer. Some large telecommunications companies like Sprint are now offering packages that include all telephone services (local, long distance, voice mail) and DSL on one set of wires.

In the table below are some of the graphics programs you might consider. They range from the one built in to FrontPage to sophisticated programs used by professional designers. You can choose the ones that best fit your ability and the style of graphics you intend to have on your Web site.

Table 5-1

Program	Features
FrontPage	Create graphics using the same Drawing toolbar as other Office XP applications (http://www.microsoft.com/frontpage).
Office XP	Gives you the basic tools to capture images in digital format, and then view and edit them (http://www.microsoft.com/office).
Microsoft Visio	Drag and drop creation of all types of business graphics, such as flowcharts, organizational charts, and office layouts (http://www.microsoft.com/office/visio).
Paint Shop Pro	Inexpensive drawing and editing tool. You can download the program at http://www.jasc.com and try it free for 30 days.
Microsoft Image Composer	Create headings and combine them with graphic images to assemble sophisticated compositions. Included with FrontPage 2002 when purchased alone (http://www.microsoft.com/frontpage/imagecomposer/imagecomposer1.htm).
PhotoDraw	Comes with the Premium version of Office XP; enables you to edit photos for the Web (http://www.microsoft.com/office/photodraw).

(continued)

Web Graphics File Formats

The two most common file formats used to display images on the Web are GIF (Graphics Interchange Format) and JPEG (Joint Photographic Experts Group). A third format, PNG (Portable Network Graphics), was developed as a replacement for GIF but never gained wide acceptance.

GIFs are best for line art, simple drawings, and illustrations. JPEGs are best for photographs. PNGs are best for Webmasters who want to avoid the licensing problems associated with GIFs (the computer company Unisys, which holds a patent on the compression method used in GIF, has decided to require royalties from any developer who writes a commercial program that uses GIF) and who want PNG's higher compression and improved color quality capability compared to those of GIF.

Table 5-1 *(continued)*

Program	Features
Adobe Photoshop	Widely used by professional designers for both print and Web publications (http://www.adobe.com/products/photoshop/main.html). Not a program for beginners or for people on a tight budget.
Macromedia Fireworks	Create, edit, and animate Web graphics, and then import the files into your FrontPage document (http://www.macromedia.com/software/fireworks).
Macromedia Flash	Enables Web developers to create sophisticated animations and presentations for Web sites as well as design Web pages. (http://www.macromedia.com/software/flash).

Learn More

Learn more about Web graphics in general by following the tutorial at http://www.dcs.napier.ac.uk/~cph/Teaching/MMT/graphics.html. Webmonkey has a good article explaining the difference between GIFs and JPEGs (http://hotwired.lycos.com/webmonkey/geektalk/97/30/index3a.html?tw=graphics_fonts).

Where Do You Find Free Graphics?

Most entrepreneurs starting a new business or moving an existing business to the Web aren't trained to create professional-quality graphics. Hiring a graphic designer to create high quality art for your logo is money well spent. But for simple graphics to use on a Web site, you might find what you need in the Microsoft Design Gallery Live. This resource, accessible to all Office users, is available from the **Insert** menu of most Office applications:

1. On the **Insert** menu, point to **Picture**, and then click **Clip Art**.
   The Task Pane appears with the heading **Insert Clip Art**.

2. In the **See also** list, click **Clips Online**.
   Your Web browser opens and automatically connects to the Design Gallery Live site, where you can choose clip art for your pages. (You can also reach the Design Gallery Live site at http://dgl.microsoft.com/mg01en/eula.asp.)

Learn More

You'll also find graphics at Barry's Clip Art Server (http://www.barrysclipart.com), Clip Art Universe (http://www.nzwwa.com/mirror/clipart), or by scouring the Web for specific types of graphics with Clip Art Searcher (http://www.webplaces.com/search).

Sticking to one style of clip art when you choose graphics can give your site the appearance of having been designed by a professional. Don't copy graphics from other Web sites; the company or the artist has probably copyrighted them. Only use graphics that are specifically offered for free download. The site where you find the clip art will have a statement of use that you should read to find out what the limitations of using their art might be.

Technical Tip

To organize your business image files, Office XP gives you the Clip Organizer, which you access by selecting **Picture** from the **Insert** menu, and then choosing **Clip Art** from the **Picture** submenu. When the Task Pane opens, click **Clip Organizer**. The Clip Organizer lets you search and retrieve not only images you've filed there yourself, but thousands of clip art images from the Web, too. From the Clip Organizer's **Tools** menu, select **Clips Online** to connect to Microsoft's Design Gallery Live and search for clip art.

Visiting Your Own Web Site

When you become a Web publisher, you need to become aware of file size and download times to keep your site from frustrating your customers. The best way to learn about when files are too big and pages are too complicated is to visit your own Web site. See Chapter 11 for more details on trying out your Web site before your customers do.

You need to acquaint yourself with more than one browser. Some browsers handle HTML components, colors, font sizes, and other elements of Web pages differently than Microsoft Internet Explorer does. You need to view your site in different browsers to make sure everything turns out the way you want. Features that might work perfectly in one browser may not even display in another. Sometimes, the same brand of browser handles things differently in one version than it did in an earlier one. You need to be aware of these anomalies and adjust your site so potential customers aren't turned away from your site.

Using Other Browsers

Netscape's browser is Internet Explorer's main competitor, and you should have a copy of it available to test your browser's behavior — opening pages in both Netscape Navigator and Internet Explorer will cover most of the users who are likely to visit you. Some features that are supported by Navigator might not show up in Internet Explorer, and vice versa.

To be really complete when it comes to testing your site, you might also want to test other browsers, which account for a small percentage of Internet users but are still important because they may display content differently.

Opening Internet Explorer from Anywhere

Browsing is easier than ever with Office XP because you can browse from within any Office application. Just display the Web toolbar, which contains icons that should be familiar to Internet Explorer users.

Figure 5-1.
Enter the URL of a site you want to browse in the Address box on the Web toolbar and press ENTER to instantly browse Web sites.

When you use any button or feature on the Web toolbar, Internet Explorer connects to the site you've specified. Internet Explorer is the most convenient of the browsers you need to have on hand to test your own Web site. It's also a convenient tool for accessing and displaying shared content on your own local network, if you have one.

Table 5-2

Browser	Where to Find It	Comments
Internet Explorer	http://www.microsoft.com/ie/	The most popular and full-featured browser around; a must-have.
Netscape Navigator	http://home.netscape.com/download/index.html	Second-most popular browser; still very popular and important for testing your site.
Opera	http://www.operasoftware.com	Third-most popular browser; considered by many to be faster than the "big two."
iCab	http://www.icab.de/download.html	Macintosh-only browser available in English, German, and other languages.
Lynx	http://lynx.browser.org	Text-only browser used by a few techies; useful for testing sites.

Technical Tip

If you need to locate browsers, find out which ones are most popular, or compare features, go to BrowserWatch (http://browserwatch.internet.com), which also includes Microsoft ActiveX and other *plug-ins* — applications designed to work within a browser window to give the program added functionality.

Keeping in Touch with Mail and News

When it comes to contacting, serving, and managing your customers, e-mail is an indispensable tool. Luckily, Microsoft Outlook Express is part of Internet Explorer and can address all your business e-mail needs. If you have a list of the names and e-mail addresses of customers, use e-mail to accomplish marketing and customer service goals. Stay in touch with your industry by subscribing to online newsletters that are delivered via e-mail.

Business Tip

Microsoft bCentral offers its users how-to instructions, as well as tips for creating e-commerce sites, through its own newsletter, bCentral Bulletin. Browse through the archive of past newsletter articles at http://www.bcentral.com/resource/articles. Or subscribe to receive a regular e-mail version of the newsletter at http://bcentralbulletin.listbot.com. FrontPage World, a site that presents extensive information about Web design in general and FrontPage in particular, has its own newsletter (http://www.frontpageworld.com/fpnewsletter.htm). CNET, the online news service, has more than 50 free e-mail newsletters to which you can subscribe, covering everything from e-commerce Web design, investments, and software you can download (http://www.cnet.com/subscription/0-16335.html?tag=cntools).

Online customers want quick responses to questions, complaints, and requests for information. Use Outlook Express to automatically respond to incoming e-mail from customers. Create a text file that sends an automatic response to incoming mail sent to a particular e-mail address, such as info@yourcompany.com. The response can tell customers you got the e-mail and that you will respond as soon as possible. The **Message Rules** command on the **Tools** menu in Outlook Express lets you set up such rules.

Technical Note

Outlook Express is primarily an Internet e-mail program. However, if you have Office and your own copy of Microsoft Exchange Server (or access to Exchange Server hosted on someone else's Web site), you can handle all of Outlook Express's messaging functions and much more, including calendars, lists of tasks, and contact lists. Find out more about Outlook at http://www.microsoft.com/office/outlook.

Outlook Express also lets you send your customers announcements about upcoming sales or events by letting you create one e-mail address, called a *group*, to reach hundreds of people with the same message. In Chapter 15, we'll discuss how you use FrontPage to set up ways for your customers to communicate with each other.

Business Tip

Mailing lists needn't be limited to customers. You can create lists for the members of your workgroup or your company so you can keep everyone in the loop about projects you're working on or announcements of upcoming meetings.

Part 2

Making It All Happen

Chapter 6

Blueprinting Your Online Store

No house builder would start laying foundations and nailing boards without first having a detailed blueprint, and you shouldn't start building a Web site without a map of where the components need to go and how the finished product will look. This chapter leads you along the steps that are involved in designing your e-commerce site. We'll start by determining how the site is structured. What goes where in the pages on your site? How do the pages relate to one another? The structure of a site is often expressed in a visual form, a computerized version of a blueprint called a "site map."

The following sections explore two ways of creating your site. First, you'll use Microsoft FrontPage to create your own site map. Then, you'll learn another approach — using FrontPage's Corporate Presence Wizard to create a site with its own ready-made structure for you. Once you have a general idea of the structure of your site, use FrontPage to help you design the visual appearance you present to the world. In Chapter 8, you'll carry what you've learned about structure and design forward to organize your site so that customers find it easy to use. After that, you'll create an interactive sales catalog.

Technical Note

You've also got a third option, one that gives you more control over your site's organizational scheme. You can create a site map outside of FrontPage — either draw the layout by hand or use a graphics program like Microsoft Visio or Paint Shop Pro. Then, you can choose to create the pages either with or without a wizard.

Designing Your Site's Structure

An e-commerce site is meant to attract and retain customers looking for a product or service. How you structure your site determines whether your customers can find what they are looking for. This characteristic of a Web site is one of the most important aspects of "usability" or "user-friendliness." Many experts have studied sites to determine what constitutes a "usable" Web site. Most agree the following characteristics are essential:

- **Simplicity.** Let each Web page concentrate on doing one thing rather than putting multiple types of content on one page. Describe your site and its offerings on the home page; provide contact information on another page; and sell items on a catalog page.

- **Organization.** Make it easy for users to find what they want and to quickly move from one area of your site to another. There are several ways to create a path through your site, and all of them involve using hyperlinks to help people navigate between pages. How your links look, and whether you use menus, buttons, or links within sentences, is not as important as whether your navigation scheme is obvious to your customers.

- **Searchability.** Giving your customers the ability to search your site by entering one or two simple keywords keeps your customers happy and encourages purchases and return visits. In addition, you can make your site searchable with the help of FrontPage's Search Form.

Business Tip

You can get more ideas on making your Web site easy to navigate and welcoming to shoppers and casual surfers alike by visiting some sites that focus specifically on user-friendliness. Check out the Best Practices area of ZDNet (http://www.zdnet.com/enterprise/e-business/bphome), goodexperience.com (http://www.goodexperience.com), and the Yale Web Style Guide (http://info.med.yale.edu/caim/manual), which contains sections on site design and page design.

Creating a Logical Page Flow

The purpose of developing a visual guide to your Web site is to help you focus on translating your customers' needs and preferred methods of absorbing information into individual Web pages. By mapping out your site, you can keep track of everything you want to do and organize the site in a way that makes sense and helps customers move from the home page to the check out area.

Professional Web designers often start a project by creating an outline, or map, of what the site will contain when completed. You need to do that, too. You can begin by drawing your map by hand, listing the pages you want to create and connecting pages to indicate how they need to link to one another. You can also draw your map by using Microsoft Word or Visio's drawing tools.

When it comes to organizing your e-commerce site, your goal is to lead your visitors in, make it easy for them to find what they want, and guide them to the check out area. Sites like Lego's Shop at Home invite visitors in as though greeting them at the front door of a physical retail outlet. Subsequent pages are like the aisles of a store, leading you from one shopping area to another. Links are like signs hanging from the ceiling, directing you to product locations.

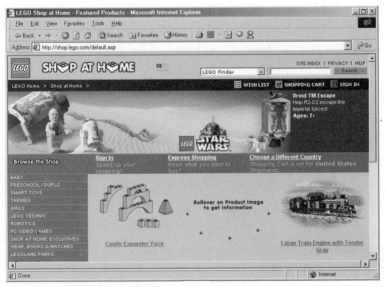

Figure 6-1.

Successful e-commerce sites like this one provide a friendly greeting and immediately provide shoppers with links to all-important areas of the site.

The creators of the Yale Web Style Guide suggest that good Web navigation includes a "consistent and predictable set of navigation buttons" that makes the logic of your site easy to understand. Jakob Nielsen emphasizes simplicity. He is critical of sites that use animations created with Macromedia Flash and that require the visitor to have a Flash plug-in to view them. He also suggests testing a site with as few as five sample users to get feedback on a prototype version of a site before going live with it. Mark Hurst of Creative Good advocates pages that aren't cluttered with promotions and that have graphics that support the user experience and give customers what they want. He describes the Page Paradigm that allows visitors to use a site effectively: "Click, get a new page with the result; otherwise, click Back" (http://www.goodexperience.com/archives/0301.html).

The formal structure of your site probably has very little to do with how most customers will get around in your site. Some follow a path you lay out for them using buttons or text links, while others meander. That's the nature of hypertext: Web surfers click on links based on associations and needs, not because they have to follow a linear sequence. Some go straight to a search box to enter the name of the item they want, while others look for an index or site map.

What's a Web site designer to do in a situation where shoppers can click around a site any way they want? You have to figure out the ways people might look for pages and how you can provide the "road signs" they need to find them. Try to imagine what your customer might do if he or she thinks, "I want to find an antique doll bed for my granddaughter." Then trace all the possible paths they could take through your site to find a doll bed or other item they might be looking for. Your visitor might just do a search, or they might click a category or look for a site map, or click each button in your link bar to see where it takes them. Just how easily they get where they are going depends on how many sign posts you give them.

The page flow might work like this:

1. **Welcome page.** This page should include links to a search page and navigation links leading to main areas of the site, such as Support, Contact, and Products. (Such links should appear on all of the site's pages, by the way.)

2. **Site map page.** This page should contain links to all pages on the Web site.

3. **Category page.** This page serves as an introduction to all of the products of a particular type. The auction site eBay (http://www.ebay.com) uses product category pages extensively. They're listed on eBay's home page and include Antiques & Art, Books, Collectibles, Home & Garden, and so on. You might get to a category page from a link right on your own home page or from your product page.

4. **Product description page**. This page is where visitors go to find out about one or more specific items for sale. You get to a product description page from a category page that contains links to all of the products in a specific category. Click a product link and you get a photo and description of the product. Include a link that allows the customer to immediately add the item to a shopping cart.

5. **Check out area**. Your customers can check items they have put in a shopping cart and add up the shipping cost and sales tax so they can decide what they want.

6. **Payment and shipping area**. This area provides easy-to-fill-out forms that customers use to provide credit card and shipping information.

The following image illustrates the organization "described" above and different paths that might lead to a purchase. This diagram is greatly simplified: In reality, you might want to put a search box right on your home page rather than on a separate page. You might have more than two category pages as well — or if you are selling only a few products, no category pages at all.

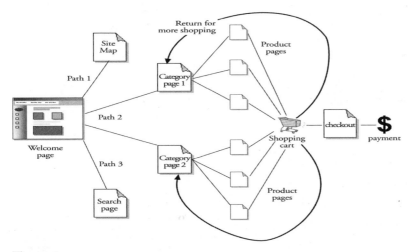

Figure 6-2.
Visualize your site's organization and create signposts that lead customers to the check out area.

Along the way, think about ways to up-sell and cross-sell. When the visitor is in one area of your site, think about other parts of the site that he or she might want to visit. When one product is described, think about related products that you can provide links to that might be of interest to the same shopper. Create links from one product page to another and include suggestions describing why the shopper might want the other items. A shopper who purchases a hairbrush might also want a comb, and someone who buys a pair of earrings might want a matching necklace, for example.

Drawing a Site Map

Since you're going to use FrontPage for your Web site, why not start the program and begin creating a framework for your e-commerce site by using Navigation view? At this point, you only need to create the primary pages for your site, so you only need to have on hand a brief list of the primary types of content and where they'll be located. FrontPage makes it easy enough to add pages or rearrange them later as new ideas come to you and you improve your site based on customer feedback.

Technical Tip

You can use the site map you create in the following steps as a design tool for organizing the actual pages in your site. A site map can be a good organizer if you plan to create all of your pages without using a FrontPage wizard. If you decide to use a wizard to create pages, print out your site map for later reference and delete the web that it creates.

Here's what you do to make a site map:

1. Start FrontPage.

    How To: To start FrontPage, click the **Start** button to display the **Start** menu. Hold down your mouse button and slide your mouse pointer to **Programs** and let it hover there a moment. The **Programs** submenu appears, displaying most (if not all) of the programs you have installed. Slide your pointer to **Microsoft FrontPage** and release the mouse button to start the program.

    The FrontPage window opens.

2. On the **File** menu, point to **New**, and then click **Page or Web**.

    The Task pane opens on the right side of the FrontPage window.

3. In the **New** section of the Task pane, click **Empty Web**.

    The **Web Site Templates** dialog box opens.

4. Click the **One Page Web** icon, and then click **OK**.

    The **Create New Web** box appears briefly, telling you that the web is being created, and then closes.

5. On the **Views** bar, click the **Navigation** button.

    The new web appears in Navigation view. A single home page icon appears in the Navigation view area to the right of the Folder List for the new web.

Let's say you want to have three pages connected to the home page: an About Us page, a Sales Catalog page, and a Contact Us page.

To create a new page that serves as a "child" of the home page (a page that's linked to the home page):

1. Click the **New Page** button on the Standard toolbar.

    A page named New Page 1 appears. A straight line indicates that New Page 1 is linked to the home page, which is displayed with the name index.htm in the Folder List.

2. Repeat Step 1 for the other child pages you want to create.

    Together, these pages represent the second level of your site. (The home page is the first level.)

3. To rename each page, right-click the name, and then choose **Rename** from the shortcut menu.

    The generic name (New Page 1, for example) is highlighted.

4. Enter the new name, and then press ENTER to make the name change.

Suppose you want to create a third level of pages under the Catalog page. Each page would represent a category of sales items in your catalog.

To create a new level of pages:

1. Click the Catalog page icon to select it, and then click the **New Page** button.

2. With the Catalog page still selected, click the **New Page** button to create as many third-level pages as you need.

After you rename the pages, you'll have a site map like the one shown in Figure 6-3:

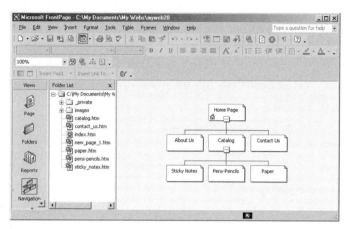

Figure 6-3.
Before you start writing text and capturing images, you can organize and name blank Web pages to get an overview of the content that you'll need to create.

The site map shown above is relatively simple. As you develop your site and add payment solutions (as described in Chapter 9), your site map can become highly complex, with multiple levels of information. An example of this is shown in Figure 6-4.

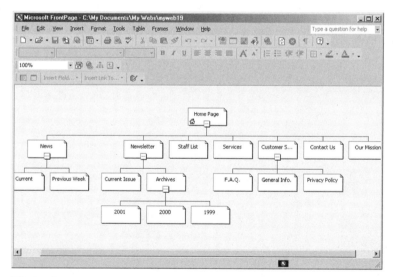

Figure 6-4.
This site is considered "shallow." It has few levels but lots of pages within each level.

On the other hand, as you develop a product catalog, your site can get very deep; visitors can click again and again as they search through more levels of information, as shown in Figure 6-5.

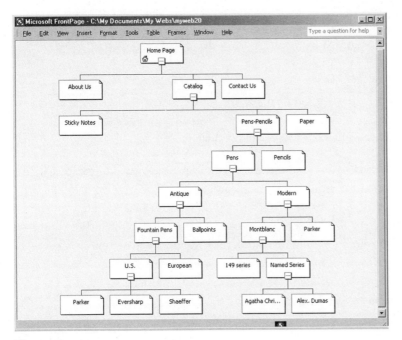

Figure 6-5.
A catalog with lots of product categories can get very deep and keep visitors clicking for more.

Creating your site map before you focus on design and content provides many advantages. You know where you are going to go (or rather, where you want your customers to go) and have a plan for getting there. You get an overview of the entire site without getting preoccupied by details. And since you're using FrontPage, you always have the option of editing your site map by adding or deleting pages or reorganizing links, as described in the following section.

Jump-Starting Your Web: Wizards, Templates, and Themes

Once you've mapped out the structure of your site, you can start building the physical pages and determining how to ensure that your site has a unique online brand. However, suppose you've never created a Web site before and don't relish the thought of having to create all the pages from scratch. Weaving a group of interconnected Web pages into a site that looks professional is a snap when you use one of FrontPage's preconfigured Web sites.

Definition

Brand A company's identity as expressed through its name, logo, or other graphic image. Branding involves the repeated use of the company's graphic image or name to establish its name and promote its activities to customers and the public at large.

In the following exercise, you'll use the Corporate Presence Wizard to create a set of Web pages that provides your customers with the content they'll need when using your e-commerce site. The Corporate Presence Wizard is a good choice when you are sure you want to create many different Web pages that address customer needs, including sales, customer service, a background page about your company, and a contact page. (Keep in mind, though, that this wizard also creates some pages you might not need, such as a What's New page. You'll need to delete these and move your product pages to a higher place in the site map, as shown in Chapter 7.)

To get started, you should have a rough idea of the types of content you want to create. You'll also need a name, address, phone number, and e-mail address for your business because the Wizard asks you to enter this information. (If you don't have some of this information, you can enter some "placeholder" information when the wizard asks for it; just make sure you enter the real details later on.) Once you create the web, you can look it over and add or delete pages as needed. It only takes a few minutes to create the web, and you'll save hours of work.

The Corporate Presence Wizard helps you by creating the organization and framework for a professional looking e-commerce Web site. Creating pages with the wizard doesn't mean you don't have to do anything. On the contrary, once the pages are generated, your work begins: You need to replace the placeholder headings and content with your own business content. The end result: a well-organized site like the one shown in Figure 6-6.

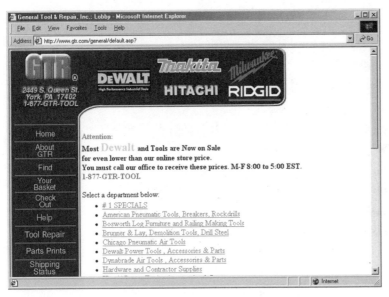

Figure 6-6.

A business Web site with many disparate sections can tie those sections together through consistent use of logos, colors, and overall design approaches.

Creating Your Core Pages with the Corporate Presence Wizard

The easiest way to design a business Web site is to use one of FrontPage's *templates*, which are Web pages with design elements already in place, or *wizards*, which create a sequence of Web pages that guide you step-by-step to complete a task. We are going to use the Corporate Presence Wizard to create a full business Web site.

Technical Tip

If you don't want to create your site with the Corporate Presence Wizard, you can either start from scratch by drawing your own site map (as described earlier in this chapter) or add to a Web site that you've already created.

With the wizard, you create page templates for your site, and then create a look and feel for your site by using one of FrontPage's design themes.

To start the Corporate Presence Wizard:

1. Start FrontPage (see the Technical Tip in "Drawing a Site Map" if you need a refresher).

2. From the **File** menu, point to **New**, and then click **Page or Web**.
   The Task pane opens.

3. In the **New** section of the Task pane, click **Empty Web**.
   The **Web Site Templates** dialog box opens.

4. Click the **Corporate Presence Wizard** icon, and then click **OK**.
   The **Create New Web** box appears briefly, and then the **Corporate Presence Web Wizard** page is displayed.

5. To move to the next page in the wizard, click **Next**.

The wizard pages are self-explanatory (such as the one shown in Figure 6-7), so the following sections only elaborate on terms or options you need to understand in order to make a selection.

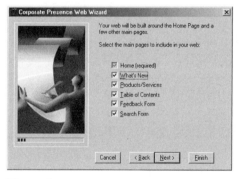

Figure 6-7.
The Corporate Presence Wizard creates a set of interconnected Web page templates that you customize with your content.

Technical Tip

Rather than follow the wizard page-by-page, you can click **Finish** at any time and the wizard creates your site. However, it's a good idea to go through each page of the Wizard in detail so you can tell FrontPage to configure aspects of your Web site, such as feedback forms, so they contain exactly the contents you want to present to your customers. Taking a few minutes now to use the wizard in detail will save you many more minutes when editing your site later.

Selecting Your Web's Core Pages

On the first few pages of the wizard, you tell FrontPage which Web pages you want it to create. These are just the core pages of your Web. After the Corporate Presence Wizard generates these pages, you're free to add new ones. First, decide which of the following pages you'll need:

- **What's New.** Only check the box next to this item if you plan to update news about your products or services on a regular basis.

- **Products/Services.** Whether you sell hard goods or provide consulting or other professional services, you need to include this page.   .

- **Table of Contents.** Consider this list of all the pages on your site as optional. You only need it if you think your site will be crowded and extensive and customers might need help finding their way around.

- **Feedback Form.** The form will only work if your Web server supports the FrontPage Server Extensions. See Chapter 4 for more information. Only create this form if you are prepared to receive feedback and respond to it.

- **Search Form.** Only create this form if you host your site on a server that supports the FrontPage Server Extensions and if you have enough content that customers are likely to conduct searches.

If you select the **Feedback Form** check box, a page later in the wizard asks you to choose to receive the information as a Web page or as a *tab-delimited text file*. In a tab-delimited text file, the information submitted by a visitor for each data element is separated by a single tab mark. This makes it easy to import the information from the text file into a database program like Microsoft Excel or Microsoft Access — each bit of data becomes a field in a spreadsheet or database.

Technical Tip

On the page of the Wizard that begins "What should appear at the top of each page," be sure to select the **Your company's logo** check box. This creates a placeholder image that you'll replace with your own logo later in this chapter.

Choosing a Theme

Once you select the core pages for your site and specify the features you want to include on each page, the Wizard asks you to choose a theme for your site. If you already have a design for your site, you can skip this step. If not, click the **Choose Web Theme** button to open the **Choose Theme** dialog box. Select an option from the list on the left side of the dialog box to see a theme's color and type selections in the **Sample of Theme** area.

A company's identity depends on many things, but consistent use of color and type is an important part of brand building. To come up with your own color and type schemes, you can browse through FrontPage's built-in themes, a selection of pages that contain suggestions for color, type, and graphics. Even if you don't use a theme exactly as planned, you can get ideas for a theme and then customize.

Try to locate a theme that matches the specific type of business you want to get online. Look at magazines and identify colors and layouts that match the look and feel you want. Remember that sometimes, simpler really *is* better. Don't load your page down with background images that make the text difficult to read. If you choose background colors for your pages, make sure they don't clash with any colors you choose for your body text.

Learn More

To help you make design decisions about your site, visit some sites where marketers examine Web branding, and where Web designers share their opinions and provide examples of what they consider to be "good" and "bad" Web page graphic approaches. Visit Click Today (http://www.clickz.com) for suggestions on branding and Mediabuilder (http://www.mediabuilder.com), which has a set of Web design tutorials you can follow.

Near the end of the Corporate Presence Wizard, you're asked whether you want to switch to Tasks view to see a list of tasks you must complete in order to finish creating your Web site. Tasks view is FrontPage's way of displaying a list of the tasks you need to work on to complete your Web site. After you select the Tasks view option, click **Finish** and the home page for your site will open in the FrontPage window.

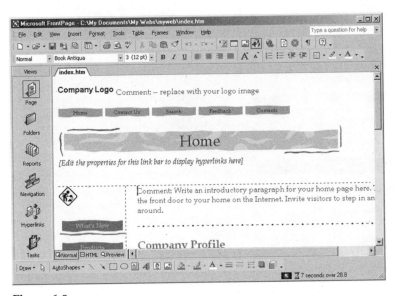

Figure 6-8.
In a matter of minutes, you've designed a complete Web site.

Congratulations! In just a few minutes, you've done the kind of Web design work that would normally require hours or even days performing from scratch.

Customizing Your Business Site

Once you've used FrontPage to create a complete business Web site, you need to customize the content to fit your own business's identity. Begin at the top of the page by adding or creating a logo.

Adding an Existing Logo

Chances are, since you already own or manage a business that you want to expand to the Web, you have a logo for your company. It makes sense to reproduce that logo so you can tie your Web site to your organization's identity.

Unless you already have your logo saved in computerized format, you'll need to scan a printed version of the image. If you don't have your own scanner, you can rent time on one at a copy shop, such as Kinko's, where the employees can help show you how to do the scanning. When you save your scanned image, save it in 72 dpi (dots per inch) resolution as a GIF (Graphics Interchange Format) file. (See the sidebar on graphics formats in Chapter 5.)

The home page you created with the Corporate Presence Wizard contains an area set aside for your company's logo. Near the top of the home page, you see the label Company Logo.

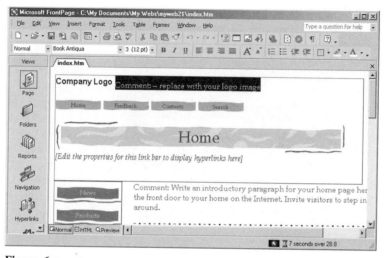

Figure 6-9.

Replace the placeholder text on the home page with a digitized version of your company's existing logo.

Technical Tip

Whether you use GIF or JPEG images, you should save them in 72 dpi resolution because that's what computer monitors display. This might seem like a low resolution to print designers who are used to working with 150 dpi or 300 dpi graphics, but on the Web, speed and compact file size are essential to keeping a site usable. The smaller-resolution graphics will appear more quickly online.

To add the image, follow these steps:

1. In Page view, click **Comment: — replace with your logo image**.

2. Delete the text, and then click **Company Logo**.

    The six black squares around the words indicate that this is an image rather than text.

3. With the Company Logo image selected, on the **Insert** menu, point to **Picture**, and then click **From File**.

   The **Picture** dialog box opens.

4. Locate your logo file and double-click the file's icon to add the file to your home page.

Technical Tip

You may need to resize the image. To do so, click anywhere on the logo to select it. Click one of the black squares, hold down the mouse button, and then drag in toward the center of the image to make it smaller. Drag out toward the edge of the Web page to make the image bigger. Release the mouse button when the image is the size you want.

Creating a Business Logo

If you don't have a company logo yet because you're starting a brand-new business, it's worth taking half an hour or so to create one with the help of FrontPage. When you're done, you'll have a logo that you can use not only on your Web site, but also in any advertisements you place or even on your business cards and other printed material.

To create a business logo:

1. Open your home page in the FrontPage window.

2. Delete **Company Logo** and **Comment: — replace with your logo image**.

3. On the **View** menu, point to **Toolbars**, and then click **Tables** to display the Tables toolbar.

4. Click the **Draw Table** button on the Tables toolbar (see Figure 5-8), and then draw a one-cell table in the **Company Logo** area in the upper right-hand part of your home page. Make the table two to three inches in width (you can adjust this later). When you have finished drawing the table, click the **Draw Table** button so that the button is no longer selected, and then click the **Close** button on the Tables toolbar.

Draw Table button

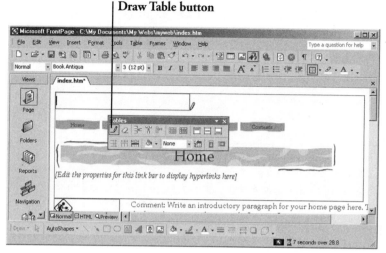

Figure 6-10.

Draw a table cell in order to provide a background color and border for your logo.

5. Type the name of your site.

6. Select the text you just typed.

7. On the **Format** menu, click **Font** to open the **Font** dialog box.

8. Assign a typeface and size to the text, and then click **OK**.

Inserting Clip Art

Now you can add some graphic interest to your logo by accessing FrontPage's extensive selection of clip art.

To insert a clip art image:

1. Position the cursor at the end of the text within the cell you drew in the previous steps.

2. On the **Insert** menu, point to **Picture**, and then click **Clip Art**.
   The Task pane lists your clip art options.

3. In the Task pane, enter a keyword in the **Search text** box, and then click the **Search** button to scan the gallery for art that matches your keyword. (You can also click **Clip Organizer** or **Clips Online** to search for choices.)
   For our example site, we are choosing an image from the Antiques group.

4. Click the image you want to use.

The image is very large when inserted; you resize it by clicking on the image handles and dragging inward to make it smaller. See "Resize an Image" earlier in this chapter for more detailed instructions.

Warning

The term "clip art" doesn't mean "free art." The creators of the artwork that you find on clip art sites around the Web, such as Barry's Clip Art Server (http://www.barrysclipart.com), hold the copyright to their work. They sometimes restrict the use of the art to nonprofit sites rather than commercial ones like yours. Read the instructions about usage restrictions or fees before you start copying.

Changing the Background Color of an Image

The clip art image's background color may not be the same as your home page's background color. To adjust this, you can make the image's background transparent (provided the image has a solid background color).

To change the image's background color:

1. Click the image to open the Pictures toolbar.

2. Click the **Set Transparent Color** button.

3. When you see the message that the image will be changed to GIF format, click **OK**, and then click the image.

Now you can customize the rest of your home page with your own content.

Adding Your Own Content

Now that you have a set of core Web pages, as well as your company logo, you need to add the words and images that will attract the attention of prospective customers and induce them to shop on your site.

First, that means deleting the placeholder text provided by the Corporate Presence Wizard and replacing it with your own text. You can either type your text right in the FrontPage window or paste it in from a word processing program. If you decide to type from scratch, remember not to press ENTER at the end of a line. FrontPage will wrap the words for you.

To use text you've prepared in a word processing program such as Word:

1. Open the file and select the text you want to copy.

2. From the **Edit** menu, click **Copy**. You can also press CTRL+C.

3. Switch to FrontPage by clicking the taskbar button for the Web page you're working on. (If FrontPage isn't running yet, you'll need to start the program.)

4. Select the text you want to replace.

   Select an entire paragraph of placeholder text by clicking anywhere in that paragraph. When you select the text, it is highlighted in black.

5. With the text selected, on the **Edit** menu, click **Paste**. You can also press CTRL+V.

   The text you selected is replaced by the text you copied from the word processing program.

6. If the text you just pasted was formatted in the word processing program with typefaces and indents that are different than your Web page uses, you'll need to choose options from the **Format** menu to change these attributes to match the rest of your page. Refer to FrontPage Help for basic information about formatting text.

The process of typing or pasting words into your FrontPage document is easy compared to actually developing the content that will help sell your goods and services. Here are some general suggestions:

- Grab your visitors' attention by writing headings that catch their eye and direct their attention to the most important contents. Don't be afraid to use terms like "New," "Free," or "Sale!" Give each heading an active verb that tells surfers what they need to do. *Buy, click, explore, shop,* and *purchase* all function as "action" verbs that encourage interaction.

- Describe yourself or your business with confidence. Emphasize why shoppers should be interested in what you have to offer. Concentrate on what makes your business unique and what distinguishes it from your competition.

- Always keep in mind the customer's questions "What's in it for me?" and "What can I gain from this?" when you describe your catalog, your shipping policies, your discounts, or other aspects of your online store.

- Consider contests, special discounts, and giveaways as strategies for getting people involved with your site and inviting return visits.

Writing for the Web differs from printed content because Web text is read on a computer screen. Keep paragraphs as short as possible, with no more than three to five sentences at the most. Don't expect readers to scan an entire paragraph or page in detail. Put the most important message at the top of a page or the beginning of a paragraph. Don't leave readers guessing. Explain the purpose of a page or paragraph in the first sentence, and ideally, in the first three or four words.

Web surfers are used to clicking from one site to another quickly. If you don't capture their attention right away, they'll move on to another location. Rather than organizing your page with a series of static labels such as *Mission, Catalog, News,* and *Service,* use active verbs and specific phrases that describe the contents beneath the heading, such as *Discover Our History and Tradition, Browse Our Complete Product Line, Learn the Latest News,* and *Questions? Get them Answered at Customer Service.*

Learn More

Writing compelling sales content for the Web is a challenge, but you can learn to do it with a little practice and some advice from informed professionals. Visit sites such as E-WRITE (http://www.ewriteonline.com) and read articles like "Writing for the Web, Parts I and II" (http://www.electric-pages.com/articles/wftw1.htm) to find out more about creating content for your e-commerce site.

Enhancing Text with Word Art

Once you have the contents in place, you can add more graphic interest with one of FrontPage's new features called WordArt. You may have already used it in other Office programs.

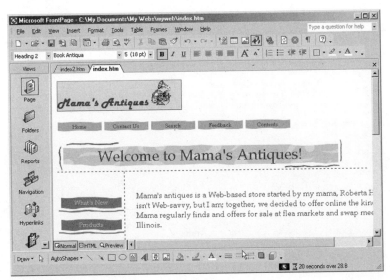

Figure 6-11.
With FrontPage's design help, you can create your own graphics, banners, and color schemes all by yourself.

An integral part of any logo is the name of the business it's advertising. Most logos present the business name in a graphically interesting way. The WordArt feature on FrontPage's Drawing toolbar lets you create typographical effects with just a few mouse clicks.

Let's step through an example of how you can do this:

1. Open your site, if it is not already open, and open your home page.

2. Select the **Contact Information** heading on the home page you created earlier in this chapter with the help of the Corporate Presence Wizard, and then press DELETE.

3. On the **View** menu, point to **Toolbars**, and then click **Drawing**.
   The Drawing toolbar is displayed.

4. Click the **Insert WordArt** button to open the **WordArt Gallery** dialog box.

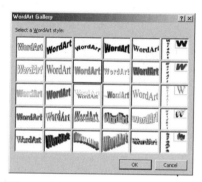

Figure 6-12.

Apply WordArt when you need to create graphically interesting typographical effects and lack experience with complex drawing programs.

5. Select a type style that fits your business's identity or the style of your home page, and then click **OK**.
   The **Edit WordArt Text** dialog box opens with the words Your Text Here highlighted.

6. Type your text. In our example, we type *Contact Mama!*

7. Click **OK** to close the **Edit WordArt Text** dialog box and return to the FrontPage window.

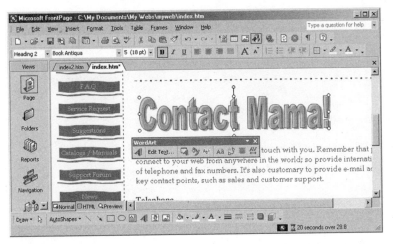

Figure 6-13.
Your transformed text now appears in the WordArt style. The WordArt toolbar is also displayed.

The text is suitable for a page heading but is too big for a logo, which is typically two to four inches wide and one-half to one inch in height.

To change the text properties:

1. Click the **Format WordArt** button on the WordArt toolbar.
   The **Format WordArt** dialog box opens.

2. Click the **Size** tab.

3. Select the **Lock aspect ratio** check box.

4. Type a new width, 263 pixels in our example, and then click **OK**.
   The text is now smaller.

5. To save your work, on the **File** menu, click **Save**.

6. To preview your new home page, click the **Preview in Browser** button on the Standard toolbar.

Other FrontPage Design Tools

The imaging, page layout, and drawing tools we have used so far are by no means the limit of the design-related tools FrontPage puts at your disposal. FrontPage can also help you:

- Create a pleasing and harmonious color scheme.

- Create shared borders so key elements are consistent from page to page.

- Manipulate images to make them bigger, smaller, or use different colors.

Selecting a Color Palette

FrontPage lets you select colors that make it easier for you to design and view your own Web pages while those pages are being assembled. You can:

- Change the colors used to display headings, individual words, or all of the text on a given page.

- Change the color of a shadow placed behind shapes.

- Change the color-coding of HTML commands in order to quickly locate and edit them.

FrontPage's color palettes are designed specifically for Web browsers. Different Web browsers, and different versions of the same Web browser, can display colors differently. Even the monitor you use can affect the colors you see in a Web browser. To maintain a consistent look, you want to make sure you are using what have come to be called "Web-safe colors."

Whenever you select a word, phrase, paragraph, or other text element on your page and try to assign a color to that text, FrontPage displays one or more of the following color palettes appropriate for your page:

- **Standard colors.** The basic 16-color palette you see when you make an initial color selection.

- **Custom colors.** A second palette of colors you have defined that is displayed below the standard color palette.

- **Document's colors.** The colors used on the current page.

- **Theme colors.** If you choose a theme, the theme's built-in colors appear in their own palette so you can extend color choices to new content you create.

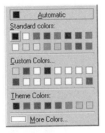

Figure 6-14.
You can save the time required to devise your own color scheme by relying on one of FrontPage's themes, which comes with its own coordinated color palette.

Technical Tip

If you are using a theme, FrontPage doesn't give you the option of changing a page's background color unless you remove that theme. If your page has text and background colors that come with a theme, you should try to stick with colors that fit the theme or you run the risk of choosing colors that clash and make some of the contents less attractive, not to mention less readable.

If you want to choose a color that isn't contained on these palettes, or if you want to change a color you've already chosen, FrontPage gives you the option to do so. Whether you are attempting to assign a color to some text or to a page's background, the same standard color selection menu appears. The menu always includes the **More Colors** option. Choosing this option enables you to make a new selection from one of the standard Windows color selection tools rather than being limited to the standard colors, the document's colors, or a theme's colors.

Setting Aside Empty Space

One of the most important design elements you can use to implement a consistent design is nothing at all — in other words, a little empty space here and there so that your Web pages aren't necessarily filled up with content. Empty space relieves eyestrain suffered by Web surfers, many of whom have been looking at a substantial number of Web sites before they come to yours. It also highlights the most important parts of a page — the viewer's eyes naturally turn to images and headings that have some blank space around them. Content buried in a sea of crowded links, text, and images that have almost no empty space give the viewer no clue where to look first. The home page of the FrontPage e-commerce site shown below has more impact because it doesn't try to overwhelm the visitor by presenting all of its contents at once.

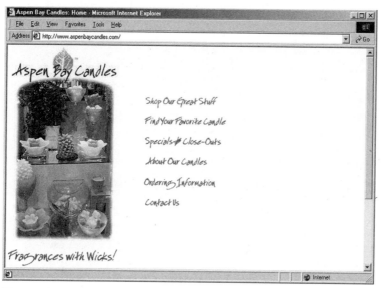

Figure 6-15.

Don't feel obligated to fill every available square inch of Web page real estate — pages that include empty space have more impact and invite the customer to explore.

FrontPage gives you a number of ways to add empty space:

- You can create a shared border that has nothing in it.

- You can set up style sheets that provide for adequate white space.

- You can use tables to lay out a page so that some of the table rows, columns, or individual cells are blank.

This might seem strange, especially since so many Web sites seem to follow a policy of filling up every bit of Web page real estate available. But white space serves a number of important purposes. It points the eye to important contents you want the weary eyes of busy shoppers to rest on. If you want to call attention to a new area of your site or a special promotion, one of the best ways to call attention to it is to surround it with empty space.

Getting Consistency with Shared Borders

You can achieve consistent placement of logos, navigation bars, and other parts of a page that are common to your Web site by creating shared borders. You can also save yourself lots of time.

Shared borders are areas at the top, bottom, or sides of a Web page that are the same on every page of a site. You create shared borders to place the same content on many pages in one step. When you change the shared border in one place, all the pages change.

Recurring content   **Recurring content**

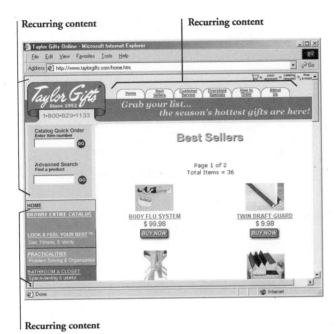

Recurring content

Recurring content

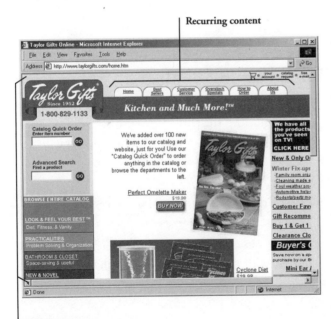

Recurring content

Figure 6-16.

Using shared borders enables you to create a series of e-commerce Web pages that contain a consistent set of content to help customers find what they want.

Creating a Shared Border

You want to quickly place a logo at the top of every page on your Web site. You can use a shared border to do that. You want to set up a shared border when you first create your Web pages.

To create a shared border:

1. Open a page in your site.

   Since it's advisable to set up a shared border when you first create a page, this should be a new page. However, you can open an existing page and add a shared border to it as well.

2. On the **Format** menu, click **Shared Borders**.

3. To include the border on all pages of the site, click **All pages**.

4. To create a top border, select the **Top** check box.

5. Click **OK** to close the **Shared Borders** dialog box and return to the FrontPage window.

   If you now want to add your logo graphic to the border, you can do this on the **Insert** menu by pointing to **Picture**, and then selecting an option from the **Picture** submenu.

Modifying Pictures with the Pictures Toolbar

Regardless of where you get a picture for your Web site, you probably need to modify it to work well on your site. For example, you might find the perfect clip in the Clip Gallery Live, but when you insert it on a page, it is too big. Not a problem! Clicking a graphic opens the Pictures toolbar and gives you the tools you need to modify any graphic.

The toolbar buttons you're likely to use most often are:

- **The Insert Picture From File button.** Insert images that you can access locally on your computer or network.

- **Contrast controls.** Increase the contrast of your image by clicking the **More Contrast** button, and decrease the contrast with the **Less Contrast** button.

- **Brightness controls.** Make your image brighter with the **More Brightness** button, and decrease brightness with the **Less Brightness** button.

- **The Crop button.** Select and eliminate parts of the image.
- **The Select button.** Select the image so you can work with it.

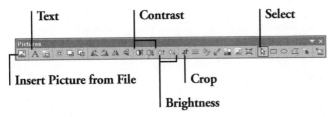

Figure 6-17.
The FrontPage Pictures toolbar lets you perform many basic image-editing functions.

Learning More About Web Design

Designing Web pages is an art that takes time, practice, and perseverance to develop. You don't have to win design awards to make your e-commerce site effective. With FrontPage's help and a little advice from Web designers, you can make your site convey the look and feel you want to the customers you are targeting.

In case the selection of more than 60 themes that ship with FrontPage 2002 doesn't include one that expresses your business's image, you can download and install themes that have been developed by others. A few sites offer themes or Web site templates that you can download free. Many other sites offer themes and templates for sale. FrontPage World (http://www.frontpageworld.com) sells templates for $15 each. Outfront.net has an extensive selection of templates for sale (http://www.outfront.net/frontpagetemplates.htm). Check out the Theme Mart (http://www.thememart.com), which sells more than 500 FrontPage themes, and FrontPage Templates.com (http://www.frontpagetemplates.com).

To get a sense of what the top Web designers consider to be good graphic sense, visit Lynda.com, the Web site of Lynda Weinman, who has written many books on Web design. She suggests that you choose colors for your Web pages that are part of the "Browser-Safe Color Palette" she has identified. This set of 216 colors (described at http://www.lynda.com/hex.html) looks more or less the same in all of the popular Web browsers your customers are likely to be using when they visit you.

High Five, an online magazine that for several years held design contests and featured innovative Web sites, ceased publication in 2000 but maintains an archive of articles and contest winners that you can browse through at http://www.highfivearchive.com. High Five was operated by David Siegel, a well-known Web consultant and author. Siegel points out that too many sites include far too much content on their home pages because they aren't targeting their customers and what those customers need. "These sites don't scale because they are trying to please everyone inside the company as well as any customers that might happen to drop by," he says on the home page of his company's Web site, Siegel Vision (http://www.siegelvision.com).

Last but certainly not least, Wilson Internet Services maintains a collection of articles entitled "Designing a Business Web Site" (http://www.wilsonweb.com/webmarket/design.htm) that are designed specifically for entrepreneurs like you. Too many graphics on a single page makes the entire contents appear more slowly, says the site's developer, Dr Ralph Wilson. "The best combination is a single sparkling graphic combined with text," Wilson says in his article "12 Website Design Decisions Your Business or Organization Will Need to Make" (http://www.wilsonweb.com/articles/12design.htm).

Chapter 7

Adding Search and Navigation Links

Form follows function, or so the saying goes. The person who first uttered this maxim wasn't familiar with e-commerce. When it comes to buying and selling online, you might say that *form follows functionality.* Good form means that you put the content your customers need where they can find it. If they can't find it on your site, it might as well not be there.

Take a moment to review what you've done to this point. You identified the purpose of your site and profiled your primary customers. You obtained an Internet connection and found a Web host. You obtained a domain name and, in Chapter 6, you created the core pages of your site using the Corporate Presence Wizard. Now, you can compare the pages you have to the site map you created in Chapter 6.

The way your site looks is important, but if the content isn't useful and the pages are not easy to navigate, no one sticks around long enough to admire your bright colors and eye-catching graphics. Your goal is for shoppers to quickly find what they're looking for and make a purchase. In this chapter, you will compare your planned structure with the real one you created, add the ability to search the contents of the site, and make sure you have provided all the possible means of moving around the site that your visitor might want.

Refining Your Site Structure

Get out the site map you created during Chapter 6 and compare it to what you created with the Corporate Presence Wizard in the same chapter. You want to determine if what you planned is what you built. Microsoft FrontPage makes it easy to see what you already have by using Navigation view. Do the pages lead into one another the way you want them to? Do you need to add pages or create new links between pages?

Looking at Your Navigation Links

Open your site's home page, then click **Navigation** on the Views bar to switch from Page view to Navigation view. In Navigation view, the list of the files currently in your web appears in the Folder List. The files and the way they are linked (or not linked) are illustrated in the main content area. As you can see in Figure 7-1, Mama's Antiques has three levels of pages. The Home page is the first level; this page links to a second level with News, Products, and Services; and these link to third-level product and service pages.

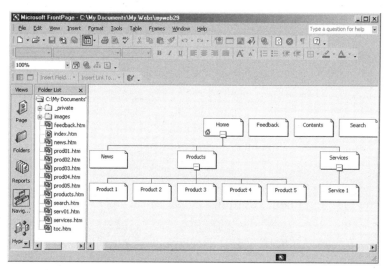

Figure 7-1.

FrontPage's Corporate Presence Wizard creates a complete Web site for you. You can add or delete pages to meet your own needs.

However, the site has some "orphan" pages — pages that aren't linked to anything else on the site. Without a link, the prospective customer will never see these pages. Once you have Navigation view open, you can adjust the structure of your site to give "orphans" links, and add content to your existing pages, as well.

Moving a Link

An *orphan* page just won't be easy to find by your visitors; it has to be linked to another page so its contents can be accessed. It's like arranging the contents of a cabinet in your kitchen. You put the things that are most important near the front, where you can reach them easily. Less important items go farther back. On a Web site, you put the most important contents — your sales products — at the top. Less essential contents go on lower levels.

To move an orphan page, click the page's icon in Navigation view, and then drag the icon, so that it's connected to the page you want. Simply "drawing a line" from one page to another in Navigation view isn't enough, however.

You then have to create a textual link on the page:

1. Enter some text on the originating page (the page that you want to link to the previously "orphaned" page) that will serve as the link text, such as "Search our Web site."

2. Select the text that you want to function as the clickable link. For the text mentioned in the preceding step, this might simply be the word "Search."

3. Do one of the following: Click the **Insert Hyperlink** button in the Standard toolbar, choose **Hyperlink** from the **Insert** menu, or press CTRL+K.

   The **Insert Hyperlink** dialog box opens.

4. In the **Insert Hyperlink** dialog box, scroll down the list of pages on your site and click the name of the page you want to link to. The page's URL appears in the **Address** box.

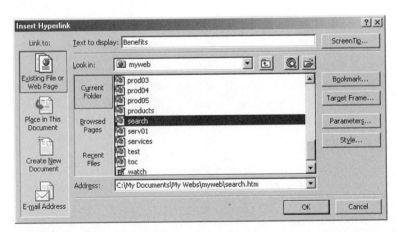

Figure 7-2.

It's easy to create a link from one page to another within your e-commerce site by using FrontPage's **Insert Hyperlink** *dialog box.*

5. Click **OK** to close the **Insert Hyperlink** dialog box and return to the FrontPage window, where the text you previously selected is now formatted as a link.

Putting Your Sales Pages Up Front

A tool like the Corporate Presence Wizard has its advantages and disadvantages. If you're in a hurry, it creates a set of Web pages in the blink of an eye. But this doesn't keep you from having to do some rearranging of those pages. The Corporate Presence Wizard has many of the elements that an e-commerce site needs, but it doesn't emphasize the selling of products and services. That part is up to you.

Once you get a set of pages from the Corporate Presence Wizard, you need to do some rearranging to put your products where they'll be noticed:

1. Go to your home page and make a prominent link to your products or catalog pages.

2. Move your product pages up so they branch right off your home page and have a level of their own.

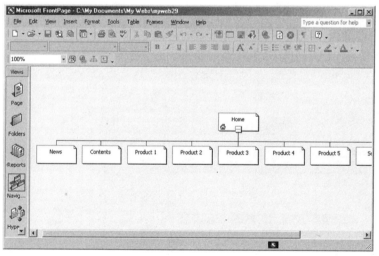

Figure 7-3.

Move your most important content — your sales items — to the top of your Web site's organization.

Make your catalog of goods and services as close to the top level of your site (your home page) as you can. Along with making your site's contents searchable (see "Adding Search" later in this chapter), putting your merchandise in a prominent location with easy-to-find links is the most important way you can improve your customer experience.

Adding Navigation Links

In Chapter 6, you learned how to set up shared borders on a Web site. You saw that such areas could include a company logo that helps unify all of a site's pages. Shared borders can also help to unify a site's organization by providing visitors with links to all of the main pages. Your customers will be able to get to your products more easily if you create a navigational feature called a link bar and put it in a shared border or other standard location on all of your pages.

A *link bar* is a set of buttons (usually four or five, though there's no rule about how many you can have) that appear at the same location on each Web page. This graphical row of buttons links visitors to important pages on your Web site.

If you use a utility like a Wizard or a template, a link bar is created for you. To edit it, right-click the link bar in Page view and choose **Link Bar Properties**. The **Link Bar Properties** dialog box opens.

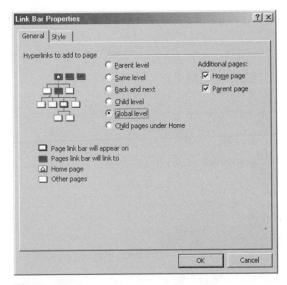

Figure 7-4.
You can edit your site's link bars to make it easier for customers to find all of the goods and services you have to offer.

The "parent level" of a site is the level above the page that FrontPage is currently displaying. The "child level" is the level below.

If you aren't using a Wizard and you want to create a link bar from scratch, follow these steps:

1. Position the cursor at the location in the currently displayed Web page where you want the link bar to appear.

    You can select the link bar later and cut and paste it to a new location if you change your mind about its placement, however.

2. On the **Insert** menu, click **Web** Component. You can also click the **Web Component** button on the Standard toolbar.

    The **Insert Web Component** dialog box appears.

3. In the **Component type** list, click **Link Bars** to select it.

    A set of link bar options appears in the **Choose a bar type** list.

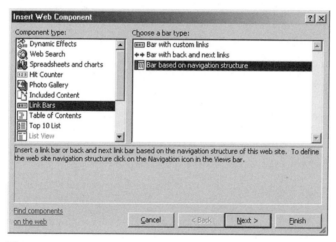

Figure 7-5.

*Graphics and links are combined automatically in the **Insert Web Component** dialog box.*

4. Select a bar type based on navigation structure.

    You can read about each link bar's characteristics, which are displayed in the bottom half of the **Insert Web Component** dialog box, when you select each option.

5. Click **Finish** if you're in a hurry and you want FrontPage to automatically assign a style to the link bar. Otherwise, click **Next** and select a theme for your link bar buttons. After you have selected a theme, click **Next**.

6. Choose an orientation. The link bar buttons can either be arranged horizontally or vertically. Click **Finish**.

The **Insert Web Component** dialog box closes and the **Link Bar Properties** dialog box opens so you can format the link bar further.

Technical Tip

If you chose the Link Bar with Back and Next links option, after the **Insert Web Component** dialog box closes you'll see a **Create a New Link Bar** dialog box displayed. Type a name for the link bar in the Name box, click **OK**, and the **Link Bar Properties** dialog box is displayed.)

7. Click **Finish** to add the link bar to your page.

Without the **Insert Web Component** dialog box, it would probably take you as much as an hour to create the buttons and links required to make a working (not to mention attractive) set of navigation buttons.

Adding and Deleting Pages

Using the Corporate Presence Wizard is great because it gives you a complete set of interlinked pages you can work with. But you have to then adjust the content of the site to meet your customer's needs by adding pages, deleting pages, or moving pages so they are linked differently.

Adding a Page

You can add pages to your site from within Navigation view or Page view. We'll do it from Navigation view. This example shows how to add a product page because that's one of the most important pages an e-commerce site can have. But the steps apply to any sort of page you want to add — a page that provides directions to your business, a page that talks about you and your experience in your field, or a page with any other kind of content.

Technical Tip

In Chapter 8 you learn how to create product listings with the Microsoft bCentral Commerce Manager. But you don't have to use Commerce Manager to create a sales catalog. You can use FrontPage to create your own catalog from scratch and publish it with another Web host, such as Verio (http://www.verio.com) or EarthLink (http://www.earthlink.com).

To add a page to your Web:

1. While in Navigation view, on the **File** menu, point to **New**, and then click **Page or Web**.

   The Task pane appears.

2. Click **Blank Page**.

   A **New Page** icon is added to your site.

3. Click the **New Page** icon, hold down your mouse button, and drag the icon.

   As you drag, a line connects the **New Page** icon to adjacent pages.

4. Keep dragging the new page until the line connects to one of your Products pages, and then release the mouse button.

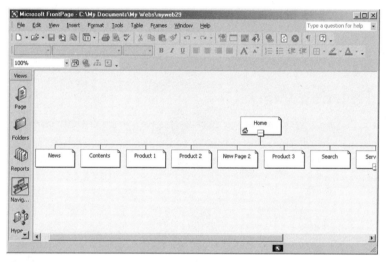

Figure 7-6.

By dragging a page's icon you can visually link that page to your site's list of products, then edit the content to describe what you have to sell.

Technical Tip

If you click **Choose page** from the **New from existing page** section of the Task pane, you can create a new page based on one of your products pages with the caption placeholders intact. The new page can then be edited by deleting the existing content. The advantage is that you'll have a new page that looks exactly like your existing product pages. If you choose **Blank Page**, you'll have to add the image, caption, and descriptions yourself from scratch.

Deleting a Page

Sometimes you might want to trim back your Web site because you don't have sufficient content to keep a page fresh. With e-commerce sites, pages that are stale and go unchanged for weeks or months at a time discourage shoppers from returning to you on a regular basis because they aren't sure they're going to find anything new when they return. It's better to have only a few pages that you update regularly rather than dozens of pages, many of which may go unchanged for long periods.

Deleting a page from a web isn't necessarily a straightforward operation — at least not with most Web page editing tools. If the page you want to delete contains links to other pages, all of the references to the deleted page will be broken. With FrontPage, however, you can safely delete a page and have all of the links updated automatically. For instance, if your home page contains a link in its navigation bar to a News page and you decide to delete that page from the web, the navigation bar will lose its News button.

To delete a page from your web:

1. In Navigation view, right-click the page you want to delete, and then click **Delete** on the submenu.

2. In the **Delete Page** dialog box, select one of the two options: Either delete the page from the Web altogether or keep the page but remove it from your site's navigation structure (that is, delete any links to or from the page). Click **OK**.

    The page is deleted — as well as any links to it.

Working with Pages in Navigation View

One of the nice things about working in Navigation view is that you not only get an overview of how your site is structured, but you can edit pages instantly. Double-click the Product 1 page, and the page opens in Page view so you can edit it.

Then follow these steps:

1. Right-click the Product 1 banner — the location differs depending on the theme you chose, but chances are it's right near the top of the page. Then click **Page Banner Properties** on the submenu. In the **Page banner** box, type a new name for the banner, and then click **OK**.

Figure 7-7.
Work in Navigation view and you can easily switch to Page view to add content to your site.

2. Click the placeholder text *Comment: Replace this image* to select it, and then press DELETE or BACKSPACE to delete it.

3. Click the image placeholder to display the Pictures toolbar, and then click the **Insert Picture From File** button to open the **Picture** dialog box. Locate the image of the product, and then click **Insert** to add the image. Resize the image by clicking the selection handles and dragging inward. See Chapter 6 for more information about resizing images.

4. Enter a caption for the product image, and then add a description of the product to the page. When you're done, click the **Save** button to save your changes. The **Save Embedded Files** dialog box appears, prompting you to save any files you have added to the page. When you click **OK**, FrontPage saves the image along with the other files in your Web.

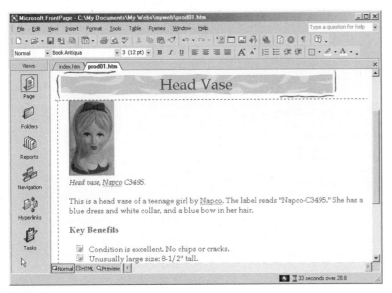

Figure 7-8.

Product pages in the Corporate Presence Wizard include placeholder images, captions, and descriptions that you can quickly replace with your own information.

Repeat steps 1 through 4 for all the products in your site. Then click **Navigation** on the Views bar so you can return to Navigation view and do some reorganizing.

Making Your Site Payment-Friendly

Encourage your customers to complete the transactions they initiate by making it easy to make the final purchase. Creating a customer-friendly environment is a necessity rather than a luxury. Your competitors with e-commerce stores may already make it easy to make purchases.

Business Tip

Include the logos of the major credit card institutions on your site to emphasize how convenient it is for shoppers to make purchases. For Visa International's logo, go to http://www.visabrc.com/doc.phtml?7,0,290. For MasterCard International's logo, go to http://www.mastercard.com/business/brand.

The following sections describe some strategies for straightening out the twists and turns of the Web sales maze.

What makes it easy for people to pay?

- Express lane to check out

- Lack of distractions to divert attention

- Easy-to-understand forms

- Secure, private environment

- Credit card payment options

- Non-credit card payment options

Providing an Express Purchase Lane

You don't want to discourage, slow down, or misdirect customers on their way to buying something from you. Customers follow two paths:

- **The purchase path.** These are the steps required for someone who has decided to make a purchase.

- **The search path.** These are the steps required to find items and prices for someone who has not yet decided to buy.

On all too many sites, the "purchase path" overlaps with the "search path." In other words, there's no express check out. Even shoppers who know exactly what they want have to do an excessive amount of searching around in order to find the item and purchase it.

One way to point shoppers in the right direction — the path to the check out page — is to make your home page do a little selling right off the bat. Show a few prices for new, specially reduced, or popular items on your home page. Make easily noticeable links to the products you want to feature. The KBkids.com home page (http://www.kbkids.com) wins praise from ZDNet's Best Practices site for its clear navigation, including the specific links in the left-hand column.

Figure 7-9.
Follow KBkids.com's example: Promote special sales on your home page and include specific links that lead shoppers immediately to the areas they'll be interested in.

Avoid providing customers with two equally prominent check out paths. Creative Good (in an article entitled "Registration Best Practices" at http://www.zdnet.com/ecommerce/stories/evaluations/0,10524,2685100,00.html) found that at many sites, new customers chose the path for return customers. Customers who get lost on the way to the checkout area are less likely to hand over payment. Make only the new customer path prominent.

Avoiding Distractions and Dead-Ends

Sometimes the best way to get consumers to make a purchase is to simply avoid obstacles and eliminate roadblocks. Stay away from:

- Distracting pop-up windows that annoy visitors who are in a hurry to search, shop, and buy on their own. They make customers feel they're not in control.

- Overcrowded home pages that leave shoppers guessing about how to make purchases or find what they're looking for. Shoppers who can't make a purchase at your site will hurry off to an online store that's easier to use.

- Hard-to-find shopping carts that slow down the completion of purchases. After putting selections in a cart, customers should be able to pay for them quickly, not hunt around for the cart itself.

Make the check out process easy. Improving the clarity and simplicity of your online forms quickly improves the user-friendliness of your check out area, as described in the following section.

Adding Search

Link bars are only one tool for making a Web site more easily navigated by prospective customers and clients. A far more important tool, and a must-have element for any e-commerce site, is a way to search your site's contents.

Studies prove that making a site searchable is the single most important navigation tool for any Web site. Your shoppers will be expecting a way to locate specific items or information based on keywords they enter in a form that lets them search the contents of your site.

Normally, it takes complex programming to index the contents of a site so you can create a search form that actually works. But FrontPage's Search Form template comes ready to work and makes use of a special programming utility called a Search bot that FrontPage uses automatically. Your job is to customize the search page and keep the index up-to-date.

Technical Tip

When you create a search page, either by using the Search template or as part of a Wizard, the Search bot will search through all the pages in your web. If there are any pages you don't want indexed, you should move them into a folder labeled **_private**. This folder is automatically created when you use a Wizard or Web site template. You might not want to enable users to search Web pages that are headers and footers in a frames layout — a set of individual pages that, together, is presented as a single Web page divided into frames.

When you create a search form by selecting it in the **Page Templates** dialog box (see the following section), you only have to link it to another page on your site in Navigation view. You don't need to customize the standard contents, except to delete the placeholder text at the top of the page.

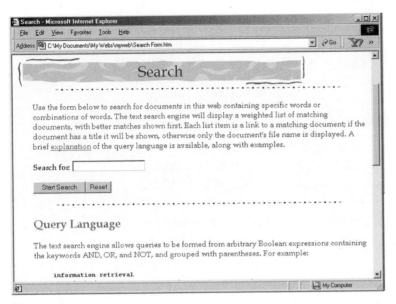

Figure 7-10.
A search form, an essential element of any e-commerce site, is automatically enabled using FrontPage's Search Form template.

How FrontPage's Search Function Works

Let's move step by step through the process of making a site searchable so you can understand exactly what's going on and, more importantly, make the search process work better for your customers.

If your Web site is hosted on a Web server running the FrontPage Server Extensions, FrontPage automatically creates a text index drawn from all of the words contained in your Web site's pages. When you save a page in your site, FrontPage adds any new words to the text index. The index is cumulative: New words are added to the index, but old ones are not removed.

Technical Note

A FrontPage search does not locate approximately 300 of the most common English words, such as "a," "the," and "or."

When a visitor enters a keyword into the search form and submits it to your site by pressing the **Start Search** button, FrontPage checks the text index and displays a list of hyperlinks to the pages containing the search text. The list of results is weighted — in other words, the closest matches are listed first.

Adding a Search Form to Any Page

You don't need to use the Corporate Presence Wizard to create a search form. You can use the Search template if you want to have a separate page solely devoted to searching. Or, you can open an existing page and add the Search Form Web component. The **Web Component** command enables you to add a simple search form to any Web page. This makes your entire Web site extra easy to navigate — from any page; the user has a simple form from which to conduct a search. The search form takes only a few minutes to configure.

To add a search form:

1. Start FrontPage, and open the page you want to contain the search form. Click inside the page at the spot where you want the search form to appear.

2. On the **Insert** menu, click **Web Component**.
The **Insert Web Component** dialog box opens.

Updating Your Text Index

Keep an eye on your site's text index periodically, especially if you delete text or entire pages. When you create pages, FrontPage automatically updates your index. But when you delete content, FrontPage doesn't remove text from the index.

You can have FrontPage notify you when your text index needs to be revised, however. First, open the web in FrontPage. On the **Tools** menu, click **Options** to open the **Options** dialog box. On the **General** tab, select the **Warn when text index is out of date** check box, and then click **OK**. Now, whenever you open the web to edit it, FrontPage will notify you if the index is out of date so you can recompile the index.

To manually recompile the text index, open the web in FrontPage. On the **Tools** menu, click **Recalculate Hyperlinks**. A message appears to notify you that FrontPage is about to check hyperlinks in the web and synchronize web data, a process that could take several minutes. Click **Yes**. That's all you have to do. FrontPage then does the updating in the background so you can go on with other work.

---

3. In the **Component type** list, click **Web Search** to select it, and then click **Finish**.

The **Insert Web Component** dialog box closes and the **Search Form Properties** dialog box opens. This dialog box allows you to change the label that appears next to the search form, the size of the search form, and the buttons that appear next to the search form ("Start Search" and "Reset" are the defaults).

Figure 7-11.
Customize your search box label and size using this dialog box.

Technical Tip

Changing the size of the text box doesn't affect how many characters a site visitor can type in the box. If a site visitor types more characters than will fit in the box, the extra characters will scroll off the left side of the box, but all of the text will be submitted by the search form.

4. Change the settings in the **Search Form Properties** dialog box if you want, and then use the **Search Results** tab to change the way the results are presented (see the following section).

5. When you're done, click **OK**.

The search form is added.

By default, the search form includes instructions on how to use the form and query language results visitors can use to find what they want (see Figure 7-10 for an example). You can cut out all the instructions if you want the search box and its accompanying buttons to appear all by themselves.

Customizing Search Results

The **Search Results** tab in the **Search Form Properties** dialog box lets you change the way search results are presented. The default selection **All** appears in the **Word list to search** box because this enables your visitors to search the entire contents of your Web. When they conduct a search by entering keywords in the search box and pressing the search button, the search engine scours the text index of your site, and then returns a set of results.

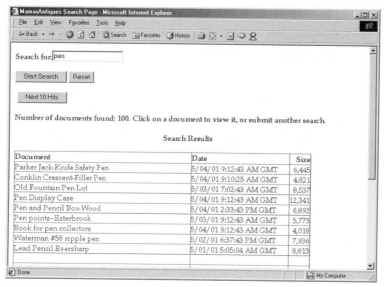

Figure 7-12.

The default search results include the titles of documents that contain the search keywords, the date the document was last modified, and the size of the document.

By clearing the options on the **Search Results** tab of the **Search Form Properties** dialog box, you can change the search results. You might want to simplify the results by removing the date, for instance.

If you want to restrict the search to a community forum or other discussion area, enter the name of the folder that contains the group's postings. Select the **Display score** check box if you want to assign a rank to the results of the search — each item on the search results page that is returned to your visitor gets a ranking based on how closely the contents match the search terms. The closest matches are ranked near 100%; matches that aren't as close are assigned lower percentages. You can also select the other check boxes if you want the search results to include the date and the file size of the file being matched. (It's an extra nice touch for visitors if they know that the file is especially large in size.)

Adding a Site Map

Web sites that contain many different products and multiple levels of information provide visitors with an additional navigation tool in the form of a Table of Contents. Many Web sites call this page a site map. It's a list of all the pages in the site, arranged by category.

The Table of Contents page that is automatically created with the Corporate Presence Wizard is relatively simple. You replace a place holding introductory paragraph and create a list of the main features of your site. If you don't use the Corporate Presence Wizard, you can create the Table of Contents page anytime by using one of FrontPage's Templates:

1. On the **File** menu, point to **New**, and then click **Page or Web** to display the Task pane.

2. In the **New from template** section of the Task pane, click **Page Templates** to open the **Page Templates** dialog box.

3. Scroll down the list of page templates, click **Table of Contents** to select it, and then click **OK**.

    The **Page Templates** dialog box closes and the Table of Contents template opens in the FrontPage window.

4. On the **File** menu, click **Save** to open the **Save As** dialog box.

5. Enter an easy-to-remember name for the Table of Contents page, such as toc.htm, and then click **Save** to save the file in your current web.

6. Click **Navigation** on the Views bar.

    The Navigation view of your site is displayed as well as the Folder List. Make sure your home page is visible so you can link to it.

7. On the **View** menu, click **Folder List**.

    The Folder List appears with your new file displayed.

8. Click the Table of Contents page in the Folder List, and then drag it into Navigation view to link it to another page in your site. (The home page is a logical choice.)

9. Right-click the icon for the Table of Contents page in Navigation view, and then click **Rename** from the submenu. Enter a new name for the file, and then press ENTER.

10. Switch to Page view, and then delete the placeholder content and replace it with your own content.

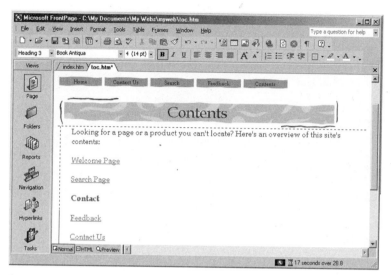

Figure 7-13.

A Table of Contents page provides visitors with an overview of your entire site.

Chapter 8
Streamlining Web Sales with an Online Catalog

Chances are you already sell your products or services through an existing bricks-and-mortar business. You may even distribute a printed sales catalog to your customers. Now you want to sell your goods or services through a *Web-based catalog* — a set of Web pages that presents merchandise for sale. A Web-based interactive catalog backed up by effective customer service provides you with the best presentation possible for selling your products or services online.

Definition

Web-based catalog A set of pages that presents sales items so customers can learn about them to make purchases. One Web page may contain a list of products. Alternatively, a single product might be presented on its own Web page. Web-based catalogs are distinguished from their printed counterparts by the fact that they are intended to appear on a computer screen, and by the use of hyperlinks to navigate from item to item or from a product page to check out.

Web sites that list phone and fax as the only purchase options no longer impress Web shoppers. Online consumers expect an e-commerce site to include a catalog, a shopping cart, and secure online payment with a credit card. They also expect to be able to find things easily and make purchases with very few mouse clicks.

A report entitled "The Art of Online Merchandising" prepared by goodexperience.com (http://www.zdnet.com/ecommerce/stories/main/0,10475,2592389,00.html) identifies six aspects of good product presentation:

- Decide why you want to sell something online. Identify the criteria that mean success for your sales effort. Do you want to clear out excess stock, maximize profit margins, introduce new products, or reach your targeted customers? Make sure your criteria match your overall online marketing strategy. Having a clear idea of your goals will enable you to decide what to sell online and what prices to set.

- Back your decisions with information. Always try to rely on demographic information to determine what to sell and how to sell it. If you don't have quantitative data available, use common sense to determine if a product would appeal to your customers.

- Rank the criteria in order of importance. A product that appeals to your target market might rank higher than unloading excess stock, for instance.

- Develop a formula that uses the criteria you've specified combined with how they rank in importance.

- Run promotions and launch sales using the formula you've developed.

- Track customer usage and evaluate what works and what doesn't. Then adjust your sales presentation accordingly.

In other reports, goodexperience.com praises Web sites like BabyCenter (http://www.babycenter.com) that present sales descriptions by placing the most important information up front — a good photo, the product name, price, and a customer rating. The marketing authority also praises catalogs that provide product recommendations or an expert who can recommend products along with descriptions (such as CustomGolf.com, http://www.customgolf.com), and whose products have a personality and are clearly differentiated from the competition (like Patagonia, http://www.patagonia.com).

Keep these and other customer expectations firmly in your consciousness when you create your catalog. An effective catalog doesn't need to contain dozens or hundreds of separate items. The accessibility of individual items and the quality of their descriptions count for much more.

Business Tip

Many Web sites give advice on creating a good sales catalog and have critical comments about catalogs that don't work. Gather some dos and don'ts from sites like BizRate.com, where you'll find research for merchants reported at http://merchant.bizrate.com/oa/research_consulting/index.xpml, or ClickZ, which has a good article about how online shoppers make decisions at http://clickz.com/article/cz.3387.html.

Web shoppers crave information. They love getting more information than they can find in a printed catalog or from a salesperson that knows the product only casually. Write lengthy descriptions of each product and include supporting information that tells the shopper why the item is desirable. You can emphasize that a product is new, discounted, or can be personalized, as you'll see in subsequent sections.

Clear images also play an essential role on the Web because the customer can't touch your items and most are unlikely to visit your bricks-and-mortar store. Some of the other qualities you should strive for when assembling your Commerce Manager catalog follow.

Designing an Effective Online Catalog

All Web catalogs contain product descriptions, prices, and photos of merchandise. Products are organized into classifications that identify the category into which the product falls, such as children's, women's, or men's apparel.

But unlike printed catalogs, Web catalogs are non-linear. Shoppers don't navigate by page numbers but by hypertext links. The more effective catalogs, such as the one shown in Figure 8-1, which was featured in a *New York Times* article, let shoppers reach all other areas of the site, as well as other sales categories, whether they are viewing the home page, a department page, or an individual product listing. (Go to the paper's Web site, http://www.nytimes.com, and search for "L.L. Bean Beats the Current by Staying in Midstream" in the September 20, 2000 issue.)

Figure 8-1.

An individual catalog listing in the L.L. Bean catalog includes links that lead you to all other parts of the site, as well as a search box.

Updating Every Day

When your site includes a catalog, you can change the content every day, depending on what you have in stock, which items are hot, or which items you want to clear out of your inventory. Because your words aren't set in ink, changes take a matter of minutes — put a different item on sale each day or reduce prices as soon as you get sales figures in. The Lands' End catalog, for example, contains regularly updated product listings and seasonal specials.

Technical Note

You'll examine how to keep track of inventory by using a database in Chapter 18.

Figure 8-2.

The opening page of the Lands' End catalog includes links to new items, special sales, and overstocked items that are changed regularly, giving customers an incentive to return to the site.

Creating a Catalog with Microsoft bCentral Commerce Manager

Creating a catalog, a shopping cart, and a check out process for a Web site is not for amateurs: It requires sophisticated programming. So rent the expertise! Microsoft bCentral's Commerce Manager gives you all the tools and technology you need and you never have to code a line. The actual product pages and server-side functions are located on Commerce

Case Study: Catalog Sales Prove Sweet for Traditional Retailer

The Chocolate Vault operates a bricks-and-mortar candy store in a former bank building located in the small town of Tecumseh, MI. But the ambience of the walk-in store isn't always sufficient to maintain the business, says owner Barb McCann. "If there is no one on the street, it's pretty tough hanging on to the business."

The Chocolate Vault finds it impossible to maintain a printed catalog. The store offers thousands of options for specialty gifts, and no printed catalog would adequately cover the store's specialty — personalization. The Chocolate Vault can mold just about anything the customer wants in chocolate. "There is just no way to put all those options in a paper catalog," says McCann.

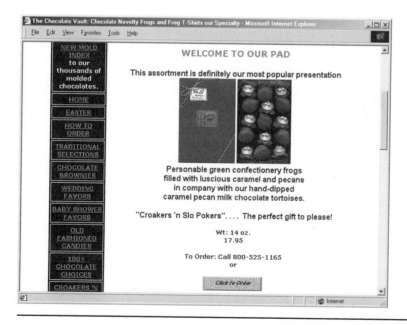

(continued)

Manager's pages. You don't have to set them up; you only link to them. But your customers aren't aware they're leaving your site to make purchases. You can keep the look and feel and brand identity of your site while integrating the catalog and shopping into your site.

Case Study: Catalog Sales Prove Sweet for Traditional Retailer *(continued)*

The company's FrontPage-created Web site and e-mail address help the company get around the lack of a printed catalog. Customers who are considering ordering molded novelty chocolate can e-mail McCann with their thoughts on the sort of gift they want to present. "We then send them a picture of the molded chocolate they are looking for, embedded in an e-mail message," explains McCann. "We do this usually within 2 to 3 hours, sometimes as soon as 15 to 20 minutes. Such e-mails serve as personalized catalog pages, complete with detailed information on sizes, weights, and costs for each chocolate novelty."

The Chocolate Vault's Web site (http://www.chocolatevault.com) also includes as much product information as possible, says McCann. "I really feel that we need to give the customer as much information as possible on our basic items, such as size, weight, or cost. However, if I have an opportunity to e-mail back and forth with a prospective customer, with or without pictures, I have an opportunity to reassure them about our quality and our service, which I feel is *the* most important part of our Web store."

Every catalog page encourages online shoppers to contact the store by e-mail or by calling a toll-free number. The catalog thus provides a means of establishing personal contact. "We've found that customers want to feel that there is a real person behind the site and the e-mails, so it is important to establish a professional, friendly, but businesslike rapport with them. If the prospective customer has to ask a question about a product, we have a better chance of selling to him or her."

"Going 'live' with the Web site was the best thing we have ever done," adds McCann. "The combination of the bricks-and-mortar and the Internet site has allowed us to continue on with our chocolate business."

Technical Note

Because you're a Microsoft FrontPage user, you can use Commerce Manager by means of a special program called the bCentral Commerce Manager Add-in for FrontPage. The add-in is available only to users of FrontPage 2000 or FrontPage 2002. It can be used with FrontPage even if your Web site is not hosted by bCentral. But if you are a bCentral customer, you can take advantage of features such as Customer Manager for managing customer contacts and Traffic Builder for increasing your site's visibility. (They're explained in Chapters 14 and 12, respectively.)

A version of Commerce Manager is also available for people who do not use FrontPage. For details, go to http://www.bcentral.com/services/cm/default.asp. For details on the add-in, go to http://www.microsoft.com/frontpage/commercemanager.htm.

Commerce Manager is closely integrated with FrontPage through the Commerce Manager Add-in for FrontPage. The add-in enables you to generate catalog pages without leaving FrontPage. The advantage of using the add-in is that you can use FrontPage's themes and Web components, together with Commerce Manager, for free. (If you don't use the add-in, you can only use Commerce Manager by signing up for a bCentral account and paying a hosting fee.)

The bCentral Commerce Manager Add-in for FrontPage gives you:

- A 25-item online catalog of your products with Buy buttons for each item
- Order management features
- A shopping cart
- Optional online credit card processing (real-time authorization and automatic payment deposit) for an additional $19.95 per month
- Access to your account from any computer that has Internet access and a secure browser, such as Microsoft Internet Explorer 4 or later or Netscape Navigator 4.0 or later

Business Tip

You can list a maximum of 25 sales items using the bCentral Commerce Manager Add-in for FrontPage. If you need to sell more than 25 items, sign up for the regular Commerce Manager service.

You don't *have* to use Commerce Manager to create an interactive product catalog for your site. And if you do choose Commerce Manager, you don't have to host the rest of your Web site at bCentral either. Rather, you can host your informational Web pages with your usual host and sign up the catalog part with Commerce Manager. The following sections examine bCentral in detail, but though the steps presented are specific to this individual service, they give you an example of how you can use any e-commerce host to give your site more sales effectiveness.

Business Tip

What if you already have FrontPage and have been using another e-commerce provider, and you want to switch to bCentral? First, check your agreement with your service provider — if you are locked into a contract, you may not be able to leave right away without having to pay a penalty. Before you do leave your current provider, copy all of your Web site files to your hard disk so you can transfer them to bCentral. Then, go to the bCentral Create and Manage Your Web Site page (http://www.bcentral.com/services/build.asp) to find out about hosting plans and payment options.

Choosing a Sales Channel

Commerce Manager lets you create e-commerce pages to include on your Web site or to include in a "marketplace." A marketplace can be an online "mall," an auction site, or a directory.

Definition

Marketplace A Web site set up to provide goods and services for sale — the site collects the merchandise offered by a number of stores like yours in one convenient location so shoppers can find them more easily. A Web-based marketplace functions like a shopping mall does in the traditional retail world.

bCentral is affiliated with several marketplace partners where you can list your items. You can find out more about each partner at http://www.bcentral.com/marketplace/buysell.asp and in the topics below.

You can list different items in different marketplaces: If you have twelve items for sale, you might want to place six up for auction, three for sale on MSN Marketplace, and three on your own Web site. You don't have to pay any charges to sell your items, but you must agree to the terms and conditions of each individual marketplace.

Technical Tip

Before you can submit product listings, you must sign up for each marketplace. The sign-up process only takes a few minutes (or even a few seconds). The steps are outlined in the sections "Selling Through a Marketplace" and "Selling an Item on an Auction" that follow.

Your Web Site

As a registered FrontPage user, you can use your own site to sell your merchandise. The E-commerce Wizard generates a set of catalog page templates, with buttons that enable shoppers to add an item to a shopping cart. You customize the templates to correspond to your site's design. You then connect to your database of catalog items on Commerce Manager. FrontPage manages merging the catalog items with the templates to create catalog pages that you publish to your site.

Auction Sites

You can list items for auction on either MSN Auctions or bCentral Auctions. You might want to do this if you're not certain how much an item is worth or if you are selling a very specialized item that appeals to a few collectors. In either case, you decide the period of the auction and whether you want to sell at a reserve price. See each site's "How to Sell" information page for more details.

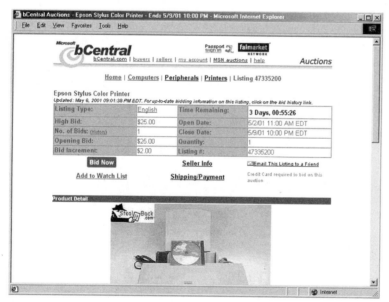

Figure 8-3.

When you use the bCentral Commerce Manager Add-in for FrontPage, you have the option of selling your merchandise at auctions like bCentral Auctions.

Marketplace Sites

You can list your merchandise on one of two Web sites that function like shopping malls: MSN Marketplace (http://marketplace.msn.com) or bCentral Marketplace (http://www.bcentral.com/marketplace/buysell.asp). Browse around either site and see how many businesses are like yours.

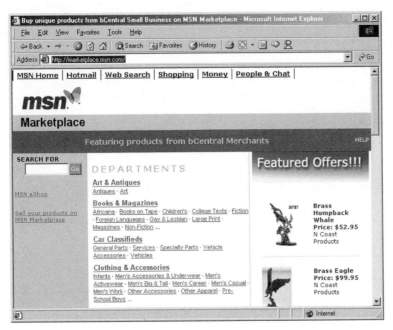

Figure 8-4.
Selling your merchandise at a marketplace like MSN Marketplace enables you to take advantage of MSN's huge customer base.

Being listed with lots of other businesses like yours might lead to more traffic because of the marketplace's pull and its advertising and marketing ability. The downside is that your items can seem lost in a sea of similar products.

Assembling What You Need to Get Started

To use the Commerce Manager Add-in, you must have a Web site built with FrontPage. You also need the following:

- Names of your products you want to sell online
- Clear digitized images of the products
- Descriptions of each product
- Pricing for each item
- The channel where you will sell the item

Installing the Commerce Manager Add-in

It doesn't take more than an hour or two to set up a fully functional catalog with the Add-in, and the following sections describe the process in detail. If you decide to accept credit cards, Commerce Manager also handles the verification of customer information, as described in Chapter 9.

When you install the Add-in, you add an e-commerce wizard and e-commerce functions to FrontPage.

To download the Add-in:

1. Start FrontPage.

2. On the **Insert** menu, click **Web Component**.
   The **Insert Web Component** dialog box opens.

3. In the **Component Type** list, click **bCentral Web Components**, and then in the **Choose bCentral Component** list, click **bCentral Commerce Manager Add-In**.
   FrontPage connects to the bCentral site and the **bCentral Commerce Manager Add-In Properties** dialog box opens.

4. In the **bCentral Commerce Manager Add-In Properties** dialog box, click the highlighted link **here** in step 1. Then follow the rest of the steps shown in the dialog box to install the Add-in.

To log on to Microsoft bCentral or set up a bCentral account:

1. On the **Tools** menu, point to **E-commerce**, and then click **Add Products**.
   The **Log in to bCentral** box opens.

2. If you have an account with bCentral, type your username and password in the boxes provided, and then click **OK**. To set up a bCentral account, select **I want to Sign up for bCentral**, and then click **OK**.

Your browser opens the Commerce Manager page on the bCentral site.

3. Click **Sign up now** for either a monthly subscription or an annual subscription.

Your browser opens a sign-up page for Commerce Manager services. If you have an existing bCentral account, you still need to sign up for Commerce Manager services.

4. Follow the instructions given on-screen to sign up for bCentral.

You'll need to:

- Enter a valid e-mail address as your user ID

- Select a password

- Select whether you want to pay monthly or yearly

5. Print out your invoice for future reference when it is shown to you on-screen.

6. When you're done, close the sign-up page and return to the FrontPage window.

Once you have installed Commerce Manager, you'll notice some new options on the **Tools** menu and in the **Web Site Templates** dialog box.

- **E-Commerce command.** This command on the **Tools** menu lets you add products, manage orders, view your settings, view the Seller Console, log out, and run the E-commerce Wizard.

- **E-Commerce toolbar.** The toolbar appears when you choose one of the options on the **E-commerce** submenu. You can insert product field information, product photos, shopping cart feature buttons, and links to other pages in your site.

- **E-Commerce Wizard.** This utility, available when you click **Web Site Templates** on the Task bar, lets you create and update your e-commerce Web site.

Creating a Catalog with the E-commerce Wizard

Now you can create your online catalog. You'll do it in five steps for each product:

1. Select a department.

2. Select the product.

3. Add a description.

4. Add an image.

5. Select a place to sell it.

You create catalog listings for one department of items at a time. If you want to sell items that fall into very different categories, such as garden tools, kitchen accessories, and clothing, first select the category for garden tools (as described in the preceding steps), and then create all of the product listings for garden tools (as described in the steps that follow). When you're done with garden tools, return to the **Tools** menu and select **Add Products** from the **E-commerce** submenu. Then identify the department for kitchen accessories and add the kitchen accessory products. Repeat the process for each department of products you want to sell.

Let's get started with the first product department.

Selecting Departments

Product departments help direct the shopper to items when they may not know the specific product name, but do know what other products it is similar to or some general characteristic of the product, such as what it is used for.

Because searching for merchandise is something many customers will do, take some time to identify the categories that most closely describe the items in your product line. Consider the Chocolate Vault Web site. On the home page shown in the sidebar "Case Study: Catalog Sales Prove Sweet for Traditional Retailer," you see a set of product categories that include "Traditional Selections," "Chocolate Brownies," and "Wedding Favors." If you click **Traditional Selections**, for instance, you go to a Web page that contains specific assortments of chocolates for sale.

To select product departments:

1. On the **Tools** menu, point to **E-commerce**, and then click **Add Products**.

A **Checking Log-In Status** message box displays briefly, followed by the **Log In to bCentral** box.

2. Enter the e-mail address and password you created earlier, and then click **OK**.

The Product Category page appears.

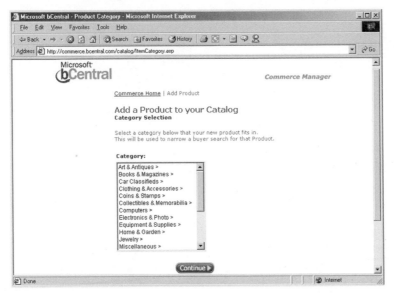

Figure 8-5.

First, select the general category that corresponds most closely to what you want to sell.

Technical Note

If you expect to have multiple sales items that fall into the same sales category, you can streamline the creation of product descriptions by clicking the **Multiple Products** link at the bottom of the Product Category page. When you click this link, a Multiple Product Upload page appears and explains how to download and fill out a Microsoft Excel template that you can use to create descriptions for multiple items that fit into the same category. Using the template, you can then transmit the descriptions to bCentral all at the same time, rather than having to create product descriptions separately for each item. Read the instructions on the Multiple Product Upload page to find out more.

3. Click a product category that describes your product.

When you select a category in the list, a new list appears to the right of the original one. For instance, as shown in the following figure, when you click the Books & Magazines category, the new list contains subcategories of the main category you just selected (including Africana, Books on Tape, and Children's).

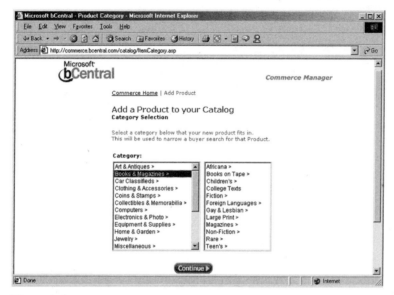

Figure 8-6.

Narrow in on the subcategory that most closely describes your sales items.

4. Select a subcategory that describes your product.

If bCentral lists any subcategories for the subcategory, a new list appears, and you may select from this list, too. For instance, if you click the **Children's** subcategory, a new list appears that looks like this:

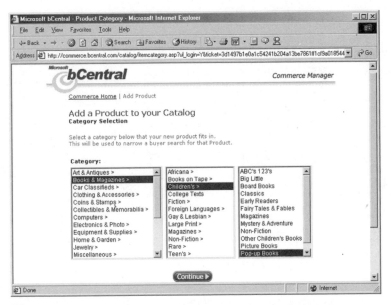

Figure 8-7.
The Product Category page shows several lists of categories and subcategories you use to identify your sales products so customers can find them more easily.

5. Click **Continue**.

   The Product Details page appears.

Creating Catalog Listings

Now you add the text and images that help your customers shop and decide to buy. You may have product identifier numbers for each item you want to sell. If you have your material ready, it takes only a few minutes to create a catalog listing.

If you have a Microsoft Word, Microsoft WordPad, or other text file containing the product description you want to use, open it now. You can copy and paste the text into the Commerce Manager — select the text you want to copy, press CTRL+C to copy it, and then switch to the Commerce Manager Product Details page. Click in the appropriate text field and press CTRL+V to paste in the text. If you want your product description to include bold, italic, and other formatting, you can format by using Hypertext Markup Language (HTML) commands.

To create a catalog listing:

1. In the **Product Name** box, type or paste in the product name.

2. In the **Description**, SKU, and **Price** boxes, type or paste in the appropriate information.

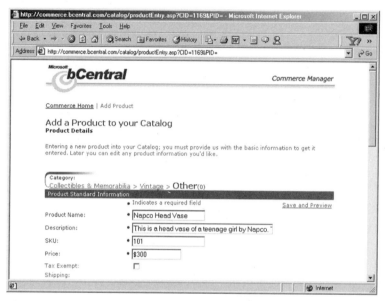

Figure 8-8.
You fill out this form to create catalog listings for your sales items in bCentral's database.

3. To add an image, click **Add/Change** next to the **Product Picture** box.
The Product Image Upload page appears.

4. Click **Browse**.
The **Choose file** dialog box opens.

5. Locate the image file you want to add, and then click **Open**.
The **Choose File** dialog box closes and the path of the image file is displayed on the Product Image Upload page.

Technical Note

A GIF or JPEG image should be no more than 4 inches tall and 4 inches wide or 240 pixels tall by 240 pixels wide.

6. Click **Submit**.

   After the file uploads, you are returned to the Product Details page, and the name of the image appears in the **Product Picture** box. This means your image file has been uploaded to bCentral.

7. To preview the image, click **View**.

8. To close the Preview page, click **Close**.

9. When you are done with this listing, click **Add Another**.

   The listing you just completed is saved and a blank form is displayed. No listings you enter now are published to your Web site until you choose a sales channel.

10. Repeat Steps 1 through 8 for each product you want to sell. When you're finished adding all of your products, click **Done**.

    The Select Products page appears and you can choose a sales channel.

Picking a Sales Channel

Once your products are added, you can view a list of them in your *Seller Console* — a bCentral page that keeps track of the items you have for sale. This page serves as a starting point for listing items, checking on sales items, and editing descriptions.

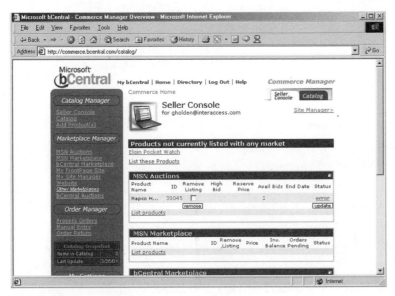

Figure 8-9.
After you have assigned departments for your sales items, you go to this page to sell them through marketplaces.

The next step is to tell bCentral where to sell your products by picking a marketplace for each item you want listed. Choose from:

- MSN Marketplace
- BCentral Marketplace
- MSN Auctions
- Your Web site
  The marketplace you select determines the steps you take next.
- If you are selling items through a marketplace, follow the instructions beginning on this page.
- If you are selling through an auction, follow the instructions on page 148.
- If you are selling directly from your Web site, follow the instructions on page 149.

Selling Through a Marketplace

For selling through a marketplace, you need to set up sales criteria, such as the length of the sale and the price for each item. You then submit your listing to the marketplace. The process of listing items for sale on the bCentral Marketplace is the same as that for the MSN Marketplace. The following steps use bCentral as an example.

To sell an item on the bCentral Marketplace:

1. On the Seller Console page, under the **bCentral Marketplace** heading, select the check box next to the item you would like to sell. (If you haven't yet sold anything on the bCentral Marketplace, you'll need to sign up by clicking the **Sign-Up** link under the **bCentral Marketplace** heading.)
   The terms and conditions of the marketplace are displayed.

2. Read the details, and then click **Continue**.
   The Select Products page appears.

3. Select the check box to the left of the product you want to list on this channel, and then, in the product's **Qty** box, change the default quantity. (If you have created product listings for multiple products, you'll see more than one item displayed on the Select Products page. You can check the boxes next to multiple items if you want to list them all at once.)

4. In the **Listing Start Date** and **Listing End Date** boxes, specify the starting point and end point for the sale or sales.

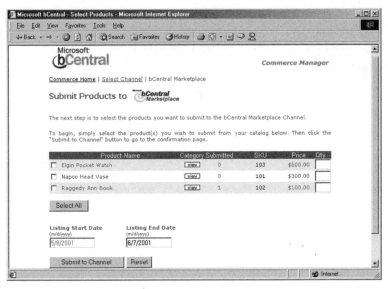

Figure 8-10.
Each item you sell on a given marketplace is assigned an end date so you control the length of the sale.

5. Click **Submit to Channel**.

    A confirmation page asks you to verify that you want to sell the item or items online.

6. To complete the listing, click **Continue**.

    A page appears and confirms that the item or items are now up for sale.

7. Click **Continue** to view the status of this and any other items you have for sale on your Seller Console page.

Warning

Do not refresh the confirmation page. If you do, your product will be listed twice.

Selling an Item on an Auction

Putting an item up for auction on MSN Auctions or bCentral Auctions is similar to selling through a marketplace, but you need to specify some additional criteria. You can select to sell using an English, Dutch, or Quick Win auction.

Definitions

English auction An auction in which a single item is auctioned off to the highest bidder and the sale ends at a specified time.

Dutch auction Often used when the seller has multiple items for sale. The seller specifies the minimum successful price for each item, as well as the number of items available. Bidders can bid at or above the minimum price for the number of items they're interested in. When the auction ends, the winning bidders are the ones who bid the lowest successful prices — in other words, the lowest bids that are still above the minimum price. MSN has an explanation with detailed examples at http://auctions.msn.com/Scripts/glossary.asp#Dutch+Auction.

Quick Win auction An auction in which the seller sets a threshold price for an item. If a bidder matches the threshold price, the sale closes immediately and that bidder is declared the winner.

To submit an item to MSN or bCentral Auctions, the process is the same. The following steps use MSN Auctions as an example. Don't be surprised: When you sign up to use bCentral or MSN Auctions, you're asked to submit a Microsoft Passport username and password rather than your bCentral username and password. Both auctions use Microsoft's Passport user identification system to register participants. If you don't have a Passport account yet, you'll be given the opportunity to sign up for one for free.

1. On the Seller Console page, under the **MSN Auctions** heading, select the check box next to the item you would like to sell.

   A page displays the terms and conditions of the marketplace.

2. Read the terms and conditions, and then click **Continue**.

   The Channel Specific Details page appears.

3. Choose an auction type (English, Dutch, or Quick Win), listing duration, and ending time, and then click **Next**.

4. On the Sign-in page, enter your Microsoft Passport username and password.
   (If you don't have a Passport or Microsoft Hotmail account, you can apply for one on this page.) Fill in your contact information, and then supply credit card information, which is needed in case you incur transaction fees or fees for preferential display.

5. Pick the start and end times, confirm the quantity of items you want to place at auction, and then click **Submit to Channel**.
   If you haven't specified all of the information needed to auction off your merchandise, you'll go to a Confirm products submission page where you'll be asked to submit more information. If you have, you'll go the confirmation page described in Step 7.

6. Click the highlighted phrase data needed to go to the Product Details page for the item you want to sell.
   The items you need to fill in are highlighted in red — if you didn't fill them in previously, you'll need to enter values for **Reserve Price**, **Opening Bid**, and **Minimum Quantity**. When you're done, click Save to go to a confirmation page.

7. On the confirmation page, click **Continue**.
   A Submission Confirmation page is displayed, confirming that your item will be put up for auction at the time specified.

Selling Through Your FrontPage Web Site

As the owner or manager of an existing business, you may feel most comfortable doing all of your marketing and selling through your own FrontPage-created Web site. In this case, you assume all responsibility for marketing and selling your products.
   Let's review what you've accomplished to this point:

- You've installed the bCentral Commerce Manager for FrontPage Add-in.

- You created an account on bCentral.

- You identified the categories that apply to the products you want to sell.

- You've created catalog listings for each item.

This information is now stored in a database at bCentral. Now you'll use FrontPage and the Add-in to generate a separate catalog Web page for each product listing. The process takes a few minutes at most. When you're done, you have catalog pages that have shopping cart functionality built in to them and are ready to publish online on your own Web site.

To generate a separate catalog:

1. On the Seller Console page, under the **My Microsoft FrontPage Website** heading, select the check box next to the item you would like to sell.

    (If you haven't yet sold anything through your FrontPage Web site, you'll need to sign up by clicking the **Sign-Up** link under the **My Microsoft FrontPage Website** heading.)

    The terms and conditions of the marketplace are displayed.

2. Read the details, and then click **Continue**.

    The Select Products page is displayed.

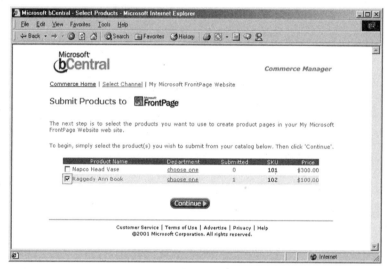

Figure 8-11.
One Commerce Manager catalog item has been specified for sale through a Microsoft FrontPage Web site.

3. Select the check box next to the name of the item you want to sell (you can select multiple items if you want). If you haven't yet selected a Department for selling the item, click to choose one link for that item. Then click **Continue**.

    A Confirmation page appears asking you to confirm that you want the item to be posted for sale.

4. Click **Continue**.

You automatically return to the Seller Console, where you can list other items if you'd like to.

5. Return to the FrontPage window.

You can bring the FrontPage window to the front of your desktop by clicking its program window, clicking its taskbar button, pressing ALT+TAB, or by opening FrontPage from the **Start** menu if it is not already open.

6. On the **Tools** menu, point to **E-commerce**, and then click **E-commerce Wizard**.

The wizard opens and displays the categories you identified for your products.

7. Click **Next**.

8. On the next page of the wizard, click **Finish**.

The **Generating Templates** message appears, followed by the **bCentral Commerce Manager Add-In** message, which asks you if you would like to view your e-commerce pages in your browser.

9. Click **No**.

(Don't worry — if you click **Yes**, your browser will open and display the pages you've created. You can then switch back to FrontPage and continue the steps that follow. Click **No** now so you can stay in FrontPage and see the files that FrontPage has created.)

10. On the **Views** bar, click **Folders**.

The Folder List opens. Notice that two new folders have been added to the files in the current web: Catalog and Catalog Templates. Within the Catalog folder, you'll find subfolders, one for each product category you identified earlier.

11. Open one of the subfolders in the Catalog folder, and then double-click one of the product pages to view the catalog page that FrontPage generated.

The name of the page is the same as the product name — in the example below, I opened a file named Marcella — a Raggedy Ann Story to view the item's Web page.

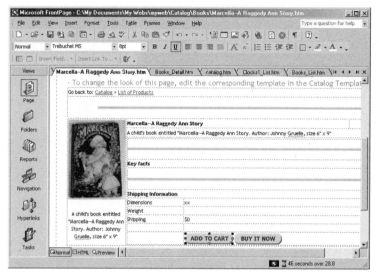

Figure 8-12.

FrontPage creates catalog Web pages, complete with a shopping cart and Buy buttons, based on products you list with bCentral.

What can you do with the product pages you've created? Publish them on your existing FrontPage Web site and start selling.

When a customer opens a product page and clicks the **Add to Cart** button, their selection is placed on the shopping cart page hosted for you on bCentral's Web servers. When your customer checks out, they see their cart and its contents.

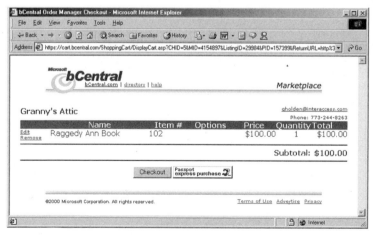

Figure 8-13.

Your FrontPage Web site uses this shopping cart, where customers verify their purchases before submitting payment.

Once shoppers review the selections in their cart, they can move to the check out by clicking the **Checkout** button (or, if they have a Microsoft Passport, the **Passport express purchase** button). The check out process is described in detail in Chapter 9.

Adding to or Changing Your Catalog

If you want to add more catalog items to a marketplace or auction site, follow the steps outlined in this chapter for marketplaces or auctions.

If you want to add or delete a catalog listing on your FrontPage Web site (because — we hope — it's been sold) you need to run the E-commerce Wizard again to regenerate all of your catalog pages. If you edit any of the product descriptions on bCentral, you also need to run the E-commerce Wizard to generate new pages with the updated information and to regenerate the old pages.

Technical Tip

Any changes you make to your sales product Web pages should be made to the templates in the Catalog Templates folder, not the Catalog folder. Each time you run the E-commerce Wizard, you regenerate the files in the Catalog Folder, thus deleting previous versions.

You might also want to sell an item that has special features not covered by bCentral's product details and that you need to highlight. In that case, you can use the **Custom Fields** option on the **Insert Field** drop-down list on the E-commerce toolbar.

This option inserts a software utility called a *bot* in your catalog page. The bot outputs custom fields for certain product categories, such as computers or televisions. For instance, if you sell a TV product, the custom fields might include the screen size (such as 24-inch or 27-inch) or whether the device offers HDTV resolution.

Chapter 9

Accepting Online Payments

You are used to receiving payment for your goods and services in the form of checks, purchase orders, or even cash. And chances are you already do accept credit card payments in your bricks-and-mortar business. But only one e-commerce feature really counts toward your bottom line — getting customers to select your goods and services and then follow through with completed sales.

As a small business owner, you don't want to worry about potential liability resulting from hackers who manage to steal your customers' credit card numbers. Even if you already have a *merchant account* — an account with a financial institution that enables you to accept credit card payments — you don't have the time to worry about verifying each customer's information and processing the payments. Microsoft bCentral gives you the option of never having to deal directly with people's credit card numbers or even having them anywhere near your in-house computers or computers you own. In this chapter, you learn how bCentral enables you to accept payments from customers who submit their credit card information to you online.

Business Tip

Credit card purchases are the safest and most popular mechanism for handling
online transactions. According to the Gartner Group, they make up 93 percent of all
online transactions.

bCentral's Order Manager is part of its Commerce Manager system for selling goods and services online. Order Manager gives you two ways to handle credit card payments:

- Order Manager notifies you when a credit card payment is made. You then process the information you receive from the customer manually by using your current credit card payment service.

- Order Manager, through bCentral's partner Cardservice International, receives the payment and validates the credit card with the credit card vendor, and Cardservice International transfers the funds to your account.

Business Tip

If you already have a merchant account and have signed up with credit card companies to receive payments from their customers, you can still use Order Manager to process payments, but you have to process orders manually. To get the benefit of automatic payment processing, you need to sign up with Cardservice International. You might consider switching to Cardservice or obtaining an additional merchant account with Cardservice to manage your bCentral transactions automatically.

In either case, bCentral's Order Manager handles the processing of orders for you. In this chapter, we'll step through setting up to accept credit card payments. Tracking and processing orders is covered in Chapter 10.

Using bCentral to Process Credit Card Payments

In Chapter 8, you learned how to create a catalog of products that's connected to a database on bCentral which stores product information. These pages have **Add to Cart** buttons on them in order for you to use bCentral's shopping cart and check out system to handle customer purchases from your catalog.

The bCentral checkout page consists of a series of forms, such as the one shown in Figure 9-1.

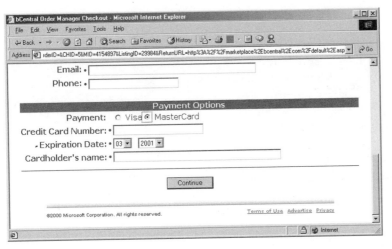

Figure 9-1.

Shoppers can submit credit card and personal information by using bCentral's secure server — note the "closed lock" security icon on the browser's status bar.

The first form requires the shopper to type their billing information. The second asks for shipping and credit card information. The third returns the data back to the shopper for confirmation so the purchase can be made.

When the customer confirms the purchase information and submits the information to bCentral, Order Manager notifies you that the purchase has been made. You then have to process the credit card information yourself, unless you've signed up with Cardservice International to do the work for you.

As a bCentral customer, you can choose one of two options for using the credit card services offered by Cardservice International:

- **Almost-free "Nano Merchant" processing.** Cardservice International will process credit card purchases free if bCentral customers have 10 or fewer sales each month. The company does charge 3.5 percent of each transaction plus 50 cents per transaction.

- **Monthly-fee "Merchant" processing.** If you opt to pay a $19.95 per month fee, Cardservice International will charge you a 2.35 percent discount fee per transaction and a $0.20 per-transaction fee. You have to choose this option if you have more than 10 sales per month.

In either case, Cardservice International processes customer data through its secure server using SSL, and handles the processing and verification of the credit card information.

Technical Tip

When you use Order Manager to store customer orders, the information resides not on one of your computers, but on one of bCentral's. By locating your customer information on the host's server, you don't have to worry about securely storing the information on your own computers. You do trade off some control, but you gain convenience: Because the information is online, you can access it from any computer with a Web browser, either in your office or while you're on the road.

bCentral Commerce Manager account holders can use Cardservice International to process the following credit cards:

- Visa
- MasterCard
- American Express
- Discover

Business Tip

You can accept payments only with Visa and MasterCard if you use the Nano Merchant service.

The following steps lead you through obtaining an account with bCentral's partner, Cardservice International. You need to know the type of account you want to start and have a check from the checking account you want credited. After following these few steps, you'll be able to proclaim on your site that you can accept credit card payments.

Supplementing Traditional Payments with a Cardservice Account

Maria Kinsey, the owner of a bCentral-hosted store called The Meandering Path (http://www.themeanderingpath.com), which is profiled in Chapter 1, already had a merchant account with Cardservice International before she decided to accept online payments. She processes payments for garden tools and accessories in her office the old fashioned way. "I have a LinkPoint 3000 terminal, as well as one of the old 'knuckle busters,'" she says.

But because there is no way to integrate the traditional payment system with payments received online, Maria decided to apply for an additional account with Cardservice so she could accept credit card payments online. "I wouldn't make any sales if I could not assure customers that processing would be instant and secure," she comments.

To set up credit card payments:

1. From your bCentral My Marketplace page (http://commerce.bcentral.com/catalog), scroll down the list of links on the left-hand side. Under the **My Settings** category, click **Edit Payment**.

   The Order Manager Payment Type page is displayed.

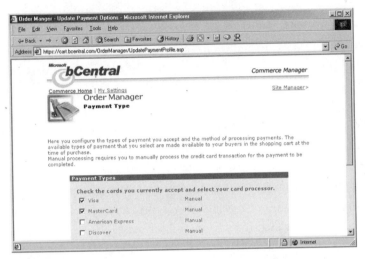

Figure 9-2.
This Order Manager Payment Type page lets you specify which credit cards you want to accept and begin the process of signing up for a merchant account with Cardservice International.

2. Scroll down to the paragraph near the bottom of the page that begins "If you do not have a way to process credit cards already bCentral already has low cost solutions," and then click the **Click here for details** link.

   The My Settings – Online Payment Processing page is displayed.

3. Click the **Sign Up Now** link next to the option you want.

4. Select the service you want to use. You can apply either as a business or as an individual.

5. In the online application dialog box, fill out the forms to sign up with Cardservice International.

   Be sure to print out the completed application form when you reach the end of the process.

You receive an e-mail from Cardservice International acknowledging the information has been received and providing you with further instructions on activating your account. In Chapter 10, we will go over how you process orders made through Cardservice International.

Not Ready for Online Payments?

Your customers probably have no reluctance to pay you when the transaction occurs face-to-face. You also have no reluctance accepting cards and numbers from individuals when they are right across the sales counter from you. When you're online, however, both you and your customers face uncertainties.

To make things easier for both you and your customers, provide options to replace or supplement credit card payment.

- **Take Telephone or Fax Orders.** Include your phone number and the hours you are available (including your area code and time zone) to take credit card orders via telephone or fax.

- **Offer an Online Payment Broker.** An online payment broker, such as PayPal, enables shoppers to buy items through a third-party who either debits their bank account (with what is called an electronic check) or debits their credit card. Numerous auction sites use PayPal (http://www.paypal.com), including eBay.

- **Support Electronic Wallet Services:** A wallet on the Internet, or e-wallet, performs a function similar to a traditional wallet. When an e-wallet carrier makes a purchase on a site that supports the e-wallet, the information stored in the wallet is passed to the site. Two of the better-known wallets are Microsoft Passport (http://www.passport.com) and Yahoo! Wallet (http://wallet.yahoo.com). Encourage customers to obtain their own wallet so they can shop with you more easily by linking to MasterCard International's e-wallet program (http://www.mastercard.com/shoponline/e-wallets).

Learn More

You can use Microsoft Passport to further streamline the shopping process for your customers. By implementing Passport on your site, you can have customers enter their Passport username and password rather than their detailed account information. At this writing, there's no fee for becoming a Passport merchant, though an annual license fee is planned for the future. To find out how to license Passport so you can use it on your business's Web site, visit http://www.passport.com/Business/Default.asp.

You might also encourage shoppers to pay you by using a credit card number especially generated for that transaction alone. American Express offers a new shopping option called Private Payments. Customers who purchase online using their American Express cards submit a special, one-time-use card number to make a purchase. American Express processes the payment and the number is then destroyed. Find out more at http://www26.americanexpress.com/privatepayments/info_page.jsp.

Chapter 10

Managing Sales and Customer Contacts

As an online merchant, making a sale is guaranteed to put a big smile on your face. (You'll be even happier when your new customer makes a subsequent purchase and sends you a glowing letter of approval.) But it is at the point of purchase that your customer gets the most anxious. This is no time to leave your customer hanging in suspense.

Think about it. To this point, you've done everything you can to help guide your customer to the point of sending in payment. You've used the Microsoft bCentral Commerce Manager Add-in for Microsoft FrontPage to create catalog pages. You've used the Add-in to generate pages that have Buy buttons and shopping cart functionality. You've published those pages on bCentral, where people can use the cart and Buy buttons to send you payment securely, and Order Manager has notified you of the sale.

This isn't enough to calm shoppers' uncertainties about shopping online, or their need for instant gratification. Customers want a quick confirmation that the order has been received. They want to know when the item will ship. Web customers don't like to wait for anything — especially deliveries.

Not to worry — once you sign up for a hosting account with bCentral or sell items by using Commerce Manager, you can also use Order Manager to track orders and send out notifications at critical stages to both you and your customers.

In this chapter, you'll learn to use bCentral's Order Manager to:

- Calculate shipping costs
- Calculate sales tax
- Process orders
- Manage customer relationships

Responding to Incoming Orders

How do you know when someone has placed an order over the Internet? There are two basic options:

- Receive an e-mail from your e-commerce provider.
- Periodically check the order directory on your Web site.

If you have a person responsible for checking order receipts, you may not need e-mail notification. If you're a one-person operation and you're frequently out of the office, an e-mail notification service can prove helpful.

Setting Up E-mail Notification

Order Manager is set up to notify you when an order is received. But it's a good idea to verify that your customers are notified, too.

To set up e-mail notification:

1. Go to the My Marketplace page (http://commerce.bcentral.com/catalog), and then click **Edit Notification** under the **My Settings** heading on the left-hand side of the page.

   The Order Manager – Notification Settings page is displayed.

2. Select one of the **Confirmation e-mail** check boxes.

   You can choose to receive e-mail when an order comes and that your customers receive e-mail to confirm an order.

3. Click **Continue**.

   The My Settings – Company Profile page is displayed.

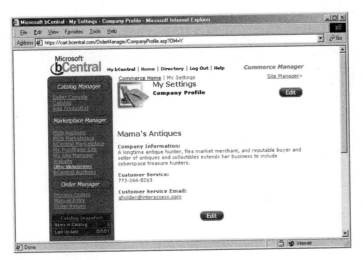

Figure 10-1.

Whenever you change how your online store presents information to your customers, this page is displayed so you can edit your company profile if you need to.

4. Click **Edit** to change the information shown on the My Settings – Company Profile page.

The My Settings – Company Profile Settings page is displayed.

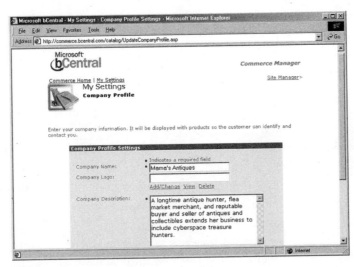

Figure 10-2.

This Company Profile Settings form contains your current description so you can edit it.

5. Edit the description by deleting text or typing new text, and then click **Continue**.

The My Settings – Company Profile page displays your new description.

Case Study: Processing Orders with Individual Attention

Dave Hagan, Jr. never lets his many work responsibilities stand in the way of giving customer orders the personal touch. He not only used FrontPage to set up a Web site for his tool supply company, General Tool & Repair, Inc. of York, Pennsylvania, but he's the president of York Internet Services, a Web site design company. General Tool & Repair's online sales catalog (http://www.gtr.com) includes 120,000 individual items that generate between 10 and 40 orders daily. When customers submit orders, employees are often notified by e-mail. In addition, several times a day, Dave joins his four employees in checking his computer directory for orders.

Dave then processes those orders himself by using a software product called Authorizer by Atomic Software (http://www.atomic-software.com). Authorizer helps check the shipping and billing addresses supplied with the order to reduce the chance of fraud (see Chapter 8). Authorizer then contacts the company's bank through a modem and transmits the sale information. The bank can't tell whether the purchase is from a card swipe or from the Internet, so it charges General Tool & Repair a lower discount rate (1.7 percent) rather than its higher rate for online purchases (3 to 3.5 percent).

By taking the time to process sales individually, Dave is able to do his own fraud checking. If he receives an order where the shipping and billing address are dramatically different, he can e-mail the card owner and notify that person of a potential unauthorized purchase. Customer information is then entered into a database so shoppers can receive notices of upcoming sales and promotions via e-mail.

Orders also get individual attention when it comes to shipping. E-mail communication with each customer helps to determine the best way to ship. Sometimes, the choice of shipper depends on the destination. General Tool & Repair likes to use United Parcel Service to deliver to crowded urban locations because their service includes the option of receiving a signature before delivery. This helps prevent shipments from being lost. The personal attention pays off: Only one in 300 items is returned, Dave reports.

Processing Incoming Orders

Once you have set up Order Manager to provide you with notification, you can wait until e-mail comes in or visit the Order Manager – Process Orders page to see if any orders have come in.

Technical Tip

On the road a lot? Have bCentral send a message to your pager, handheld device, or Web-enabled cell phone when an order arrives.

To process an incoming order:

1. In the notification e-mail message, click the URL in the body of the message.
   Since the customer order information is held on a secure part of the bCentral Web site to protect customer information from unauthorized viewers, your browser goes to the bCentral Login page.

2. Type your username and password in the appropriate boxes, and then click **Log in**.
   The Order Manager – Process Orders page is displayed.
   You see a notification like the one shown below.

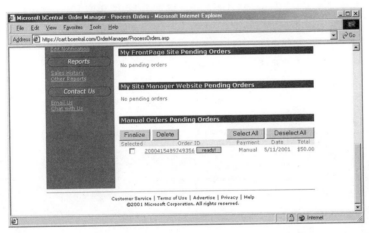

Figure 10-3.
The Order Manager – Process Orders page lists any orders you've received with an Order ID that you can click to view details about your customer and what's being purchased.

3. Click the Order ID of the order that you want to view.
   The Order Manager – Order Detail page for the order is displayed.

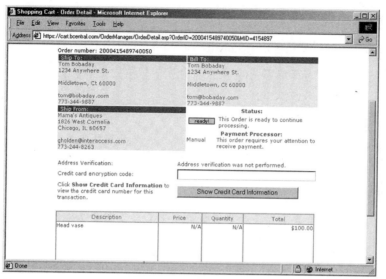

Figure 10-4.

Order Manager displays your customer's billing and shipping information in this easy-to-read format.

4. To view credit card information, enter your encryption code into the **Credit card encryption code** box, and then click the **Show Credit Card Information** button.
   You cannot view credit card information without an encryption code.

Technical Tip

What, you ask, is an encryption code? If you apply for a regular hosting account with bCentral, during the process of obtaining the account you assign yourself an *encryption code* — a sequence of 17 letters and numbers that you create. You store this code in a safe location and use it when you want to view customer credit card information. If you don't have a regular monthly account with bCentral but are using the Commerce Manager Add-in for FrontPage to sell items through bCentral, you can contact customer service to obtain a new encryption code.

5. Review the order details.

6. Once you ship the order out, return to the Order Manager – Process Orders page. Select the **Selected** check box just to the left of the Order ID, and then click the **Finalize** button.
   Order Manager automatically sends e-mail to the customer who placed the order, notifying him or her that the order has shipped. The order's ID number is

removed from the **Pending Orders** list and is stored in a list of finalized orders. A new **Finalized Orders** link appears beneath the **Pending Orders** list.

In addition to finalizing orders once you have filled them, you can perform some other actions from the Order Manager – Process Orders page including:

- **Canceling an order.** Click the **Delete** button next to an order to cancel when a customer orders a discontinued item or asks you to cancel an order before you ship it out.

- **Entering an order manually.** Use this to record orders you receive over the telephone, in person, by fax, or via e-mail.

Entering Order Information Manually

Never lose sight of the need to store customers' credit card and other personal information in a secure place where hackers and thieves can't reach it. The ideal location is a server that uses encryption to store the information and that is physically separated from your own computers. bCentral gives you such a location.

Suppose you receive credit card information and shipping/billing addresses over the phone or by fax. In addition to filing the information in a physical location, such as a filing cabinet, you'll probably want to store it in a computer database as well. You don't have to use your own computers to store the information, however. To protect yourself and your customers, you can manually enter the information on one of bCentral's secure servers using Order Manager. In addition to the extra security, performing manual entry with Order Manager sends automatic e-mail notifications to customers, telling them that you have received their order information.

To enter billing and shipping information manually:

1. On the Seller Console page (http://commerce.bcentral.com/catalog), under the **Order Manager** heading, click **Manual Entry**.

    The Order Manager – Manual Entry page is displayed.

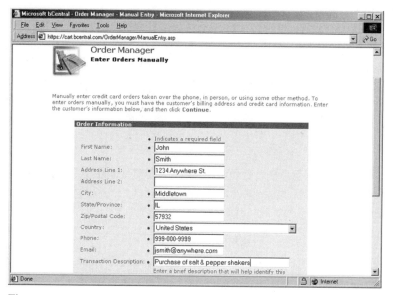

Figure 10-5.

Recording your customer purchase information manually takes a few minutes, but it protects customer privacy while reducing your liability.

2. Fill in your customer purchase information, including the credit card type, number, and expiration date, and then click **Continue**.

    The Order Manager – Process Orders page is displayed. Under the **Manual Orders Pending Orders** heading, the order appears with an Order ID assigned to it.

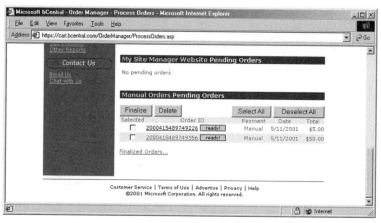

Figure 10-6.

Return to this Order Manager page when you want to review order information you've entered manually.

3. Click the manually entered order's Order ID number to review the customer's personal information.

The Order Manager – Orders Details page appears and displays the information you just entered. Like the Order Detail page shown earlier (see Figure 10-4), this page does not automatically display the customer's credit card number. You need to enter your encryption code in the **Credit card encryption code** box on this page, and then click the **Show Credit Card Information** button to view the number. It's an extra level of security for your customers.

Using Your Existing Merchant Account for Credit Card Payments

If you already use a credit card service and have a merchant account with your bank, you can use Order Manager to help you process the payments you receive from online customers. It's up to you to handle the manual processing of the actual payment — you enter the credit card number into a point-of-sale device such as a credit card terminal. The terminal transmits the data to the payment-processing network used by your bank as usual.

Here's the sequence of events: When a shopper submits credit card information to you by clicking the **Buy** button and filling out the forms provided on your bCentral site, Order Manager sends you an e-mail notification that a purchase has been received.

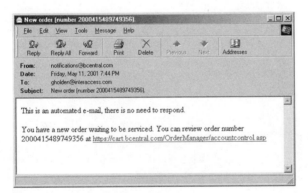

Figure 10-7

Order Manager sends you an e-mail that contains a link to a page on bCentral where you can view the purchase information.

When you click on the link contained in the e-mail, you log on to bCentral. Your browser goes to a secure page where the customer information is displayed. In order to view the customer's credit card information, you are required to enter an encryption code as described earlier in the "Processing Incoming Orders" section.

Handling Returns

Returns are an important part of doing business, both online and off. Of course we hope you won't have many returned purchases to deal with, but you need to process the transaction fairly and quickly to maintain customer satisfaction.

You don't have to refund the customer's money in full when they return an item. If the product is in good working order and the only reason for the return is that the customer has changed his or her mind, you might charge a fee for your time, trouble, and shipping costs.

Order Manager gives you the ability to process returns for any amount, up to the total cost of the order, by following a few quick steps:

1. From either your bCentral Seller Console page or the Order Manager – Process Orders page, under the **Order Manager** heading on the left-hand-side of the page, click **Order Return**.

   Your browser displays the Order Manager – Order Return page.

2. Enter the Order ID and the amount you want to return to the customer in the appropriate boxes, and then click **Continue**.

   The Order Manager – Order Return page reappears with a message stating that the return was successfully recorded.

Technical Tip

It's up to you to see that the customer's money is returned. Order Manager doesn't actually mail a check back to the customer. Recording the return in your Order Manager database ensures that your records are accurate, however.

Calculating Sales Tax

The question of whether online merchants should charge sales tax for the items they sell is constantly being debated. Check with your state's Department of Revenue or your attorney for advice. If you do decide to charge sales tax, you can have Order Manager add the tax to your customer invoices.

To calculate sales tax:

1. On the Seller Console or Order Manager – Process Orders page, under the **My Settings** heading on the left side of the page, click **Edit Tax** to open the My Settings – Edit Tax page, which you use to specify tax rates.

2. To add the sales tax to the invoices, select the state from the **States** list.
   The state's name is selected.

3. Click the **Edit** button.
   The **Enter Tax Info** dialog box opens.

4. Type the tax rate for the selected state, and then click **Submit**.
   The **Enter Tax Info** dialog box closes.

5. Click **Continue**.
   The My Settings – Company Profile pages appears and you can edit your company's description if needed.

Business Tip

bCentral recommends that you follow the tax procedures advocated by groups such as the nonprofit Internet Consumers Organization (ICO). The ICO believes that Internet sales should be treated and taxed no differently than mail and telephone sales orders, with retail merchants collecting taxes on Internet sales only if the merchant lives or works in the same state where the purchaser lives. You can keep up with the latest news on the Internet sales tax question at the NetSalesTax.Net site (http://www.netsalestax.net).

Adding Shipping Rates

Shipping rates are difficult to calculate because they change often and because they vary depending on the purchaser's geographic location. But if you use bCentral, Order Manager keeps track of these changes and calculates shipping costs automatically.

Business Tip

Before you follow the steps, you'll need to have the typical shipping charge on hand or obtain it from your shipping service(s) of choice. You can have bCentral help you calculate shipping charges through its affiliation with http://www.iShip.com. Go to the bCentral Shipping page (http://www.bcentral.com/marketplace/ship.asp). Follow the instructions on the page to quickly calculate typical shipping rates for destinations around the country.

To add shipping rates:

1. Log on to bCentral. When the My bCentral page appears, click **Manage incoming orders**.
   The Order Manager – Process Orders page is displayed.

2. Under the **My Settings** heading on the left side of the page, click **Edit Shipping**. The My Settings – Edit Shipping page is displayed.

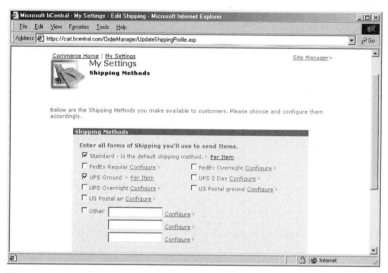

Figure 10-7.

Enter the shipping amount here for each of the options you give your customers, and Order Manager automatically adds the cost to each order you receive.

3. Click **Per Item** next to the **Standard** check box. You need to specify whether your default shipping charge is calculated on a "per item" or "per order" basis.

    Another page entitled My Settings – Edit Shipping appears.

4. Select one of the shipping options, and then click **Continue**.

    You return to the previous page.

5. Select the check box next to each of the shipping methods you use to send merchandise out to your customers. For each method, click **Configure** to specify the "up charge" you typically add to an order for shipping.

6. When you are done, click **Continue**.

    The My Settings – Company Profile page is displayed so you can edit your company description if you want to.

Any shipping methods you select are presented to the customer when he or she enters a shipping method after clicking **Add to Cart** and then clicking **Checkout** on one of your catalog pages:

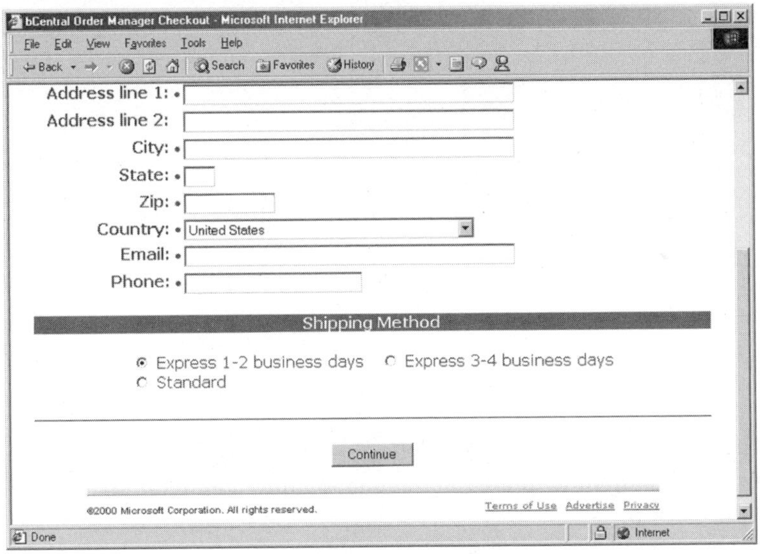

Figure 10-8.
Your shipping options are displayed on the same bCentral page that enables the customer to enter shipping information.

When Order Manager presents you with the order information submitted by the customer (as described in the following section), it will automatically add the shipping charge to the purchase price. When you e-mail a confirmation note to the customer, the shipping charge will be displayed as a line item so the customer is aware of all the charges.

Business Tip

It's a nice touch to add links to the online tracking services of the shippers you use. Your customers can go to the shipping services' Web sites and see where their orders are. FedEx's online tracking service is the best known (http://www.fedex.com/us/tracking), but United Parcel Service (http://www.ups.com/tracking/tracking.html) and Airborne Express (http://track.airborne.com/) provide similar services, as well.

Chapter 11

Testing Your Site Before the Doors Open

Beginning with your idea to create an e-commerce Web site, up to the happy moment when your catalog items went onto a Web server, you've spent many hours in planning and execution. You have assembled your site, presented your merchandise in the form of an online catalog, and set up payment and fulfillment systems. You're probably eager to get online and start selling. But first, take a deep breath before you open the doors of your online store. You need to face the shocking fact that all of your work can be undone in a matter of seconds if you fail to catch mistakes before your site goes online. A little testing to make sure your site works correctly will make your efforts pay off.

Technical Note

You might have as little as *four* seconds to get your message across. ZDNet's Best Practices site (http://www.zdnet.com/ecommerce/filters/sublanding/0,10385,6006111,00.html) suggests that if a Web page's contents take longer than four seconds to load in their entirety, visitors will go somewhere else.

Take a look at your e-commerce site through the eyes of your customers. They're not designers or programmers who are waiting to be wowed by your technical gimmicks. Most don't have fast DSL or cable modem connections. You'll reach the widest possible audience when your site is error-free and quick to load. To ensure everything works right, test your site before opening for business.

In this chapter you'll get some pointers on trying out your site before anyone else does:

- You'll identify some common problems that first-time e-business owners often confront.

- You'll learn about the importance of making sure your pages load well in different browsers.

- You'll test your site thoroughly and make sure everything works right before you open your doors and invite your customers to start shopping.

Learn more

The ZDNet article "Performance Primer: Gone in 4 Seconds" cites a survey done by the Web site host and content delivery network Digital Island. You can read the article in its entirety at http://www.zdnet.com/ecommerce/stories/main/0,10475,2682126,00.html. About.com has a series of articles and tips about testing your site for functionality (http://webdesign.about.com/compute/webdesign/library/weekly/aa042601b.htm).

Taking Your Site for a Test Drive

Making a good visual impression ranks high on your list of e-commerce goals. However, along with making sure your site looks good, you also need to be aware of some mistakes you should avoid, including:

- Overcrowded pages that download too slowly.
- Background colors that make text unreadable.
- Images that aren't cropped properly.
- Distracting sounds that play in the background.
- Web page contents that are supported by only one browser.

In addition to these general deficiencies, there are some specific rules that apply to your content:

- Do basic proofreading to catch errors in spelling or grammar.
- Make sure your text can be easily read on a computer screen — make sure the type contrasts adequately with the background and that the font size is big enough.

- Test links and scripts to make sure they function the way they should.

- Check facts to make sure all your statements are accurate.

Learn more

Check out sites that call attention to bad Web design such as Web Pages That Suck (http://www.webpagesthatsuck.com). On the flip side, visit Good Practices (http://goodpractices.com/) to get some tips about what you should be doing with your site, including testing.

When Should You Test Your Site?

At what point should you begin inviting selected "test users" to click your links, load your pages, and evaluate whether everything appears and works the way it should?

You have several options:

- You can perform some in-house "quality assurance" testing when your site is still on your computer and hasn't gone online.

- You can do some testing of content-related issues. Spelling, grammar, links, size of graphics, and similar issues can be spotted as soon as a page is completed.

- You can test the site after you move your pages from your computer to your Web server.

There's no single right answer to the question of when to test, but, in general, the best practice is to test at a number of stages. You definitely need to test your site after moving your files to the server to make sure everything arrived and is working the way it should. Testing your site before people start to visit it is essential. It's also important to keep testing and evaluating your site on an ongoing basis so you can make improvements.

Technical Tip

What's the difference between "going online" and "opening the doors of your e-commerce site?" In fact, the two events might be the same. The moment your Web pages are published on a Web server, they are online. But there are different kinds of servers: A testing server is one that exists on your own computer. Your test server can run Personal Web Server, for instance. After you do the testing, publish your files. Then, test on the remote server. If all parts of your site (including your catalog, shopping cart, and purchasing forms) are online and functioning smoothly, you're open for business. However, if you publish the site to a special directory you create for test purposes, whose URL only you know, you might be online but not open for business. You can also keep your doors "closed" while you test your site by only publishing your site's textual pages while holding back the e-commerce pages for testing.

Web site testing encompasses several vital practices:

- Content testing
- Functional testing
- Load testing
- Benchmarking

Content Testing

Once you have come up with a navigational structure for your site, written your text, added images, and made links, you can do content testing. It's often helpful to ask someone else to proofread and evaluate your work to make sure your spelling and grammar are clear. But either you or an assistant can do fact-checking to make sure your statements are accurate.

Functional Testing

In functional testing, you make sure everything works right — your images appear, your links lead to the proper sites, and your forms submit data where they need to and return confirmation pages as needed. You also need to evaluate the purchasing process. Do the Buy buttons work correctly? Are your products each ready to purchase? You might actually consider buying something from your own site to test this out.

Load Testing and Benchmarking

Some aspects of Web site testing are highly technical and best left to professionals. Load testing is only done with specialized software that evaluates how well your site can handle many customers at once. You can hire a service like Testpros.com (http://www.testpros.com) to conduct load testing on your site using its specialized testing software. But make sure you have permission from your Web host to do the testing first.

In benchmarking, either you or your testing service establishes a benchmark that represents the type of performance you consider acceptable. You should try to stick to this as your site grows in complexity and popularity.

Getting Help from FrontPage

Microsoft FrontPage provides you with one of the simplest ways to test your site before it goes online. By switching to Reports view, you can check for broken links, images that don't appear, pages that take too long to open, and other problems.

Here's how to get started:

1. Open the Web you want to test, and then, from the **View** menu, choose **Reports**, then **Site Summary**.

   The Site Summary report appears in the main part of the FrontPage window and the Reports toolbar opens.

2. On the Reports toolbar, from the **Reports** drop-down menu, select one of the following options to view a specific aspect of your site's contents: **Files**, **Problems**, **Workflow**, or **Usage**.

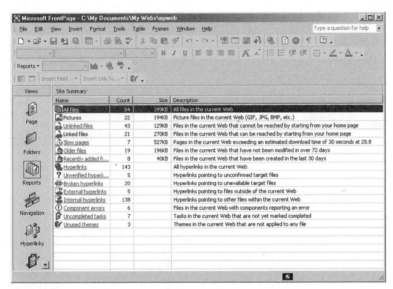

Figure 11-1.

FrontPage's Site Summary report includes lists of broken links, slow pages, and other problems you should fix before your site goes "live."

Checking Links

Links that don't go where they should make your site look unprofessional. You don't want a customer to click on a link and turn up a generic "File Not Found" page rather than the catalog, customer service, or other page they're expecting to find.

You can use the Site Summary report to track down links that don't work. After you create your site, switch to Reports view, and then open the Site Summary report.

Technical Tip

You can also verify an individual hyperlink at any time if you're working in Normal view — right-click the hyperlink, and then choose **Verify** from the submenu.

To check links:

1. Click the **Broken hyperlinks** link in the **Name** column of the Site Summary report.

   A list of all the hyperlinks in your site appears. At the same time, the **Reports View** dialog box opens and asks if you want to verify your site's links. Before FrontPage can accurately report any hyperlinks that don't work, it has to verify the links — that is, check them to make sure they go to the right locations on your site.

2. Click **Yes**.

   FrontPage checks the links one by one. Any broken links are identified with the label **Broken**. Links that work are labeled **OK**.

3. If you want to repair a link that is broken, double-click the link's path in the list of links.

   The **Edit Hyperlink** dialog box opens.

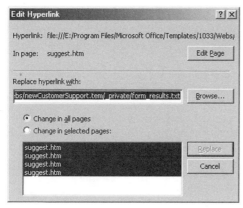

Figure 11-2.

*Repair a link that doesn't work by selecting a new page as the destination in the **Edit Hyperlink** dialog box.*

4. You fix a link shown in the **Edit Hyperlink** dialog box by clicking **Edit Page** to display the page that contains the link in Page view. You can also click **Browse** to locate a file in your Web that you want to select as the destination for the link.

5. Click **Replace**.

   FrontPage edits the link and closes the **Edit Hyperlink** dialog box. You can then repair other links listed in Reports view if you want to.

Technical Tip

Some of your site's performance isn't up to you. It has to do with the performance and reliability of your Web hosting service, and that's something you can only evaluate over a period of time, after your site has been operating for a while. It has to do with how often you encounter service outages or how slow your server is. See Chapter 17 for more on managing your site's performance.

Testing on Multiple Browsers

Smart Web designers test out their own Web pages by being the first to open them in Microsoft Internet Explorer and Netscape Navigator to make sure that the contents will look good to most, if not all, users. The two browsers are used by more than 99 percent of all Web surfers, according to a February 21, 2001 report by StatMarket (http://www.statmarket.com).

Table 11-1

Browser	Usage Share
Internet Explorer	87.71 percent
Netscape Communicator	12.01 percent
Other Browsers	0.27 percent

Learn More

BrowserWatch regularly reports which browsers are used to visit its own site as well as the much more extensive internet.com Web site. Check out this set of information at Stats Station (http://browserwatch.internet.com/stats/icstats.html).

Browsers often display some Web contents very differently. Typefaces might be different; graphics might be in a slightly different position; and some contents that are created with programming languages that are recognized by one browser might not be visible in another.

In addition to differences in browser display, different monitors and computers show Web pages with different resolutions and slight variations in color. In an ideal situation, you would have a network of computers, running both Macintosh and Microsoft Windows system software, which you could use to view your pages before they are published on the Internet.

Most likely, you only have one or two computers at your disposal. In that case, you need to make sure you have several browsers installed. Ideally, you need to view your site both on a PC running Windows and on a Macintosh. At the most basic level, fonts that are readable on one computer/browser combination might appear in a different font with another browser, or in yet another font or different size on another platform. On another level, technical features like Java applets, Cascading Style Sheets, and XML are handled differently depending on the browser and platform.

Learn More

The Browsers Toolbox area of Webtools (http://www.webtools.com/toolbox/browsers) has lots of information on different browsers and how to design your pages for them. WebReview.com has a Browser Compatibility Chart that illustrates in detail how programs differ depending on the features they encounter (http://www.webreview.com/browsers/browsers.shtml).

Testing with the Most Popular Browsers in Mind

Making sure your Web site appears more or less consistent in the browsers your customers are likely to use primarily involves staying away from things that might not show up the same in those programs. But first, make sure you're taking all the browsers into account. Don't just focus on Internet Explorer and Netscape Communicator. America Online's (AOL) browser is likely to be the lens through which many visitors view your online store — not just on the Web but also on a handheld device such as a PDA. Microsoft's Web TV Networks provides another way for potential customers to access your site. If you don't have Web TV yourself, either sign up for an account or visit a store where Web TV is sold — try it out by accessing your own site right in the store.

Technical Tip

Also remember that a small proportion of your audience uses Web clients other than the ones mentioned above. They may also choose less popular programs like NCSA Mosaic, Opera, or Ibrowse, or a non-graphical browser called Lynx, whose patrons prefer to receive only textual data rather than having to wait for graphics to appear.

At a minimum, find friends or co-workers with other browsers, such as Netscape Navigator, on their computers and view your pages in their browsers. If you have more than one computer, set up different browsers on each computer. Table 11-2 lists some Web sites where you can run your pages through a testing process that reports when you have elements that will be problematic in other browsers.

Table 11-2

Site	URL	What It Tests
AnyBrowser.com	http://www.anybrowser.com	You can see how your page looks in different screen sizes, how it looks in different browsers, and whether there are broken links.
HTML Toolbox	http://www.netmechanic.com/cobrands/workz/compat_check.htm	You can see the HTML tags that aren't supported by all the major browsers, and you can check up to 20 Web pages at once.
Web Page Backward Compatibility Viewer	http://www.delorie.com/web/wpbcv.html	You can specify exactly which Web page features you want to test, including marquees, style sheets, frames, and tables.

Web designer Veronica Taylor has developed a Web site that examines differences between the two browsers in detail (http://browsercomparison.esmartweb.com/). If you present information using Web page tables, for instance, expect the cell borders to be a slightly different width and background colors to vary as well.

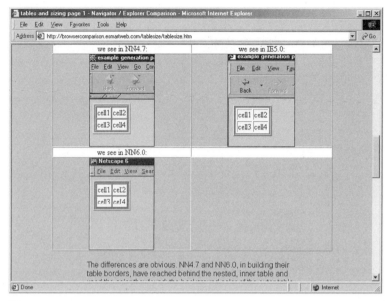

Figure 11-3.
Be aware that tables, backgrounds, text alignment, and page margins may appear differently depending on the browser in which they're displayed.

Learn More

The Webmonkey area of HotWired's Web site contains a detailed and easy-to-read chart that compares the most popular browsers and the Web page features they cover — or don't cover. Check it out at http://hotwired.lycos.com/webmonkey/reference/browser_chart/.

How Long Should You Test?

Web site testing is an ongoing activity that involves reevaluating and improving your site (see Chapter 18). CNET recommends that large-scale e-commerce sites test their services for a month (http://www.builder.com/Business/Ecommerce/ss04c.html). You, however, don't need that long of a time period.

Part 3

Open the Doors to Your Online Store

Chapter 12
Attention-Grabbing Customer Come-Ons

Traffic is usually something you fight through on your way to work. In the case of e-commerce, "traffic" refers to the number of surfers who visit your Web site.

One of your primary goals as an online merchant is to drive visitors to your site. The more visitors you get, the greater your sales. But that's only one benefit of traffic. You may also be able to attract advertising revenue. Sites that generate a high number of visitors are attractive to other sites wanting to reach the same audience.

In this chapter, you will learn about the following ways to market an online business:

- Exchange links with other Web sites.

- Advertise with banner ads on other Web sites.

- List your site in Web directories.

- Become an affiliate of sites that pay for referrals you send them.

Finding Good Company

Affiliating with other merchants whose products your customers might want is a means of bringing in some additional cash to your Web store. You don't have to scour the Web looking for sites that will pay you a commission for pointing customers their way. Once you become a Microsoft bCentral customer, you can earn commissions and referral fees by signing up for Revenue Avenue.

Definition

Affiliate program A program in which one company pays another to promote that company's Web site. Usually, the affiliate does the advertising by placing a banner ad or link on their Web site. When a visitor to the affiliate's site clicks the banner, their browser goes to the originating company's Web site. For each of these Web referrals that leads to a purchase, the affiliate is paid a fee.

Go to the Revenue Avenue page on bCentral's site (http://www.bcentral.com/services/ra/default.asp), and then click **Sign up now**. Your browser displays a list of Web site categories — click a category and browse the sites that participate in the program. When you find a site whose products or services you want to sell, you apply to become an affiliate of that site.

Being an affiliate means you display a button or banner ad for the site you're helping. The commission arrangement varies from site to site — in most cases, you earn a fee if anyone clicks on the button or ad displayed on one of your pages and then purchases something from the site you're advertising. In some cases, you get a commission if someone clicks from your site to the affiliated site and then becomes a registered user.

Putting Billboards on the Web Highway

If you host your site with bCentral, you can subscribe to bCentral's traffic building programs. Used in conjunction with Microsoft FrontPage, bCentral gives you a powerful tool to spread the word about your e-commerce Web site in a number of ways. The program includes:

- Search engine submission
- Link exchange
- Banner ads

- Banner exchange
- Directory listings
- Affiliate programs

Getting Your Site into Search Engines

One of the biggest obstacles facing e-commerce sites is simply getting your name, or a link to your Web site, before the eyes of your potential customers. The Web is an increasingly crowded place to do business. Simply having an easy-to-remember domain name and some compelling content won't do any good if your desired market can't reach you in the first place.

Think about how you find commercial outlets or sources of information on the Internet yourself. Chances are you use a directory that organizes the contents of the entire Internet by category, such as Yahoo! (http://www.yahoo.com). It's also likely that you use a *search engine*, a program that searches for specific documents on the Internet based on keywords or phrases that interest you. A search engine provides you with a simple Web page form where you submit search terms so the search engine's programs can search their databases for Web pages that match what you're looking for. The search engines have indexed the contents of huge numbers of Web pages, and they regularly scour scores of Web sites to keep their databases up-to-date.

To register with a search engine, you fill out a form that provides the search engine with the name and URL of your Web site, along with a short description of your goods and services. After you submit the information, the site sends a special indexing program to record some of your site's content, and then stores the information in the database. Then, customers who use the search engine can find your site when they are searching the Web.

Registering with all of the search engines that index the Internet can be a tedious process. With bCentral's Traffic Builder, you can register the addresses of as many as ten Web pages with your choice of the top 400 search engines and directories. First, go to the Traffic Builder home page (http://www.bcentral.com/tb/default.asp) and click **Pricing and sign-up**. Follow the instructions on the subsequent screens to complete the process. Once you've signed up, you go to the page entitled Promote Your Business Online – Traffic Builder Tutorial page.

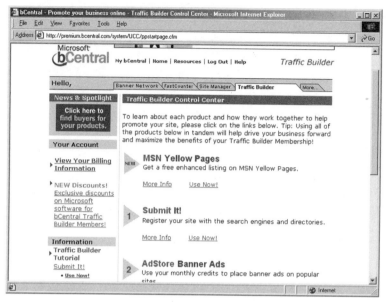

Figure 12-1.

Once you sign up to use Traffic Builder, you can click the Use Now link under the Submit It heading in the Information section to start registering your site with search engines and Internet directories.

The page shown above leads you to a variety of other services designed to increase your business's exposure online. One of the easiest and most effective strategies is similar to registering with search engines: You list yourself with Microsoft MSN Yellow Pages (http://yellowpages.msn.com), which is the directory of Web-based businesses contained on the MSN Web site.

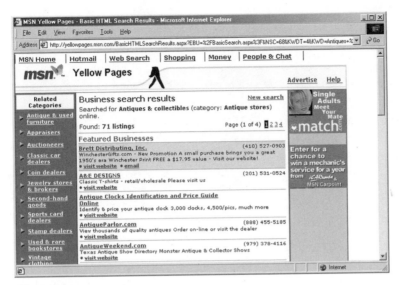

Figure 12-2.

Listing yourself in a popular business directory such as MSN's Yellow Pages enables shoppers to find you through search requests and links.

Making the Most of Keywords

While the content that's on the front of your Web pages is definitely your most important marketing tool, there's also a special kind of "behind the scenes" content you can create to help gain attention for your site. These are *keywords* — special words that you add to the HTML code for your Web pages.

In Chapter 7, you learned about a different use for keywords. When customers need to locate a particular product or other bit of information on your site, they enter keywords that represent the name or part of a description of what they're looking for. When it comes to marketing your online business, the keywords are created by you, not the user. The keywords you create help visitors locate your site from search engines on the Internet.

Learn More

Search engine placement is an important factor in directing traffic to any Web site. Two-day conferences have been held solely on the subject of understanding how search engines work and learning how to make a Web site more visible to them. Search Engine Watch (http://www.searchenginewatch.com) has a department called "Search Engine Submission Tips" that discusses how to create keywords and submit descriptions to search engines. The creator of Search Engine Watch, Danny Sullivan, was interviewed in an article on CNET's Builder.com site (http://www.builder.com/Business/SearchSecrets/). The article contains lots of good tips for making your site easier to find.

Many search engines make use of keywords embedded in the <HEAD> section of a Web page (specifically used with the META tag) when they are scouring their databases to come up with Web pages that correspond to user requests. Your job, as an e-commerce business owner, is to make sure your own site comes up in a search engine's search results as often as possible. You can increase the frequency with which your site is likely to appear by using FrontPage to add keywords to the HTML for your site's home page. You can also add a description of your site to make sure it's described the way you want; some search engines use the descriptions in the results they return to their users.

To add keywords, follow these steps:

1. Write down a number of keywords that describe your site and the goods or services you sell. You can come up with as many words as you want; a sensible range would be six to ten.

2. Start FrontPage, and then open the home page for your e-commerce site.

3. Click the **HTML** tab at the bottom of the FrontPage window to view the HTML source code for the page.

4. Near the top of the page, you see a series of HTML tags that begin with META (such as <meta name="ProgId" content="FrontPage.Editor.Document">). Position the text cursor after one of these tags, press ENTER to move to a new line, and then type the following information (make sure you duplicate the code exactly; don't add any blank spaces except after "keywords" and before the word "content"):

   <meta name="keywords" content="antiques, collectibles, vintage, art deco, watches, jewelry">

   Instead of the keywords shown in the example above, type your own keywords, separating each one by a comma followed by a single blank space.

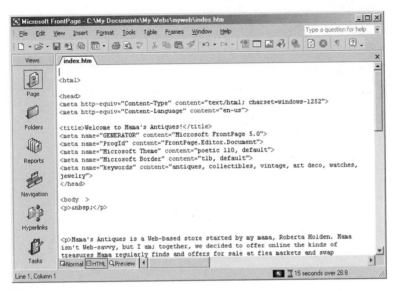

Figure 12-3.
Adding keywords to your HTML helps search engines find your site more frequently.

5. Save your changes. Click the **Preview** tab to preview the page.

You should not see the keywords visible on screen — if you do, go back and check your HTML.

Business Tip

Another program available to bCentral members, KeyWords, automates the process of choosing keywords and writing descriptions. You submit search keywords and descriptions to the search service GoTo, and then suggest an amount you will pay each time someone goes to your page because of a search on GoTo. The higher you bid, the higher your site appears in the search results list. Find out more at http://keywords.bcentral.com.

Exchanging Banner Ads

Ads have kept newspapers and magazines going for many years. The Internet, with its ability to provide interactivity and animation, is proving a fertile ground for developing new approaches to the staid old banner ad.

Some new trends in Web-based advertising take interactivity to a new level. While they're probably a bit expensive and technically complex for you to produce yourself, it's good to know about them because they indicate how hot a medium the Internet is to advertisers and retailers. One new type of ad, an *interstitial*, appears while a requested page is downloading. A *takeover ad* is even more intrusive, using animation to get attention; if the viewer clicks on the ad, it is replaced by a Flash animation that takes over the entire Web page. Pop-up windows and Flash animations are proliferating as advertising tools. There's no doubt that advertising on the Web is becoming big business.

Learn More

Interstitials are discussed in an article on internet.com's Electronic Commerce Guide (http://ecommerce.internet.com/solutions/ectips/article/0,1467,6311_771181,00.html). Takeover ads are described in an article at http://www.turboads.com/richmedia_news/2001rmn/rmn20010516.shtml. The ChannelSeven Web site (http://www.channelseven.com) presents news and trends in online advertising.

Whether you're working with a Web designer to create an animated ad or you are just looking to create a simple banner, ads on the Web work best under certain circumstances:

- **The ads are targeted.** Rather than broadcasting information about an e-commerce business on sites with a wide range of visitors, such as a portal, an effective banner ad is targeted — in other words, it's placed on a page where people are likely to see it.

- **The ads are cost-effective.** Banner advertising on popular Web sites such as Yahoo! can cost thousands of dollars. Often, such advertising drains a dot-com startup's available resources. Don't spend too much on advertising.

To ensure that your banner ad placements are both targeted and cost-effective, you can use bCentral's Link Exchange Banner Network program. Banner Network is accessible either as one of the Traffic Builder services or as a free service. You don't have to sign up for Traffic Builder to use Banner Network, but if you have signed up for Traffic Builder, the following series of steps explains how to get started with the banner exchange program:

1. Under the **BannerNetwork** heading in the **Information** section, click the **Use Now** link.

    The Banner Network – Traffic Builder Banner Advertising page appears.

2. Read the terms of use, and then click **I agree to these terms** at the bottom of the page.

    The Banner Network – Join Form appears.

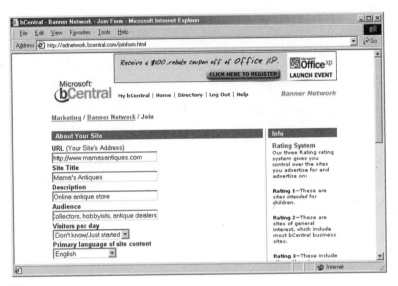

Figure 12-4.

By describing your site's contents and specifying the types of sites with which you want to exchange banners, you target the audience for your online advertisement.

3. Fill out the form with information about your site and the sites you want to advertise on, and then click **Continue**.

   A page appears that presents the information you just entered.

4. When you have read and confirmed that the information is correct, click **Submit**. (If the information is not correct, click your browser's **Back** button to return to the previous screen and make corrections.)

   A page appears with your account information.

5. Click the **Log in** link.

   The Banner Network Statistics Summary page appears.

6. In the **Complete Sign-Up** section, click the **Select your site's content category** link to identify the type of content your site presents, so the banner network service can provide banners that your audience might be interested in.

7. Click **Create and submit your own banner GIF to us** to identify your banner ad.

   It takes a day or two for the banner network service to approve your banner ad and begin placing it on other sites. Return to the Banner Network Statistics Summary page to see if it has been placed and view statistics about how many visitors have seen your ad.

Business Tip

Banner Network's Targeting feature allows you to direct where your banner shows, when it shows, and, to some degree, who can view it. A banner for a site selling a certain magic trick is going to get more interest on other magic sites, fantasy sites, and gift-oriented sites than it would get on a computer hardware site. Be aware, though, that targeting too narrow a field can actually decrease your click-through rate by reducing the population viewing your banner.

Creating Your Banner Ad

A *banner ad* is a rectangular graphic that contains information about a Web business and that is a link to the advertised business's Web site. When a viewer clicks on the ad, his or her browser goes to the site.

The first step is to create the graphic image that serves as your own banner. Although you can make the banner ad any size and shape you want, it's often a good idea to follow the conventional rectangle (about an inch tall and two to four inches wide) to enhance your professional appearance.

Technical Tip

If you want to spread your banner ad far and wide using the bCentral Traffic Builder Banner Network feature, it needs to conform to specific requirements. It must be a GIF file (see Chapter 5 for more on GIF images); it must measure 468 pixels wide by 60 pixels high (which is roughly 6-1/2 inches wide by one inch high); the GIF image must not be transparent; and the file size must be no bigger than 10K.

To create the graphic, you have several options:

- Hire a designer to create the banner ad. Also consider having the designer create a logo for your company.

- Use a graphics program such as Microsoft Image Composer or Paint Shop Pro to make the banner yourself.

- Secure the services of a bCentral customer who volunteers to help others create ads (see http://www.bcentral.com/help/bannermakers.html).

Exchanging Links with Other Sites

Banner ads are only one type of content that you can exchange with other Web sites in order to do cost-effective online advertising. You can also ask other sites to exchange links with you — you'll place a link to their site on your page if they'll place a link to your site on theirs. Such arrangements work especially well if the sites involved complement one another and aren't direct competitors. If you sell antiques, for instance, you might exchange a link with an online publication that discusses collecting and antiques, such as Antiques Bulletin Online (http://www.antiquesbulletin.com).

Create Free Banner Ads

Using the Banner Generator, an online do-it-yourself graphics creation service, you can create a banner for free. This site gives anyone free access to a program that creates banner ads based on your specifications.

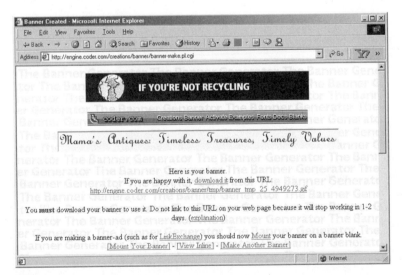

Figure 12-5.
Enter your banner ad text, choose colors and typefaces, and then submit your choices to this Web site's program, which generates a banner for you.

The Banner Generator is itself an e-commerce success story: You don't pay to create graphics because the popular site makes money selling banner ads to advertisers!

Enlisting Your Own Affiliates

Affiliate programs are a way for you to earn money by directing visitors from your site to sites that pay you for sending them business. If you have a few extra dollars to spend, you can turn that around and pay others to send business *your* way, too.

bCentral's marketing program, ClickTrade, enables you to find sites that will affiliate with you. You pay the affiliates if a visitor on their site clicks your ad or makes a purchase from you. ClickTrade handles the payments for you. The Lobster Net, a company that ships live lobsters anywhere in the country (http://www.thelobsternet.com), has more than 1000 affiliates ranging from home and garden sites to gourmet cooking sites.

Reaching Customers with Direct E-mail

E-mail is one of the most popular means of communication using the Internet. Not surprisingly, it's also one of the most effective tools for marketing an e-commerce organization, even though it is easy to overlook in the face of flashier strategies available on the Web.

E-mail can be used to publicize your business in two important ways:

- **Mailing lists.** A *mailing list* is a group of individuals who either receive announcements via e-mail or conduct discussions by exchanging e-mail messages that are shared among the whole group.

Learn More

Creating a mailing list for a group discussion and then moderating and maintaining the list is a lot of work. A number of Web sites will help you set up such a list, including VP Mail (http://list.to/srv/Homepage). Setting up the list is one thing; the really labor intensive aspect is suggesting topics for discussion, keeping discussions on topic, and being an active and regular participant in the list yourself. About.com published a three-step guide to creating your own mailing lists (http://email.miningco.com/internet/email/library/weekly/aa113098.htm) that's a few years old but still relevant today.

- **E-mail newsletters.** An *e-mail newsletter* is a publication distributed to a group of subscribers who submit their names and e-mail addresses to the Web site that produces it.

Don't create a newsletter if your only goal is marketing or assembling a list of e-mail addresses that you can use for soliciting business. Consider creating a newsletter if you really have some useful information or advice that you want to communicate to people. Make sure your newsletter is a value-added feature that provides "insider" tips that visitors won't find on your Web site. You can't use your newsletter to sell directly — if you do, you'll lose subscribers.

Learn More

The best e-mail newsletters give readers a glimpse into trends and tips about a particular industry or Internet technology. Dave Burstein sends out a weekly newsletter called DSL Prime that covers the Digital Subscriber Line (DSL) Internet access industry (http://www.dslprime.com). CNET, the online news service, offers 50 free e-mail newsletters on topics including new software, hardware recommendations, and technology trends (http://www.cnet.com/subscription/0-16335.html?tag=nl_all). Internet.com's ECommerce Guide (http://ecommerce.internet.com/) offers six free newsletters that give daily news headlines, tips, and technical advice.

You can create mailing lists and e-mail newsletters on your own, but you can save time and trouble by using bCentral List Builder. List Builder assists you with the tasks involved in running a mailing list. It is available to you when you subscribe to Traffic Builder.

List Builder helps you create a customizable subscription page so customers can indicate that they want to receive your e-mail announcements or newsletter. The service also helps you keep track of undeliverable e-mail you send and messages asking you to unsubscribe someone from the list. It's up to you to create the newsletters and announcements that you want to send customers. Such e-mails may include news about upcoming sales, special promotions, or breaking developments within your organization.

Business Tip

Don't forget about Usenet newsgroups when you want to publicize yourself or your Web site. Locate groups that discuss topics related to your own area of business. Participate in the groups by providing advice, answering questions, and making suggestions that draw upon your own business expertise. Add the name of your business and the URL of your Web site in your signature. Be careful, though, many newsgroups have rules about blatant advertising.

Chapter 13

Keeping Track of
Your Customers

The Web can be a remarkably personal place despite the fact that individuals use it to share information and conduct sales transactions and never see one another face-to-face. A successful e-commerce business continually gathers data about its shoppers — both those who simply browse and those who go on to make a purchase — to try and get to know them better. Successful research and site management can turn a stagnant e-business into a successful one.

Microsoft FrontPage can provide you with information about your customers through reports of Web activity. FrontPage can also create input forms so your customers can contact you and tell you about who they are, what they think of your Web site, and what they need from you. You don't want information for its own sake, though. You want to analyze and act on it. By learning about who is visiting your Web site and what they are doing while they are in your online store, you can better tailor your goods and services to meet their needs.

Learn More

Need some help interpreting what log file statistics mean for your business? An article called "Beyond the Log" in CIO WebBusiness describes how Northwest Airlines, Andersen Consulting, and other companies track Web site visits to improve their business (http://www.cio.com/archive/webbusiness/100198_main.html). An article called "Evaluating Web Traffic" in Internet World (http://www.internetworld.com/031501/03.15.01webtraffic.jsp) explores new options for tracking Web site usage and applying the knowledge to doing better business online.

Where Do They Go?

The first place to look when you want to find out about the number of visits you've had to your Web site is to check the list of all the site's visitors. Web servers are configured to record every visit made to a Web page, image, or other object on a site. The visits are recorded in an electronic document called a *log file*.

Most Web hosting services let you look at the log file for your Web site. Log files are not a perfect tool for doing market research, but they give you a rough idea of where your visitors are from and which resources on your Web site are the most visited. When used with other strategies described in this chapter, they help you get a good idea of how well your site is working.

Business Tip

If Microsoft bCentral is hosting your site, you can keep track of how many people are visiting by installing FastCounter. You can install FastCounter to visibly display the number of times a particular page has been viewed. When you sign up for FastCounter, you can also ask to receive weekly or monthly e-mails containing information about how often your site has been accessed. FastCounter is free; find out more about it at http://www.bcentral.com/services/fc/default.asp.

Viewing Web Site Logs

Chances are you have to either ask your host to set up log file viewing for you or activate log file viewing; most hosts don't provide the service automatically because log files consume large quantities of disk space.

Once the service is activated, you should be able to view the information in a format that organizes the numbers and makes them easy to read, such as a table or a graph. One of my own Web hosts uses a table to display data.

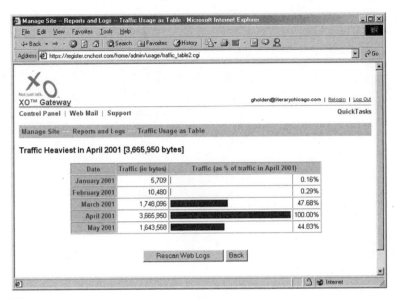

Figure 13-1.

A Web host should present log file information in a format that makes it easy to read and interpret.

If you look at log file information in its "raw" text form, you're probably mystified by page after page of numbers and techie gibberish. Log files typically record information such as the IP address and the domain name of the computer that accesses a Web page. They don't tell you the name and address of the person using the machine at the time. They give you an idea of where the computer is located geographically, based on the suffix at the end of a domain name (such as .de for Germany or .fr for France). They can't tell you more about the individual user.

Many Web hosting services also use log file analysis software that displays the log file in a graphical format you can grasp more quickly. Some companies give you a special URL, such as http://www.mysite.com/reports, to look at your log file.

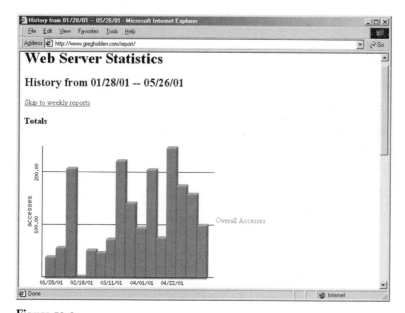

Figure 13-2.
Most Web hosts give personal and business customers the option of viewing access statistics in a
graphical format.

Some hosting services let you choose the options you want to view in your log files.
You can view information for a particular month, week, or other period. You might also
be able to choose options such as:

- **Domain reporting.** Tells you which domains the requests are coming from.

- **File type reporting.** Lets you track the kinds of files that are being accessed —
  whether people are looking at images, text files, and so on.

- **Referrer reporting.** Tells you the site the user was accessing just before coming
  to your site. By tracking referring sites, you can tell which links or ads are
  getting results.

- **Browser reporting.** Lets you track which browsers your customers use. If 90 percent
  use one browser, you can safely consider adding a feature that only that browser
  can display.

Once you have the information from your hosting service, discuss it with your coworkers
and colleagues to see which parts of your Web site are gaining lots of visits and which
aren't. For instance, if a substantial number of visitors come from a particular country,
consider translating content into that country's language.

Adding a Hit Counter

A *hit counter* records the number of visits made to a Web page. The counter resides on the Web server that hosts your Web pages. You make a link to the counter on each page you wanted counted.

For sites hosted on bCentral, you can add a counter to one of your pages free. Your home page is a likely place to put a counter if you will have only one page counted. bCentral's counter is called FastCounter.

To add FastCounter to a page:

1. Go to the FastCounter sign-up page at http://www.bcentral.com/services/fc/default.asp/.

2. Click **Sign up now**.

3. Read the terms of use and click **I agree to these Terms and Conditions**.

4. Enter the URL for your bCentral site, choose the type of counter you want to add, and specify whether you want your statistics to be sent to you weekly or monthly.

5. Click **Submit**.

   The Welcome to Fast Counter page is displayed.

6. To add the counter, copy the HTML code and paste it on the page.

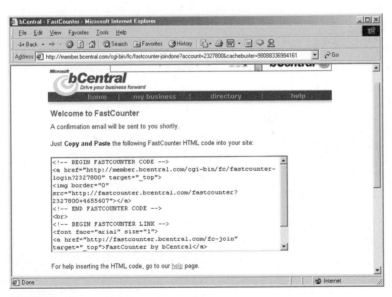

Figure 13-3.

FastCounter lets you track visits to your pages when you host with bCentral.

An e-mail message is also sent to you from bCentral containing the code. If you didn't copy the code from the Welcome to Fast Counter page, you can copy the code from the e-mail message and paste it onto your page:

1. Open your e-mail program, and then open the e-mail message from bCentral.

2. Select the code within the body of the e-mail message, and then on your browser's **Edit** menu, click **Copy**.

3. Open FrontPage, and then on the **File** menu, click **Open Web** to open your bCentral Web site.

4. When the **Open Web** dialog box opens, enter the URL for your site (such as http://mysite.com) in the **Web name** box, and then click **Open**.

5. Open the page in your bCentral web where you want to add the counter.

6. Click the **HTML** tab at the bottom of the FrontPage window to view the HTML source code for your page.

7. Scroll to the place on the page where you want to paste the counter, and then click to position the text cursor.

    Usually, hit counters are placed at the very bottom of a page, before the final </BODY> and </HTML> tags.

8. Press ENTER to insert a new blank line.

9. On FrontPage's **Edit** menu, click **Paste**.

10. Click the **Save** button to save your changes.

11. Preview your page in your browser window to see the counter in action:

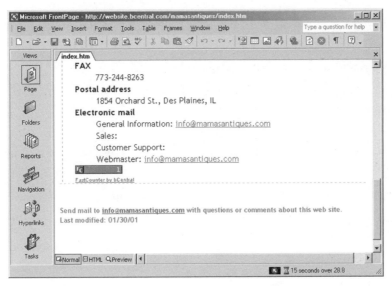

Figure 13-4.
You can use FrontPage to cut, paste, or reposition your counter like any other Web page element.

Reading Usage Reports

Usage Analysis Reports, a feature new to FrontPage 2002, give you another level of control over the information about the visits your site receives. You, not a service, gather the data by using FrontPage. You can then process and present the information any way you want in order to understand it better.

To make the reports work, a number of conditions need to be in place:

- Your Web site needs to be hosted on a server with the FrontPage Server Extensions 2002 or SharePoint Team Services installed and running.

- The server needs to support data collection and usage analysis.

- You have to have some usage statistics to gather — you won't get any numbers until visitors actually access your pages.

Technical Tip

Usage Reports aren't supported by bCentral hosting accounts. However, if your ISP hosting account supports the FrontPage Server Extensions, you can probably take advantage of Usage Reports — ask the host's technical support staff if they can be activated. Usage Reports are ideal for tracking the usage of a Web site on a corporate intranet. When you have Administrator rights on the server that hosts the site you want to analyze, you can activate the Usage Reports feature yourself as explained in the steps that follow.

Once you have the required software and some visitors, follow these steps to create a report:

1. Start FrontPage, and open the Web you want to analyze.

2. To make sure Usage Reports are active, on the **Tools** menu, point to **Server**, and then click **Administration Home**.

   A Web page opens with settings that let you administer your server.

3. Under **Configure Usage Analysis Settings**, click **Change usage analysis settings**, and then click **Submit**.

4. On FrontPage's **View** menu, point to **Reports**, and then point to **Usage**.

5. Select an option from the **Usage** submenu and wait a few seconds for FrontPage to gather the data.

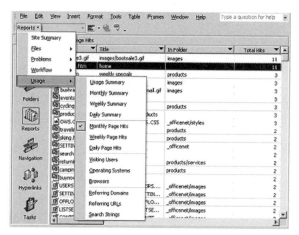

Figure 13-05.

FrontPage lets you gather your own weekly, monthly, or daily Web site data.

One of the benefits of FrontPage's Usage Reports is being able to export the results to a program like Microsoft Excel so you can view and analyze them in depth.

Technical Tip

The following steps work with all reports except Usage Summary and Site Summary.

To export a usage or other report to a Microsoft Office application such as Excel, you only have to follow a few simple steps:

1. Display the report in **Reports** view.

2. Right-click anywhere in the body of the report, and then click **Copy Report** from the submenu.

3. Open Excel.

4. On Excel's **Edit** menu, click **Paste**.

   The report opens as a new Excel file.

Looking at Your Top 10 Lists

They're not just for David Letterman and his Late Night show: Now, any time of the day or night, you can compile your own Top 10 Lists to track the usage of your e-commerce site.

Definition

Top 10 List A way of measuring your Web site's usage. The list is added to a Web page and visibly displays the number of visited pages, referring domains, referring URLs, search strings, visiting users. The information contained in the list is drawn from the server on which the site resides and gives the viewer "live" usage information.

Use Top 10 Lists to steer customers to the most popular pages in a product catalog, the most read articles on a news site, or other types of content you offer and want to highlight. Top 10 Lists are public rather than private. Top 10 Lists are displayed on a page only when the page is viewed with a Web browser. The lists change each time a page is opened or refreshed.

Technical Tip

Top 10 Lists only work if the server that hosts the site supports the FrontPage Server Extensions and the Usage Analysis Reports feature is activated. See the preceding section on Usage Analysis Reports for more information.

If your site supports the use of Top 10 Lists, you can add them to your pages by using the following steps:

1. Start FrontPage, and then open the page where you want a list to appear.

   You might want to create a separate Statistics or Lists page to hold the information. But store the page in a location your visitors won't be able to access, such as the **_private** folder.

2. On the **Insert** menu, click **Web Component** to open the **Insert Web Component** dialog box.

3. In the **Component type** list, select **Top 10 List**.

   A set of the lists available to you appears in the **Choose a usage list** list.

4. Click one of the lists to view a brief explanation in the bottom section of the dialog box.

   You can specify one of the following lists:

List	*Contains*
Visited Pages	Shows the top 10 most frequently visited pages on your site.
Referring Domains	Displays the domains that users visit before they come to your site.
Referring URLs	Tracks the Web sites visitors came from immediately before your site.
Search Strings	Lists the most frequent keywords or phrases entered in search engines that display links to your pages.
Visiting Users	Identifies the computers that visit your site most frequently.
Operating Systems	Specifies the operating systems (such Microsoft Windows, Mac, or UNIX) that your visitors use.
Browser	Tracks the browsers your visitors use.

5. Click **Finish**.

The **Top 10 List Properties** dialog box opens. You can replace the default text in the **Title Text** box.

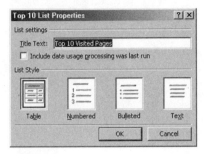

Figure 13-6.
Use this dialog box to configure the format of your Top 10 List.

6. Select one of the four **List Style** options.

The first option encloses your list in a box; the other three are more "open" in appearance.

If you don't like the style you selected or want to change the list heading, right-click the list, click **Top 10 List Properties** on the submenu, and then change the settings in the **Top 10 List Properties** dialog box.

7. When you're done, click **OK**.

The **Top 10 List Properties** dialog box closes and you return to the FrontPage window, where your list is displayed.

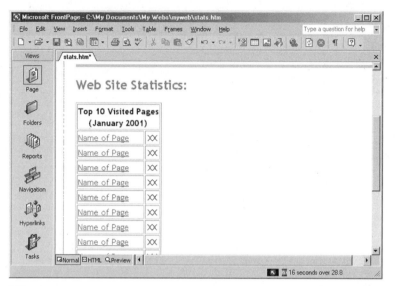

Figure 13-7.

When you initially add a list, placeholder statistics appear. When you preview the page, the "live" statistics are gathered from the server and presented in the browser window.

8. Save the page and preview it in your browser window in order to see the current statistics for your site.

If your server doesn't support the FrontPage Server Extensions, you'll see only the label **FrontPage Usage Component** rather than live data. Ask your Web host's technical support staff for help with setting up usage analysis for the server.

Chapter 14
Keeping the Customer Satisfied

Attracting potential customers or clients to your online business is only half the battle. The key to making an e-commerce site a success is to turn casual browsers into purchasers — and even more importantly, into *return* customers.

One way to ensure return visits and turn your site into a recognized resource is by providing effective customer service. Using Microsoft FrontPage and Microsoft bCentral options for gathering feedback, providing helpful information, and making contacts, you can develop ongoing relationships with your customers, improving the chances that they'll return to your site to make more purchases.

FrontPage and bCentral tools for customer service are described in detail in this chapter. They include:

- A FrontPage Web site template for creating the typical pages of a customer support section on your site.

- bCentral's Customer Manager tools for responding to customer requests, creating a customer database to help track customers and increase sales, and tools to help you and your staff work better together to provide terrific customer support.

Adding Customer Support Pages

Customer service sets one business apart from another on the Internet. It plays an essential role in building credibility, developing customer loyalty, and ensuring return visits that help develop a loyal customer base.

A customer service area is where visitors go to get questions answered and problems resolved. You can put any number of customer contact options on your Web site, but the most common elements are:

- A place where customers can get common questions answered anytime of the day or night
- A contact page that tells shoppers how to get in touch with you
- What's New
- Products
- FAQ
- Service Requests
- Suggestions
- Catalogs/Manuals
- Support Forum

The Customer Support Web site template helps you create pages that you can customize — you may want to eliminate some pages and add others, for example.

Creating the Customer Support Area

1. Start FrontPage, and then open the web in which you want to include the customer support pages.

2. On the **File** menu, point to **New**, and then click **Page or Web**.

3. In the **New from template** area of the Task pane, click **Web Site Templates**.

4. In the **Web Site Templates** dialog box, click **Customer Support Web**.

   Select the **Add to current Web** check box if you want to add the customer support pages to the currently open web.

5. Click **OK**.

   A message is displayed saying that "The file you submitted, index.htm, already exists" and asking if you want to replace it. The index.htm file is the home page for your Web site; unless you want to replace your home page, click **No**. If you click

No, you won't replace your site's home page; however, you won't create a home page specifically for your Customer Support Web set of pages, either. You may see subsequent messages asking if you want to replace files that already have the same name as files that the Customer Support Web site template wants to create.

6. On the **Views** bar, click **Folders** to see a list of the newly created files.

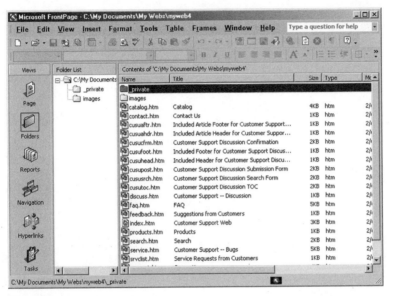

Figure 14-1.
The Customer Support Web template creates an extensive set of Web pages providing customer support options that you can customize.

Technical Tip

In Folders view, the **Title** column tells you which pages in the current web are part of the customer support set of pages. Expand the **Title** column to read the entire contents.

7. Double-click one of the Customer Support Web pages to begin editing it.

Technical Tip

If you created a home page for your Customer Support area (see Step 5 above), this page will be named Customer Support Home. If you did not, click another one of the Customer Support pages, such as the Customer Support page named index.htm.

Customizing the Support Pages

The Customer Support home page has a series of links along the left side of the page. Each link connects to a subcategory of the Customer Support area including: What's New, Products, F.A.Q., Service Request, Suggestions, Catalogs/Manuals, and Support Forum.

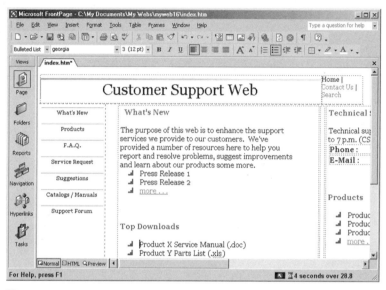

Figure 14-2.

The Customer Support Web contains many common Web pages, but some are applicable only to companies with extensive product catalogs.

Some of the pages may not be applicable to your business. You may not have instruction manuals, for example. Nevertheless, some of the pages are universal, such as the Contact Us page or the Service Request page

Web shoppers crave information. Customize the customer support pages to fit your business's offerings and give your customers the choices and supporting data to help close sales. The following table includes details about each page that FrontPage creates and ideas about how you can make them better fit your business.

Table 14-1.

Page	Purpose
What's New	A What's New page tells visitors about new products, new staff, articles in the media about you or your company, and any press releases you've issued. Of course, the content on this page has to actually be *new*. It's worse to have a What's New page with old information than to have no page at all.
F.A.Q.	A Frequently Asked Questions or FAQ (pronounced "fack") page is commonly used to provide answers to the questions your customers ask most often. The default FAQ page in FrontPage is divided into subcategories that you can customize.
Service Requests	A Service Request page allows users to submit a form to you that describes the problem they're having and ask you to get back to them with help.
Contact Us	A Contact Us page needs to be as complete as possible. Include all relevant e-mail addresses, phone numbers, fax numbers, street addresses, and any other options you have, such as a chat area. You can also include a map to help visitors reach your store's physical location.
Suggestions	You can increase the chances customers will ask questions and make suggestions if you give them a place to do so.
Search	The Search page allows visitors to search the files within the Customer Support area only. You can create pages of content and FrontPage will update the Search index each time the content changes. This can be a useful alternative to a FAQ page.
Products	The Products page is for customer support information for specific products, such as instruction manuals or data sheets. The Products page may contain the content that Search pages search and may also include an index of items.

Changing Placeholder Text

Like any set of predefined Web pages, the Customer Support Web contains lots of placeholder text that you need to edit. Some of the text won't apply to your e-commerce site at all, and you should simply delete it.

You can't miss placeholder text: It's displayed in a different color than the body text around it. Not only that, but it begins with the telltale word "Comment" or "Comments." For example, the Customer Support area's Products page contains a phrase that explains its purpose.

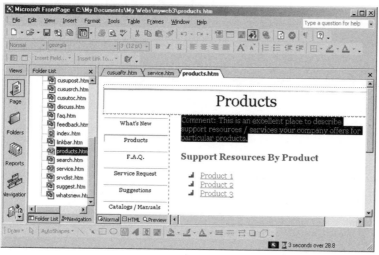

Figure 14-3.

Simply click placeholder text to select it all at once, and then press DELETE to remove it.

You can regard all of the text that comes on the Customer Support pages and that is not explicitly a comment as placeholder text that you can edit. For instance, after you delete the Comment at the beginning of the Products page, you can and should change the list that follows (Product 1, Product 2, and Product 3) to refer to your own specific products.

Adding Pages To a Support Area

When you're in Navigation view, you can also easily add a page to the web. Just follow these steps:

1. Right-click the icon for the page that you want to link to the new page.

2. On the submenu, click **Add Existing Page** if you want to add a page to the Customer Support Web that has already been created. If you want to create a new page, point to **New**, and then click **Page**.

3. If you select **New** and then **Page**, the new page appears in Navigation view and is named New Page 1. To assign the page a name, right-click its icon, and then click **Rename**. The page's name is selected. Type the new name, and then press ENTER.

When you open the Customer Support home page, you'll see that the name you just assigned to your new page has been added to the list of links on the left-hand side.

Business Tip

What could you possibly add to FrontPage's Customer Support Web that isn't already included? You'll find some good ideas on the Ben & Jerry's Web site which, along with lots of ice cream-related sales information, offers an unusually wide variety of customer support resources and background information. Scan the list of links on the left side of the site's home page (http://www.benjerry.com/indexg.tmpl) for options such as a Gift Shop, a Research Library, a Legal and Privacy information page, Employment Opportunities, Factory Tours, and even more resources that you can include to enhance your customers' experience.

Deleting Pages from a Support Area

If you need to delete a page from the Customer Support Web, you need to be careful because the pages are part of a larger web and you don't want to end up with broken links. Say, for instance, you want to cut one of the other Customer Support pages, the Catalog/Manuals page, because you don't have a product catalog. Follow these steps:

1. With the Customer Support Web open, click **Navigation** on the Views bar.
2. In either the Folder List or the Navigation view area of the FrontPage window, right-click the icon for the page you want to delete, and then click **Delete**. The **Delete Page** dialog box opens.

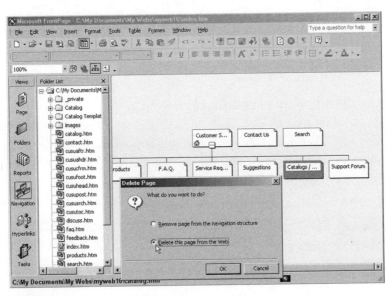

Figure 14-4.
When you delete a page from a web using this dialog box, FrontPage automatically deletes any links on pages that were linked to the deleted page.

3. Select the **Delete this page from the Web** option, and then click **OK** to close the **Delete Page** dialog box.

> The page is deleted from Navigation view.

Once you have added or deleted the pages that come with the Customer Support Web, the next step is to customize the other pages in the web. Suggestions for how to edit the existing Customer Support Web pages follow.

Learn More

An article on the LocalBusiness.com site called "Providing Good Customer Service" (http://www.localbusiness.com/Story/Print/0,1197,NOCITY_282888,00.html) is a good introduction to providing quality customer service. About.com's Small Business Information Customer Service page (http://sbinformation.about.com/smallbusiness/sbinformation/cs/customerservice/index.htm) has links to good articles, including "Old Customers are Cheaper than New."

Adding bCentral Customer Manager to Your Site

According to a report by Cahners In-Stat Group, nearly 70 percent of small businesses identify "managing customer relationships" as a key challenge in 2001 and into 2002. Small business owners often find it difficult to keep track of customer contacts when they're attempting to juggle all the other responsibilities that go with running an e-commerce site.

Customer contact management can be handled for you by a bCentral service called Microsoft bCentral Customer Manager, enabling you to focus on processing orders and updating your catalog and other information. Customer Manager is an extra-cost service, but works well to make your entire online business run smoothly.

Customer Manager enables you to:

- Receive notification when a customer tries to contact you.

- Capture information from your Web site and automatically save it in a customer contact database.

- Track how and when a customer last contacted you, and whether a sale was completed or not.

- Set up contact information so you can receive notifications through a mobile device, such as a Web-enabled cell phone.

- Set up templates so you and your coworkers can send standardized e-mail to every contact depending on the inquiry.

Customer Manager is a service that carries its own monthly or yearly fee — see the Customer Manager home page (http://www.bcentral.com/services/csm/default.asp) for an overview of features. To check on pricing, go to the Features and Pricing page (http://www.bcentral.com/services/csm/pricing.asp), and then click **Sign up now**. You can try the service free for 30 days and then decide whether to continue with it.

Definition

Customer Relationship Management (CRM) All activities that keep you in contact with your customers and potential customers. CRM activities include: keeping track of names and addresses, maintaining records of how your company responded to a customer, and helping you develop standard response templates that everyone in your organization can use.

Customer Manager stores the contact information and keeps track of your company's responses by storing the information online at bCentral so you can access it easily. You could install CRM software on your machine, but having the information online as a hosted application service enables you to access the information anywhere from any computer.

Technical Tip

To use Microsoft bCentral Customer Manager, you need Microsoft Internet Explorer 5.0 or later, Microsoft Windows 95 operating system or later, and 800x600 or greater screen resolution.

When you sign up for this service, Customer Manager gets you started by automatically importing customer information from your Web site. You don't have to go through the time-consuming process of creating a record for each customer. (You can add customers on your own if you want to, however.) Every time you contact a customer by e-mail or by faxing a message from your computer, Customer Manager stores information about the contact in the record that it previously created for that customer. The record is presented in the form of a Web page so you can keep track of the individual's contact information as well as any responses that you need to make.

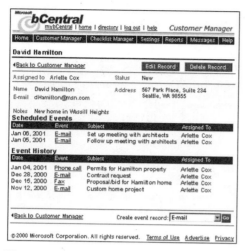

Figure 14-6.

Create a database record for each of your customers by using Customer Manager.

You can set up your bCentral FrontPage Web site to send names, addresses, and other customer information to Customer Manager. In FrontPage, you can create a form that submits customer data and inquiries from your Web site to your Customer Manager account. To create the form, download the FrontPage template from the **Downloads** area of Customer Manager Help. (You need to be a bCentral Customer Manager subscriber to access the **Downloads** area.)

Creating a Form to Capture Customer Information

You can set up your bCentral FrontPage Web site to send customer sales or contact information to bCentral Customer Manager. In FrontPage, you can create a form that submits customer data and inquiries from your Web site to your Customer Manager account. To create the form, download the FrontPage template from the **Downloads** section of the Customer Manager Help page. You need to be a bCentral Customer Manager subscriber to access this template.

Learn More

bCentral's Special Reports area (http://www.bcentral.com/resource/articles/special/archive.asp) offers reports such as the one called "Customer Tech 101" and an article called "Capturing Customers: The Web Way" that give you advice on attracting, contacting, and keeping customers.

Tracking Orders

It's important for an e-business to be able to track orders so it can work better with current customers. As part of bCentral's Commerce Manager, you get sales history reports that help you determine where to sell your products in the future. Customer Manager can also help — it records purchases made by each customer as well as e-mail messages, faxes, and other contacts made by that customer.

It's also good customer service to inform customers when their orders are shipped. You can purchase and install a software package called UPS OnLine WorldShip by United Parcel Service (http://www.ups.com/bussol/solutions/office.html). It includes a feature called E-mail Ship Notification, which alerts customers of incoming shipments.

In addition, UPS and FedEx give you codes for tracking shipments. If you use UPS, you can download a free set of online shipping tools that help your customers track their shipments — find out more at http://www.ups.com/tools/tools.html. If you use FedEx for shipping, one of the FedEx eShipping Tools (http://www.fedex.com/us/ebusiness/eshipping/), called FedEx Ship Manager, can send automatic e-mail notifications to your customers when a package is shipped.

Chapter 15
Building a Customer Community

Every e-commerce Web site needs scores of new visitors. But real success comes when you see lots of familiar faces, too. Ultimately, your profitability depends on customer loyalty. A single customer experience is better than no customer experiences, but you really want to keep people coming back. One way to do that is by encouraging them to connect with one another.

The previous chapter examined how customers can get questions answered regarding your products and services in a support area. Another communications tool — a community forum — helps your members get to know one another and gives them another reason to visit your site more frequently and for longer periods of time. In this chapter, you will learn about the three types of community forums you can establish on your e-commerce site to build connections between customers: Web-based discussion areas (sometimes called message boards), e-mail-based mailing lists, and chat areas.

When you turn your site into a meeting place, you make your customers feel that they are part of a group. They then return to your site again and again, bringing you more business in the process. That's your ultimate goal, after all.

Do Your Customers Need a Community Forum?

A community forum makes sense if your products or your field of expertise (politics, medicine, off-grid living, roses) sparks strong interest and concern in your customers. The benefits might not seem obvious at first if your immediate e-commerce goal centers on product sales. However, experience shows that providing a gathering place for customers with common interests can lead to a big return on your investment. Chris Phillipo, bicycle sales manager at Ramsay's Cycle and Sport store in Nova Scotia, Canada, has run discussion groups for mountain bike enthusiasts and set up a mailing list for the store at http://www.ramsays-online.com. He knows that online forums can contribute to sales and keep Web surfers returning to the store. "The mailing list we use has about 180 members, and when a special or new product announcement is mailed out, it usually does generate a few orders. I believe many customers forget to return to the site after their initial visit, but those who take the time to subscribe to the list usually return if prompted."

A 1998 story on the Oregon Live Web site (http://www.oregonlive.com/technw/9810/tn98101902.html) illustrated how an online discussion group helped contribute to the success of a new product: Amgen, a pharmaceutical company, hired Sapient Health Network to create a virtual community of Hepatitis C sufferers, who are the likely users of its newly developed drug, Infergen. The goal was to learn about possible side effects and compliance problems that patients might have with the medication. In only three weeks, 500 Hepatitis C patients had joined. Before long, membership jumped to 10,000, and Amgen was projecting that it would soon have a large percentage of all Hepatitis C sufferers connected to its new online resource. It would have been virtually impossible to do the same market research without the Internet.

What exactly *is* a community forum, and how do Web-based communities differ from those in the bricks-and-mortar world? In your everyday life, you have clubs of members who meet in church basements or coffee shops to share their enthusiasm for photography or collecting a certain type of antique. Similarly, members of an online community might share ideas on a daily, even hourly, basis. They can "meet" anytime, day or night, to pose questions about the product they've purchased or compare notes with fellow consumers. They "converse" by typing messages to one another on the Web, through e-mail, or in a Web-based chat room. Their discussions are not only more frequent, but also tend to get more passionate than those of their offline counterparts.

Definition

Online Forum Any place on the Internet where groups of individuals can post messages and hold online discussions. Discussion groups (sometimes called *newsgroups*), mailing lists, and chat areas are all varieties of online forums.

I recently purchased a Volkswagen and began visiting a Web site set up especially for Volkswagen owners (http://www.vwvortex.com). There I read messages posted by other VW owners, ask questions about parts, find out news about upcoming models, and engage in discussions with other drivers who love to express their love for their cars.

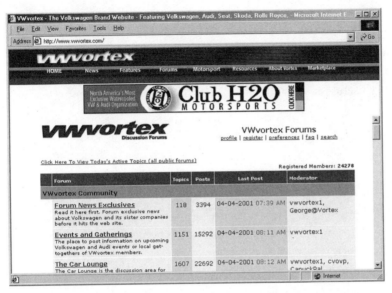

Figure 15-1.
The VW Vortex community adds value to Volkswagen's product and reinforces consumers' sense of loyalty to this brand.

What sets a customer support forum apart from a customer service discussion area is the intent. Before you do anything, be sure your customers want this feature and will use it. How do you know they *want* a community forum? Do your products or services inspire many technical inquiries, outbursts of enthusiasm, or questions like "Do other customers come to you with the same questions I do?" If you already hear such inquiries or comments, a community forum is in order.

Business Tip

Your site can include both a support forum and community forum. A community forum works whenever your customers have questions or thoughts they want to share with others. If you sell products that a person has to build or install, such as computer hardware or software, then a support forum make sense as well.

The physical steps involved in setting up a community forum with Microsoft FrontPage are the same as a customer support discussion area. Once you've decided a discussion area is right for your Web site, you can set it up by using FrontPage's Discussion Web Wizard. See "Adding a Discussion Forum" later in this chapter for details.

What Do You Gain From a Community Forum?

Establish your goals for a community forum before you go through the effort of setting one up. After all, it takes a lot of work, not just to organize the forum, but also to maintain it so the discussion is useful for your customers. You might set up a forum to achieve goals such as:

- **More hits for advertising revenue.** If you can show advertisers that some of your community forums have hundreds, or even thousands, of messages from participants, you make a strong case to them for purchasing ad space on your site.

- **Visitors who turn into purchasers.** To make a purchase online, shoppers need to be reassured that what they're buying is desirable. A forum that attracts enthusiastic individuals who have already purchased the products encourages the casual shopper to make a purchase.

- **Greater loyalty.** A community forum lends a sense of professionalism to an e-commerce site. It differentiates your site from those of your competitors.

A community forum makes your site a more valuable place for your customers to visit. It tells visitors that you aren't just interested in selling your products, but that you are also interested in *them*. When customers feel you want to strike up a one-to-one relationship with them, they'll trust you and purchase what you have to sell.

Organizing a Community Forum

Once you are certain that a community forum is a useful addition to your site, you need to organize it. Again, you can break the discussions into specific topics, as you did with the support forums described in Chapter 14. The topics that are common to community forums differ substantially from support forums, however. They often include topics like these:

- Announcements
- Tips
- Questions

- Ratings

- New Products

- General Talk

- For Sale or Trade

Start out small with a single forum and expand as needed. Create a welcome page that introduces your forums, sets terms of use (see "Making Your Forum a Success" later in this chapter), and contains a link to each forum. You can use tables to organize this "directory of forums," such as the one shown on the FrontPage-created MicroWINGS Web site (http://www.microwings.com).

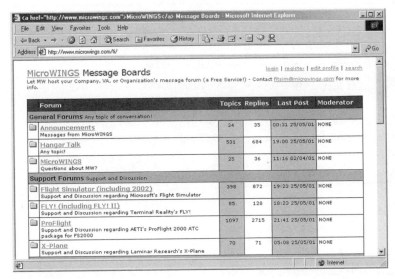

Figure 15-2.

If you have more than one discussion forum on your site, create a welcome page that points visitors to all of the offerings.

Business Tip

You're likely to encounter a major difficulty faced by virtually all Web-based forums: They require a reasonably high level of traffic (by one estimate, at least 2,500 visitors a day) before large numbers of new visitors will join them. A forum that only attracts a handful of postings might give customers the impression that your site isn't popular at all. You can help get your forum off the ground by identifying regular customers and encouraging them to post often and interact with new members who join the group. If it doesn't seem like your forum is drawing lots of users, remove it from your site. A forum that doesn't attract a lot of users or message postings will make your entire site seem less lively.

Setting Up a Discussion or Support Forum

A discussion forum is a great way to let customers voice their opinions, ask questions, or simply to visit with other customers. Why not set up a discussion group hosted on your site so visitors can converse without leaving your "premises"? A forum makes your site "stickier" — you give visitors a reason for sticking around. You also give them a reason to return.

Technical Tip

FrontPage's Discussion Web Wizard only works if the server that hosts your site supports the FrontPage Server Extensions. Make sure your hosting account includes such support.

Case Study: Customers Plus Community Equals Loyalty

When it comes to community, look no further than eBay (http://www.ebay.com), the well-known and popular online auction destination. eBay's community-building features provide strong evidence that when customers feel they are part of a group with shared interests, they return to a site more frequently and spend more money there.

A NetRatings Top Properties survey by the Internet measurement service Nielsen/ NetRatings in April 2001 (http://209.249.142.27/nnpm/owa/NRpublicreports.toppropertiesweekly) indicated that the average eBay user spends more than 47 minutes on the site during a typical visit. This is far beyond the usual time (10 to 20 minutes) spent on most Web sites.

What inspires such loyalty? The ever changing content and the lure of good deals is certainly one factor. Another is the emphasis eBay places on community building among its members. eBay enables its customers to deal with one another not only as buyers and sellers but also as friends and colleagues. Community-building venues such as the Community area and special features help bring visitors together. This area includes the following community-building features:

- **Feedback.** eBay buyers and sellers are encouraged to post comments about their dealings with one another in a Feedback forum. Positive feedback comments from other users tell prospective customers that an individual is trustworthy. Negative feedback results from slow delivery, nonpayment, or general lack of responsiveness.

- **Message boards.** Many eBay users collect the same objects. The eBay Café and other message boards provide venues where they can discuss their common interests. Users regularly meet and greet one another — often at the same time each day.

- **Web pages.** Buyers and sellers whose eBay usernames are accompanied by a "me" icon have created personal Web pages using eBay's software so other visitors can find out more about them.

(continued)

Making Your Forum a Success

Online forums carry a number of pros and cons for the individuals who create them and make the commitment to manage them on an ongoing basis. You need to know what's involved in making a forum successful before you go through the effort of creating it. If you fully understand what you need to do and you're willing to put forth the effort to cultivate your forum, you can make it an important asset to your e-commerce site.

Case Study: Customers Plus Community Equals Loyalty *(continued)*

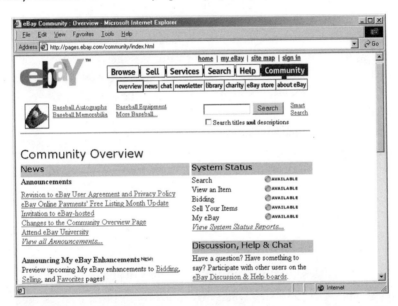

- **Newsletter.** The *eBay Insider,* distributed by e-mail, contains profiles of individual users as well as success stories.

- **Charitable activities.** Giving back to society at large is part of being a member of a community. eBay gives users the chance to bid on charity items to benefit organizations that help others.

eBay culture has evolved to the point where members have their own slang and greet one another like old friends on the message boards. Your own community offerings need not be so elaborate. But the same sense of customer loyalty is a goal worth attaining. For simple e-commerce sites like yours, discussion boards and mailing lists make the most sense.

First, you need to be ready to moderate discussions. Post the first message on your own forum. Make it a welcoming message that also establishes rules of use for your forum. You might say something like the following:

The Antique Pen Collectors' Community Forum is a gathering place for experienced pen collectors and novices alike who want to talk about this exciting hobby. News of upcoming conventions, descriptions of items for sale or trade, and questions are welcome. Anyone who contributes unsolicited advertisements, uses profanity, or abuses other members will be banned from further participation.

You should also post a statement of policies to which people are agreeing when they join the discussion and which are the bases of any action that you as the owner take. (If you don't do this, you could encounter legal problems.)

A moderator also suggests topics of discussion to get things going. One great thing about discussion forums on the Internet is that everyone can participate and post just about anything they want. That's also a downside of forums — they can easily be abused with off-topic, profane, and abusive postings. A moderator keeps discussions focused by deleting messages that are inappropriate. FrontPage gives you the ability to delete messages or edit messages to remove inappropriate comments. (Such editing takes place after the message has been posted online, not before.)

The level to which you moderate discussions and weed out unsuitable messages is up to you. But maintaining the forum is a must. At the very least, you need to delete old messages to save disk space. FrontPage can warn you when text in the discussion area is out of date:

To have FrontPage check for out-of-date discussions:

1. Open the discussion web in FrontPage.

2. On the **Tools** menu, click **Options** to open the **Options** dialog box.

3. On the **General** tab, select the **Warn when text index is out of date** check box, and then click **OK**.

After you follow these simple steps, FrontPage will alert you when the index of text files in the discussion area is out of date. You can then delete old messages.

Having a forum that has old, outdated messages or no activity at all can hurt your business — it makes it look as though nobody visits your site. Making the commitment to maintain the forum and encourage discussion increases the chances that you'll get plenty of activity and the forum will attract regular visitors to your site.

Case Study: MicroWINGS takes off

MicroWINGS, the online home of the International Association for Aerospace Simulations, includes an online store where visitors can purchase back issues of a bimonthly magazine (also called MicroWINGS) as well as flight simulation CDs. The FrontPage-created Web site also provides a variety of other community-building features for flight simulation enthusiasts, including a chat area, a directory page where commercial members can post contact information and links to their Web sites, an extensive set of message boards, and a guest book.

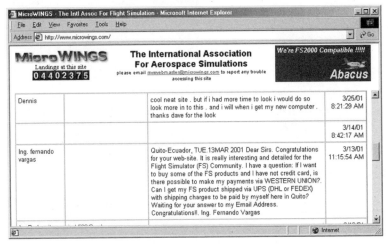

Figure 15-3.

A guest book enables visitors to sign their names and post their comments so other visitors can read them.

Robert MacKay, the site's owner, enjoyed a big technical advantage when it came to creating his own chat area. MacKay used his computer programming knowledge to write his own chat software, and then formatted the chat pages with FrontPage.

MacKay emphasizes the importance of moderating community forums to make sure postings are on-topic and generally up to the community's standards. Anyone who posts inappropriate messages is prevented from posting further messages by marking his or her e-mail address as "banned," which means the site will not accept further messages from that address.

He goes on to say that community building is the key to building up the site's base of loyal return visitors. "There is no doubt in my mind that community building is key," he comments. "Another key is very frequent updates — you have to give people a reason to keep coming back to your site."

Learn More

Find out more about the benefits and responsibilities of maintaining online forums at the Moderators Web Page (http://www.cais.com/cfs-news/moderators.html). Although the page refers to Usenet newsgroups and mailing lists, the general issues apply to any online forum.

Publishing Your Files

If your e-commerce store is hosted on Microsoft bCentral or another Web host site, make sure you have the remote web open in the FrontPage window when you create the discussion web. On the **File** menu, click **Open Web** and then in the **Web name** box in the **Open** dialog box, type the URL for your site, such as http://www.mysite.com, and click **Open**.

If, on the other hand, you create a discussion web on your local computer, you'll need to publish the new files on your "public" Web site so others can start using them. On the **File** menu, click **Publish Web**, enter the publish destination for your site, and then publish the files.

Adding a Discussion Forum

FrontPage makes it easy to set up a discussion area using the Discussion Web Wizard. The wizard is easy to follow:

1. Start FrontPage, and then open the web that you want to contain the discussion web.

2. On the **File** menu, point to **New**, and then click **Page or Web**.

3. In the **New from template** section of the Task pane, click **Web Site Templates**.
   The **Web Site Templates** dialog box opens.

4. Click **Discussion Web Wizard**.

5. Select the **Add to current Web** check box if you want to add the discussion area to the web that you currently have open, and then click **OK**.
   The first Discussion Web Wizard page appears.

6. Click **Next**.
   On the next page, you need to identify the main components of your web.

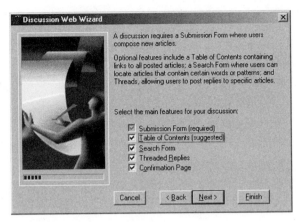

Figure 15-4.
You can add a Table of Contents or a Search form to your discussion area to help people find comments on specific products or subjects.

Technical Tip

"Threaded replies" refers to a series of comments that focus on a single topic. By threading replies, you organize the comments on your web according to topic, rather than chronologically. You might only need a Table of Contents if your discussion web gets really extensive and contains many different topics. A Search form will help individuals find comments that include a particular keyword or phrase. A Confirmation page lets participants know their messages have been received.

7. After you select the main features you want for your discussion web, click **Next**.

8. On the next page, assign a name for your web and name the folder where the articles will be stored. Enter a title, change the default folder name if you want to, and then click **Next**.

9. On the next page, select the main input fields you want your form to have — if you plan to sell products or categories of services on your site, pick the options that let users enter data in fields labeled Products or Categories, and then click **Next**.

10. On the next page, specify whether the web is to be protected — that is, whether users need to enter a username and password to view or post a message. Select one of the options, and then click **Next**.

11. On the next two pages, specify how the messages in the Table of Contents (if you have one) are to be organized, and whether you want the Table of Contents page to be the home page for your site. Select the appropriate options, and then click **Next**.

12. On the next page, specify the fields you want included in your discussion area's Search form when it returns results. Select the options you want, and then click **Next**.

13. The next page enables you to select the design of each page in the discussion web. You can decide to have questions and replies in a single frame (the first option) or divide the page into multiple frames (the other three options). When you select an option, the corresponding page layout appears in the miniature page layout area to the left. Click **Next**, read the final page of the wizard, and then click **Finish**.

    The discussion area is created.

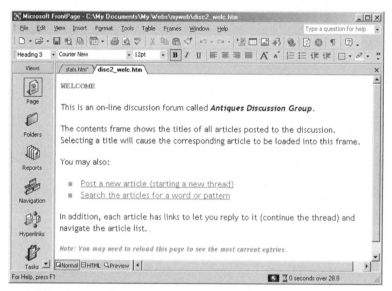

Figure 15-5.

You can divide discussion web pages into separate frames that hold the name of the discussion area in one frame, the contents of the site in one frame, and individual messages in another frame.

14. If you are connecting your discussion web to the current web, it doesn't appear automatically in Normal view. On the Views bar, click **Folders**, and then find the discussion group pages, which have disc in the filename.

15. Double-click the Welcome page, disc2welc.htm.

    The Welcome page opens in the FrontPage window.

Managing Your Discussion Group

Once your discussion web is online, you need to perform ongoing maintenance. You can delete old messages to conserve disk space or edit individual messages if you find them to be unsuitable, such as if a participant is being profane or abusive.

You open the folder containing the discussion group messages (which has the default name _cusudi unless you changed it to something else when you created the discussion area). Each message has a name that follows the form ########.htm; each # is a digit. Right-click the message you want to remove, and then, on the submenu, click **Delete**.

To modify a message, double-click its name to open the message in a text editor, and then edit the file and save the changes. It's a good idea to let the individual who posted the message know that you changed it and explain why you did.

Business Tip

Remind your customers that when participating in online discussions, it's important to remember the unwritten but widely observed set of rules for online communication collectively known as Netiquette. These guidelines encourage good manners in discussion forums and e-mail messages. To find out more, consult the Netiquette Home Page (http://www.albion.com/netiquette).

The Support Forum for Customer Service

FrontPage's Customer Support web contains its own discussion area called a support forum. If you want customers to also have a community forum, it may be best to have two separate forum areas.

The pages that make up the support forum are:

- Table of Contents page (cusutoc.htm).
- Search form (cususrch.htm).
- Submission form to submit comments to the discussion area (cusupost.htm).
- Confirmation page sent after submitting a message (cusucfrm.htm).
- Two sets of header and footer files (cusufoot.htm and cusuhead.htm for the discussion area pages, and cusuaftr.htm and cusuahdr.htm for individual articles).

If you have given your customer support area a specific name, be sure to edit the text in the header files for the support forum because they contain the Customer Support placeholder heading.

Another aspect of ongoing discussion group maintenance is paying attention to new participants. If a new member posts a message that receives no response, acknowledge it and reply to it yourself. Make an effort to identify and encourage participants who emerge as natural leaders or people who post often and try to help other, newer users out.

Business Tip

Keep community members returning on a regular basis by introducing new discussion topics. You can set up one or two discussion forums and leave future topics to your participants. They might suggest new categories. Be receptive to their suggestions and update the site to match their needs.

Setting Up a Mailing List

Web-based community forums work best when participants think through issues before responding, and when community members develop ideas or follow conversational topics over time. If communications tend to be simple and brief, or if you need more privacy, an e-mail discussion forum called a *mailing list* will do the trick.

Definition

Mailing list A list that enables group discussions over the Internet in which participants communicate by means of e-mail messages. Each member of a list subscribes to it by sending an e-mail message to the list's operator or to a program set up to add or delete list members.

Discussion-based mailing list A mailing list in which members post messages that go to everyone else who has subscribed. Anyone can then post a message in response. That response can generate its own responses, and a discussion results. A series of messages on a particular topic is called a *thread*.

Announcement mailing list A mailing list in which the owner sends out periodic announcements to members, but members don't have the ability to "talk back" to one another. In either case, participants can join or remove themselves from the list whenever they choose.

Unlike Web-based discussion forums or chat rooms (see below), mailing lists don't have to be accessed on the Web. Depending on how you configure your list, messages can go directly to members' e-mail inboxes or to a Web site that members can only access with a username and password. The e-mail option works well in terms of privacy but has the disadvantage of substantially increasing members' e-mail traffic. Mailing lists, like discussion forums, benefit from close moderation from their owners.

In contrast to discussion forums, mailing lists can't be assembled with the help of FrontPage. You can set up a simple announcement list with your e-mail program by assembling the e-mail addresses of your customers, and then grouping the addresses into a single list. You then send a single message to all the members of the list at once.

Technical Tip

If you put the names of your list's recipients in the CC: address box, the recipients won't see each other's names. This maintains their privacy.

Community building, though, results from discussion-based lists in which participants type messages to one another. When it comes to setting up a discussion-based list, you have three options:

- **Install your own mailing list software.** This only makes sense if you have lots of technical experience and access to a server on which mailing lists are permitted. (Most Web hosts won't serve mailing lists because they create so much traffic.)

- **Hire a list administrator.** If you have the money, you can pay a mailing list service like SkyList.net (http://www.skylist.net) to handle subscriptions and cancellations, track down e-mail addresses that don't work, provide digests and searchable indexes, send out instructions to members, and all the other responsibilities that go with running a list. You would pay a $250 setup fee plus $50 per month to SkyList.net for a list with 250 members or less.

- **Take advantage of a free list administration service.** If you need to save your pennies yet don't have the time or expertise to administer a mailing list yourself, consider signing up with ListBot, the free community mailing list administration service provided by bCentral. In exchange for the free administration, you display advertisements, which are inserted into the e-mail messages circulated by your group.

ListBot is easy to use and set up. Go to the ListBot home page on the bCentral Web site (http://www.listbot.com), scroll down to the **ListBot Communities Email Groups** section of the page, and then click **Learn more**. On the bCentral Listbot page, click the **Click here to sign up** button, and then follow the instructions presented on subsequent pages.

Figure 15-6.

When you set up ListBot, you add HTML to your Web pages that displays a text box and button, which enable users to add themselves to your mailing list.

Busier lists benefit from setting up a searchable archive of all previous discussions. Those with heavy traffic can be set up to send a single e-mail message called a *digest* that contains all of the messages sent to the list on a given day. Members get one digest message instead of many individual ones. Ask your mailing list host to give you a digest option if your list receives heavy traffic.

Learn More

Another bCentral mailing list service, ListBuilder, costs $19.95 per month but doesn't include advertising. If you already have a small-scale list that you've started yourself and want to hire a service to handle future expansion, you can easily import the addresses to ListBuilder, too.

Setting Up a Chat Area

A discussion area or mailing list provides you with an effective tool for community building, but neither one enables participants to converse in real time. There's always a gap of a few minutes or more between the time a message appears on a discussion area Web page and the time required for another participant to compose and post a response. If your customers begin to post messages within minutes of one another and it seems they would be eager to conduct a real conversation, consider providing them with a chat area on your site or scheduling conversations using MSN Messenger. Using MSN Messenger requires that all participants download and install the software and obtain a Microsoft Hotmail account.

Definition

Chat areas Space where participants can conduct real time discussions via the Internet by typing messages to one another in a special chat window. Participants connect to a chat server that allows users to type messages to one another. Everyone who is connected can read each message at the same time. Chat messages, unlike discussion board postings, appear online in a matter of seconds, and participants can respond to them by typing and posting their own messages almost immediately. Once the chat session is closed, the conversation "disappears."

As you probably know, chatting is extremely popular with teenagers who use it primarily for fun and recreation. Because chatting *is* fun and immediate, it can be useful to your customers as well. The downside is that chat areas are complex to set up and manage. You can't set up chat areas using FrontPage. If you know a computer programming language like C++ or Perl, you can create your own chat room as Robert Mackay did with his MicroWINGS Web site (see the Case Study earlier in this chapter).

It's much simpler to set up a chat room on someone else's Web site, and then link to it from your site. You can set up a chat area through the Webchatting site (http://www.webchatting.com/addchat.htm) for instance. You can also go to everyone.net (http://www.everyone.net) and click the **Plug-in-Community** link to read about the benefits of setting up discussion boards and chat areas on your site. On the Plug-in-Community Intro page, click the **Customization** link to view a series of screens that describes the kinds of community features you can create.

With everyone.net, you sign up to use the service. There is no fee to use it, but you commit to displaying advertisements on any community forum or chat room pages that you set up using the service.

You need to select how many areas you want. You can either have one general community area, or you can have multiple ones. You might set up one for customer service, one for community, and so on. You can even have subcategories within each area. Each community forum you set up can have a chat area where people can communicate in real time. Exercise control over how you configure your chat room or discussion room by selecting colors in which messages and responses will be displayed to make them easier for participants to read. You can also display your own images to add visual interest to your community forum or banner ads to generate revenue. Find out more by clicking the **SIGN UP NOW** link that appears on each everyone.net page and then following the instructions.

Chat areas work best if discussions are controlled. Set up and publish a schedule for chat sessions and keep them to an hour at a time. Many of the community discussion areas on the HealingWell.com Web site (http://healingwell.com/), which were set up using everyone.net, include chat sessions that occur at specific times.

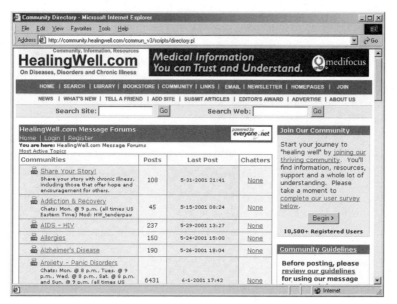

Figure 15-7.
This health-related site includes discussion forums on various topics, some of which include regularly scheduled chat sessions.

Be sure you or a coworker participates and moderates the discussion by suggesting an initial topic, and then monitoring comments to make sure no conflicts erupt. Chat moderation represents a substantial time commitment. On the other hand, it's a great way to meet your visitors firsthand and learn about their needs and thoughts.

Technical Tip

Chat areas are easy to set up and use with everyone.net, but participants must have the latest browsers that support Java as well as plenty of free memory. Chat areas require Java 1.1 and Microsoft Internet Explorer 4.x or later, Netscape Navigator/Communicator 4.x or later, or AOL 5.x or later. Microsoft WebTV is not supported at this time. Mac OS users are advised to allocate a preferred memory requirement size of at least twice their browser's suggested size.

Chapter 16

Keeping Your Content Fresh

Online shoppers are continually searching for something new. They surf the Web on their lunch hour, during study breaks, or as a reward for completing a housekeeping chore. Whether casually browsing or looking for a specific item to buy, they are subject to a phenomenon called *churn*. Visitors churn through one site after another, clicking, scanning, and moving from page to page. They may pause briefly if something catches their interest, but then they continue their pursuit of sites with fresh and different content.

For an e-commerce Web site developer like you, the message is clear. You can't afford to spend too much time congratulating yourself on developing a community of visitors. To retain your clients, your material must be continually reworked.

It takes a lot of effort to keep updating a Web site — especially when you're preoccupied with serving your customers and marketing your products. But it's essential that customers have a reason to return on a regular basis. Old or outdated content is one of the kisses of death for commercial Web sites. You need to make a commitment to add fresh and compelling content to your site, such as frequent promotions and new products. This chapter will help you develop a plan for refreshing your Web site's content on a regular basis. That's one of the keys to keeping customers satisfied and coming back for more shopping and purchasing.

Doing a Regular Tune-Up

You make appointments with your mechanic for tuning your car — if you don't, your machinery doesn't run smoothly and you end up in the repair shop. Your Web site's machinery (specifically, your text, images, and links) benefits from regular examinations as well. Links to other sites become useless when those sites change their addresses. Any content that depends on specific times or events, such as seasonal sales or products that are tied to holidays, needs to be removed or changed when it is out of date.

Andrea Milrad, president of LittleBIG Man, a Coral Springs, FL custom card and announcement maker, regularly updates her Web site (http://www.littlebigman.org) using Microsoft FrontPage. Her site averages 30 sales per month — ranging from invitations for 24 birthday party guests to 4,000 trade show attendees.

"I update the site's content whenever it's needed — sometimes every day, sometimes every other month," says Milrad. "Usually, I add new content when I have a new ticket idea to share, or when the pricing or contact information changes. But just as often, changes of content result from customer inquiries. When customers ask the same questions, I realize that the site is probably not giving enough information."

Although keeping her e-commerce site's content fresh takes time, it's an essential part of doing business online. "I have to make time for this," she says. "The Web site is my only store and if it doesn't properly display my products, pricing, and philosophy, then my store is a failure."

Customers generate some of her site's new content. "My customers are often my greatest source of creative input," says Milrad. "They come up with great ideas and uses for my products." After customers repeatedly said they were using some of her cards for bar mitzvahs, for instance, Milrad added a new line of placecards to her online catalog.

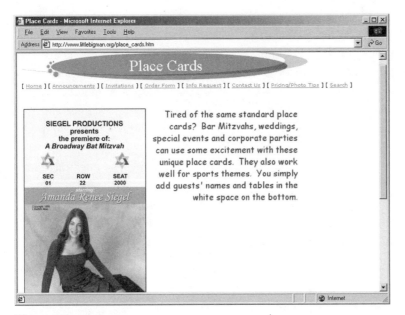

Figure 16-1.

Listen to customer suggestions and comments, and respond by adjusting your sales content to meet their needs.

Business Tip

If you have a few extra dollars, consider hiring someone to update your site. You might know of a Web-savvy student who would enjoy checking links on your site and suggesting new content on a weekly or monthly basis. Such services need not be expensive, and you'll get the benefit of an outside opinion of what makes your site attractive. Consider posting an ad for such help on eLance (http://www.elance.com) or FreeAgent.com (http://www.freeagent.com).

Setting a Maintenance Schedule

When you're in business for yourself, you know that your income depends on generating new content. That makes it all the more difficult to get around to revising earlier work. Evaluating your site should periodically be on the top of your "to do" list, however. The exact interval between check-ups depends on how quickly your content becomes outdated — you can plan to return every week, every month, or every few months. What's important is having a regular plan for revising your site's content.

FrontPage automatically creates a list of tasks when you use one of the templates or wizards to create a web. You can also create a task list from scratch.

First, determine which areas of your site you want to update, and decide how often you want to update them. Then, identify the best person to do the work: In most cases, it might be you, but if you have coworkers to help you, you can delegate the job to them.

Then draw up your task list as follows:

1. Open the Web page that you want to associate with a task in FrontPage.

2. On the **File** menu, point to **New**, and then click **Task**.
   The **New Task** dialog box opens.

3. Enter a name, select a priority level, and then enter a description for the new task in the appropriate areas of the dialog box.

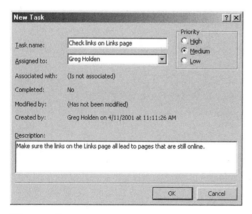

Figure 16-2.

FrontPage can help you keep track of regular updates you need to perform to keep your content fresh.

4. Click **OK**.

      The **New Task** dialog box closes.

5. Repeat the preceding steps for each task you need to add.

6. When you want to view your tasks, open the web and click **Tasks** on the **Views** bar.

      FrontPage displays the Tasks view list for the web. The Web page that is associated with each task is listed in the **Associated With** column.

7. You can edit a task's description by right-clicking the task in Tasks view, and then choosing **Edit Task** from the submenu.

      The **Task Details** dialog box is displayed so you can change the description.

8. To start performing a task, right-click the task in Tasks view, then choose **Start Task**.

      FrontPage opens the page associated with the task so you can edit it.

9. When you edit the page and save your changes, you are prompted to mark the task as completed. If you click **Yes**, the task's status is changed to **Completed** in the **Status** column in Tasks view.

Technical Tip

You can also add a task from within Tasks view. Right-click the blank area beneath the list of tasks, and then click **Add Task** from the submenu to open the **New Task** dialog box.

Updating Links

One of the most important aspects of updating a site's content is checking links to other pages, either on your own site or on the Internet. Take the time to visit your site periodically and follow any links to see where they lead. Better yet, save some time by having FrontPage update the links for you:

1. Open the site you want to check in FrontPage.

2. On the **Tools** menu, click **Recalculate Hyperlinks**.

      A message box notifies you that the process may take several minutes and asks if you want to continue.

3. Click **Yes**.

      On FrontPage's status bar, a message appears notifying you that the links are being recalculated. When the process is complete, the message in the status bar disappears. Don't be surprised to find that links lead to pages that no longer exist or that they are at another location. Web pages move around frequently as their owners perform their own revisions.

Technical Tip

Performance problems with hosts can cause temporary lapses in service. If a Web site or page that you've linked to disappears one day, return the next day to make sure the absence is permanent, rather than the result of a brief glitch.

Listening to Your Customers

As stated earlier, some of the best ideas for fresh content come from your customers. But you can't simply unlock a suggestion box to find out what they are thinking. Sometimes you realize content needs to be revised when you receive a series of inquiries on similar topics. Other times you need to provide customers with a convenient form to encourage them to tell you about new features they want or information they need.

In earlier chapters, we examined FrontPage's Web site templates for establishing an effective corporate presence and a customer service area. Your business may be so small in scale that you don't feel the need to create entire web pages for either of these purposes. You can still use some of the individual pages within the wizards and templates to help you present new material or request feedback. You have a couple of options for doing this:

- **Add a single-page template.** From the FrontPage Task pane, click **Web Page Templates**. When the **Page Templates** dialog box appears, select a page such as **User Registration**, **Table of Contents**, or **Feedback Form**.

- **Use a wizard or template.** Some wizards or templates (like the Customer Support Web template) add a group of pages all at once. Others lead you step-by-step through the process and give you the option of creating only one or two pages.

Here's an example of a wizard or template that lets you create a single page if you wish: The Corporate Presence Wizard includes a Feedback page. Once you determine that you want to invite suggestions from visitors (maybe they've been posing lots of questions, some of which lead to improvements on your site), you can use this wizard to add only that individual page rather than the entire web. Follow these steps:

1. Start FrontPage, and then open your Web site.

2. On the **File** menu, point to **New**, and then click **Page or Web**.
   The Task pane opens.

3. In the **New from template** section of the Task pane, click **Web Site Templates**. The **Web Site Templates** dialog box opens.

4. Select the **Add to current Web** check box, click the **Corporate Presence Wizard** icon, and then click **OK**. The first page of the wizard appears.

5. Click **Next**. The second page of the wizard appears.

6. Clear the check boxes for all of the pages except the one you want to create. Since you only want to create a page that customers can use to make suggestions, on this page of the wizard, only the **Feedback Form** check box should be selected.

7. Click **Next**, and then follow the wizard through the rest of the steps involved in creating the page. When you click **Finish** on the last page of the wizard, the wizard closes and the Feedback Form page is created.

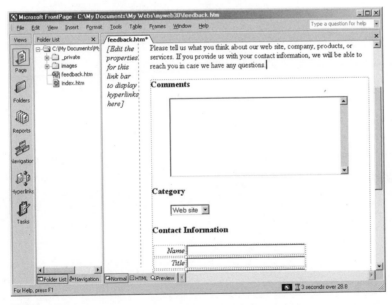

Figure 16-3.
You can use one of FrontPage's wizards to add a single page to your e-commerce site so customers can provide feedback and suggestions.

Notice that when you add the page to a current web, it takes on any themes you've already used to give your web a graphic identity. You then need to edit the navigation bars and the main body of the page. Don't forget the shared footer at the bottom of the page — replace the text in brackets with information about your own company. Make sure the new page is linked to your other pages by switching to Navigation view and then adding the new page to the web (as described in Chapter 7). Save your changes and upload the new files to your Web server, and then test your site to make sure the new material appears correctly and the links work the way you want.

Technical Tip

For a feedback or suggestion form to work, your site must be hosted on a server that supports the FrontPage Server Extensions, such as Microsoft bCentral.

Update One Thing Per Day

Some Web sites make it obvious that their content has been changed so visitors know immediately that they'll find something different. One of the author's favorite Internet radio stations, WFMU (http://www.wfmu.org), includes a new humorous slogan and a "sound bite of the day" on its home page. Much of the rest of the site stays the same, although new radio shows are added frequently to the station's extensive archives. But regular visitors know there's a little surprise waiting for them each day.

Consider posting a date-based series of events. A calendar of upcoming events will keep visitors coming back for future offerings or news on your site. Some sites feature a chronological record of the content added recently. The Husker Fever Web site (http://www.huskerfevercard.com), created with FrontPage, includes a What's Up series of updates on the right side of its home page. The updates don't need to be significant — even e-mail messages received from fans of the Nebraska Cornhuskers are included as they arrive — but just the fact that there's a list of updates tells visitors that the site's content is refreshed on a regular basis.

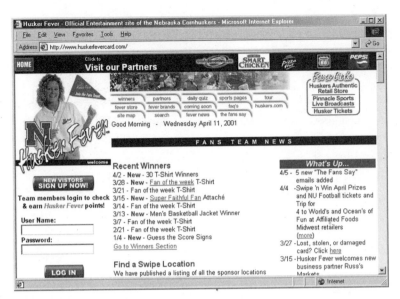

Figure 16-4.

List any revisions, messages, or new advertisers or partners on your site to make it clear that you're actively revising and improving it.

Business Tip

If you host a Web site with bCentral, you get periodic reevaluations and updates with the help of a professional. Sign up for a Web Site Manager Custom Site for a one-time fee (http://www.bcentral.com/services/wsm/default.asp). After your site has been live for 30 days, your Web consultant checks with you to see how your Web site is doing. You go over what is working, as well as where there is room for improvement. Then it's time to make a plan of action to help continue your Web success. Every six months, your consultant discusses ways to improve your online presence and helps you set goals for the upcoming six months.

Borrowing Third-Party Content

Even professional designers don't do all their work themselves. Those who aren't illustrators make frequent use of artwork that others have created called clip art. Similarly, news of interest to your customers is available online for you to add to your site. The key is to determine which content gets a good response from your audience.

If you sell hardware or software related to the Internet itself, you'll find no shortage of Internet-related news services that let you add headlines and newsbytes to your pages. If you're in the field of finance, your customers may be interested in stock price tickers added to your pages. Only add news content to your pages if you're sure it meets the needs of your visitors. If so, make use of the convenient services described in the sections that follow.

Case Study: Keeping a Sports Site Flying High

Sports fans don't cheer for cobwebs. The advantage of having a sports-oriented Web site is that details about games, matches, and meets are available online for die-hard fans to follow. However, that means updates must be made constantly to keep up with the winners and losers.

Mark Cramer updates his FrontPage-created eBalloon.com site (http://www.eballoon.com) every day about the relatively new sport of competitive ballooning, and new information comes in constantly during the season.

"During the months of May through October, we update every two to four hours," says Cramer. "The reports are sent to us from individuals who are covering events, and we edit and publish the information ourselves. Sometimes we will offer fresh content from three different places in United States using the site where I'm located as the hub. It is not unusual to have reporters at events returning from their "assignments" handing off to a spoke site (event headquarters) so that coverage can be transmitted to the hub (us) for editing and loading. Our content is always changing during events because of the needs or wants of our audience."

The emphasis on up-to-the-minute content corresponds to audience needs. "Pilots and their teams (and sponsors) want to know how they did and see themselves on eBalloon.com. And the spectators at the events visit to get more insight into the sport," Cramer explains. "Content is everything and eBalloon.com is focused on timely reports

(continued)

Adding Automatic Web Content

Automatic Web content allows FrontPage Web site authors to insert ready-made business or other content into their Web pages. You can add news headlines or weather forecasts from MSNBC. If you need to insert directions to your office or store, you can copy a map from the Microsoft Expedia travel site. Such tools are provided to you as Web components.

You add them from FrontPage's **Insert** menu, by following these steps:

1. Connect to the Internet, start FrontPage, and then open the page where you want to place the Web component.

2. On the **Insert** menu, click **Web Component**.
   The **Insert Web Component** dialog box opens.

Case Study: Keeping a Sports Site Flying High (continued)

during each of the events it provides coverage of during the year. Our traffic will swell to 50,000 unique visitors in a weekend during many of our events and 51 percent of that traffic will repeat each day."

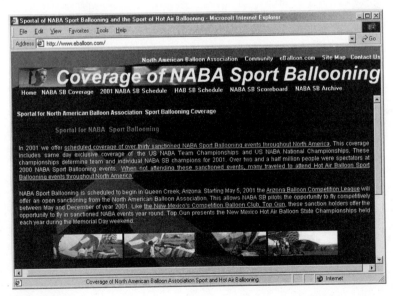

Figure 16-5.
The eBalloon.com site is built around a schedule of events that requires constant updating of information.

3. Scroll down the **Component type** list on the left side of the dialog box. Click an option to view specific components on the right side of the dialog box.

   For instance, if you click **MSN Components** in the **Component type** list, two options appear on the right: **Search the Web with MSN** and **Stock quote**.

4. Click the component you want to add, and then click **Finish**.

   The component is added to the currently open Web page. Because you are connected to the Internet and you added an active headline component, the contents that appear in the FrontPage window are real, current headlines. Some examples of different components are shown below.

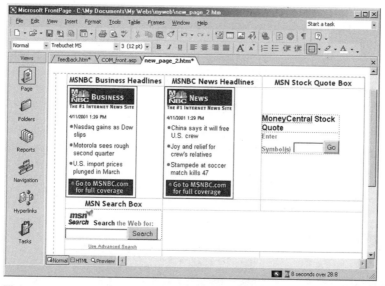

Figure 16-6.

You can preview Web content components in the FrontPage window and cut and paste them as needed.

Other components, such as the MSNBC weather forecast component, display sample information — when you publish the file online, a link is made to MSNBC and "live" information is displayed on your site.

Linking to Online News Services

The content provided by MSNBC's Web components provides general news or business headlines. For most e-commerce sites, they won't be appropriate for your visitors. However, you can take advantage of other news services that offer more narrowly focused content.

Try the following:

- **iSyndicate.** This online content provider (http://www.isyndicate.com) will work with you to gather news headlines that are related to your site's content. Services begin at about $1000 per month, however. The iSyndicate Express program lets you add content for free (http://affiliate.isyndicate.com).

- **ScreamingMedia.** This site (http://www.screamingmedia.com) gathers content from providers that cover specific topics like cooking, travel, law, business/finance, and education.

- **News Index.** This news service provides you with free, customizable news headlines you can add to your site (http://www.newsindex.com/freenews.html).

- **AUTO Content.** Fill out a short survey on this site (http://certificate.net/wwio/syndicate.shtml) and you gain access to two lines of JavaScript that you add to your Web pages. The JavaScript displays customized content culled from this service's articles. Topics include parenting, pets, hobbies, sports, and religion.

You can also sign up for ChangeDetection (http://changedetection.com). This service lets your visitors receive an e-mail notification each time your site changes. Stealth Promotions (http://www.stealthpromotions.com/suggest.htm) provides you with free code that you can add to a page to let visitors tell their friends about a site. The code produces a simple form on the page. A visitor enters his or her name and e-mail address as well as the e-mail address of a friend. Submitting the information allows Stealth Promotions to send a message to the friend suggesting they visit the site.

Business Tip

In the race to freshen your e-commerce site with new content, you might overlook stale sales notices and other outdated content. Be sure to purge such content from your site. Rather than delete the notices, save them to a directory on your local computer. They can provide you with a record of promotions and notices you've held in the past, and a source of content you can reuse if needed.

Chapter 17

Managing Traffic, Outages, and Performance

Getting your Microsoft FrontPage e-commerce Web site online is an accomplishment, but keeping its virtual doors open around the clock and its catalog and check out areas running smoothly is necessary for success.

Traditional retailers have faced a host of problems resulting from service outages and slowdowns when traffic was heavier than their servers could handle. Wal-Mart, for example, suffered several outages during the 1999 holiday season and was forced to completely shut down its Web site for more than a month to re-launch it. Toys "R" Us encountered numerous problems setting up its Web site before finally teaming up with Amazon.com in Fall 2000.

You don't hear all that much about monitoring Web site performance when you read about setting up e-commerce sites. That's because this step comes after the site is established. Yet, outages and hosting problems must be tracked or your work to this point will be undone. You also need to monitor the capacity of your server to handle the traffic that comes to your site and any others that are hosted on the same machine. In this chapter, you will learn about monitoring and improving your site's performance, and coping with services outages and other shortcomings posed by Web hosts that aren't doing their job.

Why Monitor Your Web Site?

Ask yourself: Now that I've got my e-commerce business up and running, should I really spend some of my valuable time monitoring how often service outages cause it to go offline? After all, you pay someone good money to keep your site online and make sure it's operating smoothly at all times so you can concentrate on selling and marketing.

One answer: The time your site is offline due to problems with your hosting service can cost you money and hurt your reputation. Internet Week reported back in 1999 that if Dell Computer's site was down for just one minute, it would cost the hardware giant $10,000. A 90-minute outage would cost the company nearly a million dollars — and the rate is probably even higher these days.

Your site must be accessible whenever visitors want to shop, day or night. A single attempt to access your site that results in a "file not found" or other error message can send customers to another online location — perhaps never to return. In addition, your pages need to load quickly and your links need to lead where they're supposed to, as described in Chapter 11.

Learn More

Keep tabs on your e-commerce site's technical behavior, but also monitor and evaluate where your customers come from, which resources they use most frequently, and when they visit you. FrontPage can help you keep track of your site's usage without having to look at technical log files or wade through complex lists of data. See Chapter 13 for more information.

Monitoring Web Site Performance

If your site doesn't work well, another site whose pages load more quickly can be found just a few mouse clicks away. That's the harsh reality you need to keep in mind when your site goes online and you begin to attract customers. Put your energy into retaining those customers by providing them with a positive experience, beginning with their first visits and continuing for initial page views. By maintaining some simple quality control procedures, you guard against dissatisfied customers who may seek out other venues.

Installing Site Monitoring Software

A number of programs are available for $30 to $200 that continually keep an eye on your Web site and notify you of any problems. Such programs take some effort to install, but the minimal effort required to get them up and running lets you know about setbacks at least as soon as your customers, if not before.

WebCheck is a utility that monitors the performance of your Web site. It automatically checks your web and notifies you when your site goes down or if a page has been accidentally renamed or deleted. You can be notified by any number of communications methods — for instance, e-mail, fax, pop-up browser window, or taskbar icon.

Learn More

You can download WebCheck from the ZDNet Web site (http://www.zdnet.com/downloads). Another application, SiteScope, by Freshwater Software (http://www.sitescope.com/SiteScope.htm), runs on Microsoft Windows NT or 2000 and checks sites every five to ten minutes.

Hiring a Monitoring Service

Software programs are limited by operating systems and they require some installation and learning that you may not have the time to perform. In that case, you can pay a periodic fee to a site monitoring service that will keep an eye on your site's performance.

For example, @watch (http://www.atwatch.com) provides an online service that checks your site periodically to see if everything is working correctly. The company offers several levels of service. The @watch Lite version costs $19.95 per month and checks your site once every 60 minutes. Other versions can check your site as frequently as every five minutes.

Andrea Milrad, who maintains the LittleBIG Man Web site (http://www.littlebigman.org), uses a similar service called AlertSite (http://www.alertsite.com) to notify her when some of her Web site files become unavailable or when the entire site goes offline due to server crashes.

"If my Web site is not up or is not running properly, then my customers cannot visit my store," she explains. "I actually left my former Web hosting company because I got so many alerts notifying me of server problems. When I called the host, I was told that the server my site was on. When I asked to have my files moved to a more reliable server, my request was turned down. So I moved myself to another ISP."

Learn More

Keynote Systems (http://www.keynote.com/adv/wrn.html) lets you sign up to use its site monitoring service free for a week. You can specify the locations in the U.S. or around the world that you want your site to be tested from. You also get access to diagnostic tools to pinpoint and resolve performance delays.

Dealing with Web Site Outages

When you run an e-commerce Web site, the time that your pages are offline can detract from your potential income. This is where your Web host needs to be cooperative and forthcoming about problems with its equipment or with the network. You, for your part, need to be patient but firm in dealing with technical problems that impact your business.

Ideally, your Web host will provide a page on its Web site that keeps track of its network status and records any recent problems.

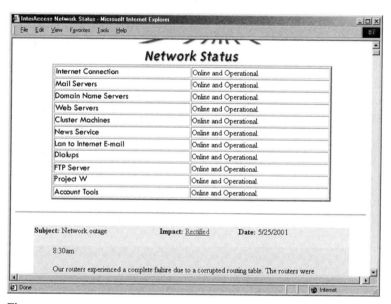

Figure 17-1.

My own Internet access provider, which also provides Web hosting services, maintains a record of recent service outages.

Talking to Your Host

One notification from either a site monitoring program or service probably shouldn't be cause for concern. However, when you receive a series of notifications, call your Web hosting service and talk to their technical staff. Be courteous, but be specific. Tell them exactly what the problem was. You might even want to print out the reports you receive so you can be aware of the exact nature of the problems.

Business Tip

You may be dissatisfied with your Web host, but that doesn't mean you can escape your service contract. You may have to wait until the contract expires before you switch hosts.

Ask the host what kind of server the site is hosted on. How fast does the server run, and how much memory does it have? Also, ask about the provider's own Internet connection — how far is it to a Network Access Point (NAP)? If the host is one or two more "hops" from the backbone, the quality of its own connection to the Internet is potentially weak. Don't let the host tell you this happens to everyone. You're in the e-commerce business, and it shouldn't happen at all. If you get resistance, it's time to move on.

Definition

Network Access Point (NAP) Part of the so-called Internet backbone; a high-speed part of the Internet that is maintained by some of the major telecom companies. Ask the vendor who their backbone provider is. If it's a big player that has a good network backbone connection, such as PSI, UUNET, or MCI, the provider has a good Internet connection, and any problems are likely due to the server that hosts your site.

Exploring Better Hosting Options

If your current host provides service that you find to be less than satisfactory, look for one that has a better connection to the Internet or one that offers you more robust server set-ups (that is, multiple servers that have enough memory and processor speed to handle all the traffic that your site generates). If your site proves especially successful, you might consider hosting setups such as these:

- **Co-Location.** You own the server on which your files reside, but the machine is located at your Web host's facility rather than your own location. Your site is the only one on your machine. You also get the reliability of the host's technical support and high-speed Internet connection.

- **Dedicated Web Server.** You rent space on a machine that is dedicated to serving your site. This arrangement is far more expensive than sharing a Web server, and should only be chosen if the number of visits to your site at any one time becomes too great for a shared server to handle. You'll know a shared server is becoming over-taxed if your site is slow to load. Discuss the situation with your host to see if a move to a dedicated server makes sense.

Business Tip

Telocity (http://www.telocity.com) offers Web hosting space as part of its DSL Internet access service on a month-to-month basis rather than as an annual contract.

If You Do Have to Move...

Once you make the decision to move your site from one server to another, don't rush. Keep your eye on your ultimate goal — maximizing your site's "online time." A smooth and deliberate transition keeps your site online during the move. Make a checklist of tasks to ease the transition, including:

- **Operating system.** Chances are you want to stick with the same operating system you had before. Be sure you know what system your previous host used, and be aware of any extra costs for Windows NT hosting with your new host.

- **Forms and search boxes.** If your FrontPage site uses forms, search boxes, or other features that require the FrontPage Server Extensions, move to a host that supports the extensions. Be aware of any extra costs that you may incur to use the extensions.

Technical Tip

Discuss with a technical support person exactly which features are supported before you sign on the bottom line. Some hosting services say they support the FrontPage Server Extensions but don't immediately make it clear that some features, like discussion groups or sub-Webs, cost extra.

- **Make backups.** Before you move any files, make sure you copy your data to a secure location on one of your in-house computers so nothing gets lost.

- **Save a mirror.** Save a mirror image of all of your site's files. A mirror keeps all the files, folders, and subfolders in the same location, mirroring the site structure, so that the browser can find the links and images.

- **Keep documents.** Make note of everything you've done and everything that remains to be done so you don't forget any files.

- **Test.** Once your files are relocated, be sure to test them in different browsers to ensure everything works correctly. See Chapter 11 for more information about testing your site. Also test any e-mail addresses, such as auto responders; you have on your site.

- **Stay online.** While you are setting up your new site, keep your domain name pointed at your original server. You'll have to pay monthly hosting fees to two locations for at least a month, but you'll have your site online at all times.

Once you've gone online at the new location and performed all the necessary testing, your host should contact the DNS you used when you first set up your site and point the domain name to the new location. After the move, notify your Web host that you're discontinuing service. The notice period will depend on your contract with the old hosting service. One month's notice is common.

In the meantime, periodically check the old server logs. You'll probably find that a small number of users or robots (programs that automatically scour the Internet indexing the contents of Web sites so the contents can be stored in search engines' databases) are still using the IP address of your old server and not your domain name. Identify the pages they're accessing and replace them with a page that redirects traffic to the new server.

If you do all the steps right, your customers won't experience any outages. In fact, they won't even know you've moved your site. Only you will know that a change has taken place.

Technical Tip

While you are testing your pages on your new host and your site is still up and running on your old host's server, you can block search engines from indexing your pages. Go to the home page on the new server, and enter the following in the HTML: <meta name= "robots" content="noindex, nofollow">. This keeps some search engines (those that support a search-blocking protocol) from indexing your pages during the testing phase. Don't forget to remove the code when your site goes online from its new location.

Chapter 18

Adding New Features to Your E-commerce Site

Once you begin to achieve the goals you originally set for your e-commerce site, a new set of goals arises. The customers you attract to your store may raise questions and suggest new features. The hoped-for large number of visitors might slow down your server's response time and necessitate a move to a new host server. The need to keep track of items sold and items in stock may make a database "back end" for your business a necessity also.

After your site has been online for a while, the next step will be to upgrade it to handle more traffic and serve a larger number of customers more efficiently. It is a sign of success when an online business needs to "scale up" — in other words, to grow in capacity and efficiency in order to handle more requests and fulfill more sales.

Microsoft FrontPage is flexible enough to accept new components and applications that add strength and functionality — and popular enough that software developers continually create new features, such as shopping carts, that should be of interest to e-commerce site managers. This final chapter looks ahead at ways to improve your online business so you can maintain a high level of service and remain in business for many years to come.

When to Redesign Your Site

Revisit the goals you established for your e-commerce business in Chapter 1. Also review the profiles you drew of the customers you most hope to attract. Evaluate whether your site, as it currently stands, accomplishes what you set out to do. Are the customers you're reaching the ones you'd hoped to reach? In the process of appealing to some customer personas, are you inadvertently excluding others? If the answer to either of these questions is yes, some adjustments to your site can help to widen your customer base.

Another reason to revise your site is to increase sales by selling more aggressively. Don't be reluctant to promote yourself and your products. Too many people put their sites online and are too bashful to effectively tell people how good they are or why their products stand out from those of their competitors. They also fail to point out with sufficient earnestness that some of their content is new and timely.

Learn More

Get tips from the experts about evaluating your site's effectiveness and upgrading your Web presence. Read "Improving Web Site Usability and Appeal" on the Microsoft Developer Network Web site (http://msdn.microsoft.com/workshop/management/planning/improvingsiteusa.asp).

You're Overwhelmed by Success

Every Web site needs to plan ahead and be prepared for success. "Success" in technical terms means lots of computers around the world visiting your site and requesting files from you, all at the same time. You've probably heard horror stories about Web sites that crashed under heavy loads because they received more visitors than they could handle. The wise site owner will be ready for upcoming promotions and talk to his or her hosting service's technical support staff to prepare for jumps in visitor volume.

For example, *U.S. News & World Report* publishes its annual rankings of U.S. colleges each September. Its Web site might receive as many as 2 million visits just after the results are published online. The site went through extensive testing to make sure its server could handle the load. Web sites that consistently receive thousands or even millions of visits each week have their contents copied (or mirrored) onto as many as 20 Web servers. Each request goes to a hardware device called a network content distributor that functions as a traffic director — the server directs requests to the least busy server so that the load is balanced between each one.

Definition

RAID Redundant Array of Inexpensive Disks, a big computer containing many disks, each storing a copy of your data, so multiple computers can gain access simultaneously. If your site gets really busy, you might start talking to your host about implementing a RAID.

You Just Need a Makeover

A *makeover* is a graphic redesign of your Web site: You redo your use of color and change your logo or other graphics to achieve a new look in order to keep your site fresh and attractive to your visitors. Store makeovers in the real world aren't all that different from those on the Web. This book's author worked in the local corner drugstore when he was in high school. Every few years, the walls would be repainted and the shelves next to the entrance to the store would be rearranged and made to look more inviting. New sets of "impulse" items were placed near the cash register. Over time, the store became less cluttered rather than more crowded — redesigning was as much a matter of clearing out items that didn't sell as adding new merchandise.

You, too, can change your site's colors periodically. Pay attention to your front entrance — make your home page less cluttered and more inviting. One of the easiest periodic revisions you can make is to place a few "impulse" items for sale right on your home page. Change the items every week or two, and your customers will get a feeling of constant activity and sales promotion that will encourage them to hit the Buy button.

How do you know when it's time for a makeover? Opinions vary: Some advisors recommend as many as four redesigns each year, while others say that keeping the site's current graphic design as long as possible gives customers a predictable, comforting experience. The opinion that really counts is *yours*. But make yours an informed opinion — gather input from your customers and get to know them well enough that you'll be able to predict what they want and need.

Perhaps your site isn't generating as many visits as it used to. Perhaps sales are dropping off. Perhaps you just aren't as excited about your site's public face as you once were — if you're getting a ho-hum reaction from your own site, it's a safe bet your customers are, too.

Business Tip

Chances are you can find a company in your local area that will perform usability testing of your site: Some test consumers are hired to shop at your site, and you can follow their eyes on your page and the movements of their cursors. Ask your chamber of commerce to suggest a local company that performs such tests for small businesses at an affordable price.

Strengthening Your Business Presence

If you've decided that your site needs a facelift or if you need new functionality to cope with higher traffic, you need to take only a few simple steps to do better business online. Listen to your customers; ask your first and best customers why they came to your site in the first place, and why they continue to return. Place your "best sellers" in a special featured area on your home page or on a page devoted to best sellers. Take the items that don't sell well, reduce prices as much as you can, and put them on a "Reduced" or "Specials" page.

Changes don't always have to center on specific sales items. You can also upgrade your site's content in other ways:

- "Seed" conversations by introducing topics on your discussion boards, if you have them (See Chapter 15).

- Provide timely content that you advertise as being recently updated or added to the site (see Chapter 16).

- Reach out and provide links to additional high-quality information in your articles or topics or to other Web sites to improve your site's usefulness. While you don't have to ask for permission before you make such links, it's often helpful if you do so, because you might get the owner of the site you're including to mention your site in return.

- Make your site easy to use. Are your visitors immediately aware of the point or theme of your site? They also need to know how and where to get started with the site's primary features. As they move around your site, they should intuitively be able to sense where they are, where they need to go, and how to return to a "safe" home base.

Business Tip

One of the best ways to bring lots of traffic to your Web site is to be picked as a "hot" or "cool" site by an influential authority like Yahoo! or *USA Today*. You don't necessarily need to have lots of technical tricks to get the thumbs-up. Your site should be well designed, family-oriented, and frequently updated. Check out Yahoo!'s "Picks of the Week" (http://www.yahoo.com/picks/) for ideas on what can gain you the coveted "Hot" designation.

Joining a Business Community

The importance of community might at first seem paradoxical when viewed in regard to e-commerce. Web surfing is, for the most part, a solitary activity. So is dealing with customers and business colleagues over the Internet: You exchange e-mail messages, download files, and post discussion group or bulletin board messages sitting by yourself at your computer.

But online businesspeople also thrive if they reach out to join communities of other online sellers and managers. If you deal in business materials rather than consumer goods, online marketplaces like Commerce One MarketSite (http://www.commerceone.com) and VerticalNet (http://www.verticalnet.com) can help you find a supplier or group of related supply companies who already provide the goods and services you are looking for.

You can also join the Small Business Discussion List (http://www.talkbiz.com/bizlist/index.html) where you can share your experiences with fellow online entrepreneurs. Feel free to ask for advice — the list members will be glad to help.

Becoming a bCentral Business Customer

If you use the Commerce Manager for FrontPage Add-in, you can only sell 25 catalog items on Microsoft bCentral. Before long, you'll want to move up to a full Commerce Manager account, not only so you can sell 26 or 126 sales items, but also so you can take advantage of the other business services provided for free to bCentral small business customers.

When you sign up for a Business Web Services monthly hosting account with bCentral for $29.95 per month, you get a branded e-mail account (that is, an e-mail address that matches your site's domain name, such as owner@mysite.com). You also get access to marketing and promotional tools like banner ad and search engine placement, the ability to create e-mail newsletters, and more.

Taking Stock with a Database

Before long, keeping track of your merchandise as it's purchased and restocked becomes increasingly difficult. A database that works with FrontPage provides a perfect interface between your sales items and your Web-based store. FrontPage 2002's ability to work easily with Microsoft SQL Server, Microsoft Access, or Microsoft Excel counts among its strongest features. For most applications, you'll use FrontPage's Database Interface Wizard to connect to a database, create a Web page form that lets your customers search the database's contents, and filter and sort records.

Technical Tip

In order to display database information on your Web site, your site must be hosted on a Web server that supports Active Server Pages (ASP) and Microsoft ActiveX Data Objects (ADO). Your Internet service provider (ISP) or Web administrator can tell you whether your Web server supports ASP and ADO. When you publish your site, the database connection will transfer to the server. You won't need to create a new database connection on the destination Web site.

Adding a Spreadsheet to a Web Page

Suppose you purchased the stand-alone version of FrontPage and don't have a copy of Excel that you can use to create or modify spreadsheets to keep track of your sales or inventory. Or suppose you're on the road a lot and want to make changes to your inventory from your laptop or a computer in another location. In that case, you can add an Office Spreadsheet Web component to your site. You connect to the Web page that contains the spreadsheet and by using your Web browser, you can enter new data or make changes to the spreadsheet.

Definition

Web Component Self-contained programs that add complex functionality to your Web site without requiring you to know programming. An Office Spreadsheet Web component enables you to add a fully functional, interactive spreadsheet to a Web page without installing Excel on the computer that you're using.

To begin, make sure you know what data you want the spreadsheet to contain. Draw out your spreadsheet on a piece of paper so you can enter the data easily when you begin to work with the component.

To add a spreadsheet to a Web page:

1. Start FrontPage, open your web, and then open the page that you want to contain the spreadsheet.

2. On the **Insert** menu, click **Web Component**.

    The **Insert Web Component** dialog box opens.

3. In the **Component type** list, click **Spreadsheets and charts**, and then in the **Choose a control** list, click **Office Spreadsheet**.

4. Click **Finish**.

    The spreadsheet is added to the page.

5. Click in one of the spreadsheet cells to select it, and then enter the data you want to track.

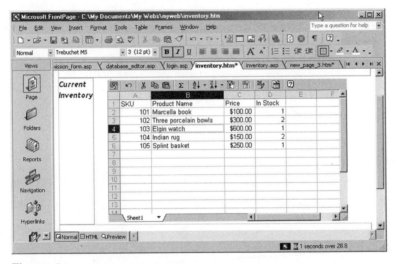

Figure 18-1.

Web components let you add dynamic Web content to your Web pages. The Office Spreadsheet component lets you create a spreadsheet you can edit in your browser.

6. Save the page to your local web, publish it to your Web server, and then preview the page in your browser window. You can continue to edit the spreadsheet while viewing it with your browser.

Warning

If you add a spreadsheet component to your Web site to monitor and adjust inventory, you probably want to be the only one able to view and edit the file. Be sure to place the file in a directory that only you, and not your customers, can access, with an URL that only you know. The spreadsheet component you add to your Web site doesn't *have* to be a private one, however. You can create a spreadsheet that enables your customers to calculate shipping costs and sales tax on sales items, for instance.

Publishing an Excel File to Your Web Site

Web-based catalogs are really powerful when they are linked to databases. You and your customers can get pages that draw on active data sources so your site displays current, reliable information. FrontPage 2002 makes connecting to databases easier than ever before. Suppose you've already created a database with Excel and you want to add it to your web. First, you need to import the database into your web.

Adding Your Database to Your Web

To add your database:

1. Start FrontPage, and then open the web that you want to contain the database.

2. On the **File** menu, click **Import**.
   The **Import** dialog box opens.

3. Click **Add File**.
   The **Add File to Import List** dialog box opens.

4. Navigate to the Excel file you want to import, select the file, and then click **Open**.
   The **Add File to Import List** dialog box closes. The database file is added to the **Import** dialog box.

5. Click **OK**.
   The file is added to your web.

6. Click **Folders** on the **Views** bar, and then scroll down the list of files in the web to verify that the file is present.

Create a Database Connection

Once you have made the database part of your FrontPage web, you need to make a connection to it by using FrontPage's Database Results Wizard.

Technical Tip

The Database Results Wizard enables you to gather live information from a database that resides on your own computer. That doesn't mean visitors to your e-commerce Web site can make the same connection. If your Web host already operates a relational database program such as MySQL (http://www.mysql.com) and will host the database for you, you can set up a live database connection that your customers can access. You'll need to discuss with your host exactly how to do this.

Live Versus Static Database Connections

You can display information from an Access database or an Excel spreadsheet on your Web site in one of two ways: Make either a "live" connection or a "static" connection to those files. The option you choose depends on the size of the database you want to present online, the capabilities of your Web server, and your own technical abilities.

Static database information is easier to get online. You simply save your Access or Excel file in Web page (HTML) format. You then publish the Web page on your Web site along with your other documents. The information is static because it never changes — unless you edit the Web page manually or update your database file, save it again as a Web page, and then re-publish it on your site. If your database is small (say, less than 50 items), if your Web host won't host a database along with your Web server so you can have a "live" connection, and if you don't mind the frequent updating of Web pages, go with a static connection.

If your database if big (containing hundreds or even thousands of individual items) and your host is open to running a database along with your Web site, opt for a live connection. In a live connection, the database is stored on a server that is connected directly to the Web server that hosts your site.

A live connection works like this: Your visitor makes a request for information — in technical terms, your visitor's browser makes a request to your site's Web server to view a catalog listing. The Web server passes the request to the database server, which gathers the information from the database. The database server passes the information to the Web server, which sends it out to the visitor's browser. The important thing to remember is that in a live connection, the information is generated fresh with every request. The information is not coming from a static flat file, but from a database that is continually being updated.

Another important distinction is the one between a FrontPage web that resides on your local computer and a public Web site that resides on an external Web server. A web that you run on one of your computers can make a "live" connection to a database file on your computer or another machine on your local area network. But only you can gather the live information. For a live connection to be available to your customers, your Web host must do two types of hosting. It must host your Web site on a Web server and your database files on a database server. The two servers must be connected to one another. Not all hosts permit such connections; check with yours before you start trying to link to your own database.

To create a database connection:

1. Either create a new page or open a current page in your FrontPage web that you want to connect to the database.

   The page appears in the FrontPage window.

2. On the **Insert** menu, point to **Database**, and then click **Results**.

   The Database Results Wizard opens.

3. Select the **Use a new database connection** option, and then click **Create**.

   The **Web Settings** dialog box opens.

4. Click **Add**.

   The **New Database Connection** dialog box opens.

5. In the **Name** box, type a name for your connection, select the **File or folder in current Web** option, and then click **Browse**.

   The **Database Files in Current Web** dialog box opens.

6. In the **Files of type** list, select **Microsoft Excel Driver (*.xls)**.

7. Locate the database file you just added to your web in the previous series of steps, select the file, and then click **OK**.

   The **Database Files in Current Web** dialog box closes, and the name of your database file appears in the **New Database Connection** dialog box.

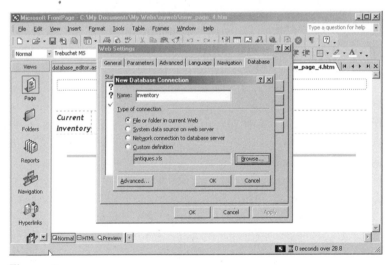

Figure 18-2.

Use the Database Results Wizard to make a connection to a database file.

8. Click **OK** to close the **New Database Connection** dialog box and return to the **Web Settings** dialog box.

9. Click **Verify**.

   A check mark appears next to the database connection you just created to verify that the connection is working. If the check mark is not there, reopen the Database Results Wizard and try again.

10. Click **OK** to close the **Web Settings** dialog box, and then follow the steps in the rest of the wizard to set up your database connection.

    When you click **Finish**, the database page opens in the FrontPage window.

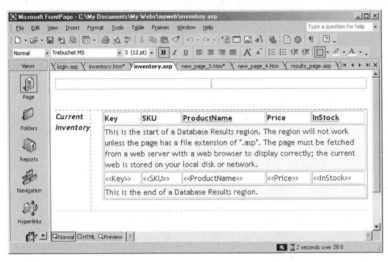

Figure 18-3.
When you make a database connection, the page that contains the connection looks like this. The instructions highlighted in yellow don't appear when viewed in a browser window.

11. On the **File** menu, click **Save As**, and then save the file with the extension .asp.

    This page must be saved with the filename extension .asp in order to function correctly.

12. Publish the file to your Web server, and then preview the page in your browser window.

Technical Tip

ASP is a technology that enables a Web server to run programs and display dynamic Web pages. ASP will only work if the server runs an ASP interface program. Check with your host to make sure your server is ASP-compatible.

Working with an Access Database

If you already have an Access database, you can get its contents online by making either a live or static connection (see the earlier sidebar on this topic). You can import it into your Web, and then make a connection to it by following the same steps outlined in the preceding section.

If you don't have an Access database, you can use FrontPage's Database Interface Wizard to quickly create one and link it to your Web site. Use the following steps:

1. Start FrontPage, and then open the web that you want to contain the Access database.

2. On the **File** menu, point to **New**, and then click **Page or Web**.
   The Task pane appears.

3. In the **New from template** area of the Task pane, click **Web Site Templates**.
   The **Web Site Templates** dialog box opens.

4. Click **Database Interface Wizard**, select the **Add to current Web** check box, and then click **OK**.

5. Complete the wizard.
   Once the database is created, the wizard asks you to choose which pages to display. If you select the **Database Editor** check box, you'll be able to add records to your database or edit it from the Web using your browser.

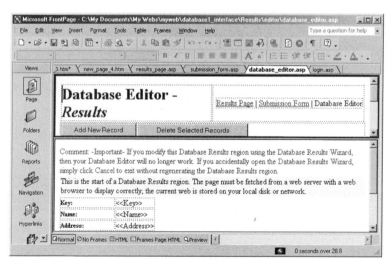

Figure 18-4.
The Database Interface Wizard can create a data entry Web page you can use to edit your Access database.

The database pages are placed in a special folder named Results, which is located within a folder that is named after your database. To locate this folder, open your web in FrontPage, click **Folders** on the **Views** bar to display the folder list, and then scroll through the current web to take note of the location of the Results folder. You need to publish this folder and its contents to your Web server in order to make the database's contents accessible from your Web site.

Technical Tip

If you import an Access database into your Web, you will be asked to create a database connection and to store the file in a folder within your Web site named Fpdb. Permissions for the Fpdb folder specify that the folder can't be viewed in a Web browser. You can protect the privacy of your database by moving it into the Fpdb folder.

Using Third-Party Resources

Some third-party companies function as e-commerce affiliates for FrontPage users. These companies have developed integrated solutions for FrontPage that you can't get elsewhere.

Go to the page on Microsoft's site that lists such resources (http://office.microsoft.com/assistance/9798/frontpageassociates.aspx) to find out more about them. Some of the utilities listed on this page offer services that you can obtain from bCentral (such as a shopping cart) or from within FrontPage 2002 itself (such as Table of Contents and Navigation Bar Web components). The following list contains brief descriptions of other available services:

- **Customer management.** StoreFront 5.0 by LaGarde Software (http://www.storefront.net/sf5/sf5se_new.htm) allows returning customers to retrieve and reorder from previous orders and recall customer profile data to speed the check out process with built-in CRM (customer relations management) tools. It's specifically designed to work with FrontPage.

- **Jump menus, floating windows, and more JScript tricks.** Webs Unlimited (http://www.websunlimited.com/j-bots_plus_2000.htm) has created software packages called J-Bots 2000 and J-Bots Plus 2000 that enable you to add dynamic Web page effects without having to enter the JScript commands yourself.

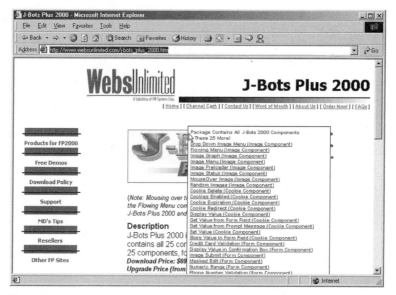

Figure 18-5

Add clickable menus that drop down from images, as well as jump menus and other special effects, with one of the JBots add-on packages for FrontPage.

- **Improved search engine standings.** SiteTagger, a utility created by Office Power! (http://www.office-power.com/products/stagger/index.htm), improves your site's search engine standings. New options added to FrontPage's **Tools** menu enable you to prepare reports describing your site's search engine readiness.

Business Tip

If you need help expanding your business, don't assume you have to do everything yourself. The Small Business Administration (SBA) of the U.S. government can help independently owned and operated businesses with training, advice — and loans. Visit their Web site (http://www.sba.gov) to find a location in your area.

Improving your site is the culminating step in the business plan you began creating in this book's first chapter. You identified your ideal customers and focused your marketing and sales efforts toward meeting those customers' needs. You've either expanded your traditional brick-and-mortar business to the Internet or created your first successful commercial endeavor — and that's what essential e-commerce is all about. Congratulations, and happy online selling!

Glossary

Active Server Pages (ASP): A Microsoft technology that adds small scripts to HTML Web pages; the scripts are processed on the Web server that hosts the pages.

Affiliate program: A marketing program in which one company pays an affiliate to place a banner ad or link on the affiliate's Web site. When a visitor to the affiliate's site clicks the banner or link, their browser goes to the originating company's Web site. For any such "referrals" that result in a purchase, the affiliate is paid a fee.

Auto responder: A utility that automatically e-mails a reply to a request for information about a product or service that you offer.

Benchmarking: The process of testing something (such as a Web site) to establish the level of performance (in other words, *benchmark*) you consider to be acceptable.

Branding: The repeated use of a company's graphic image or name to establish its name and promote its activities to customers and the public at large.

Cascading Style Sheet (CSS): A set of markup instructions that let you precisely position content and achieve a consistent presentation from page to page across a Web site.

Certification Authority (CA): A company in the business of certifying someone else's identity on the Internet. The CA issues a digital certificate to a company or individual and assumes responsibility for stating that the owner of the certificate is actually the individual or company identified on the certificate.

Chat: An Internet communications technology that enables participants to conduct real time discussions by typing messages to one another in a special chat window.

Churn: The process of clicking, scanning, and moving from Web page to Web page and from site to site.

Cookies: Bits of electronic data left behind on a computer after the browser on that computer has opened a Web site. The cookie typically enables the Web server that owns the cookie to identify the client browser on subsequent visits.

Customer Relationship Management (CRM): Activities that enable you to manage contacts with your current and potential customers.

Digest: A single e-mail message that contains all of the messages sent to a mailing list on a given day. ·

Digital signature: A means of authenticating an individual's identity as a signer of e-mail or documents.

Domain name: The "microsoft.com" or "internet.com" part of Web addresses like http://www.microsoft.com or http://www.internet.com. Domain names are part of the *domain name system,* which is the way servers on the Internet are identified in order to facilitate distribution of data across the Internet. Domain names are used as substitutes for IP addresses because they are easier to remember.

Dutch auction: A form of auction used to sell multiple items. The seller specifies the minimum successful price for each item as well as the number of items available. Bidders can bid at or above the minimum for the number of items they're interested in. When the auction ends, the winning bidders are the ones with the lowest bids that are still above the minimum price.

Electronic wallet: Software that stores someone's personal information and credit card number for later use.

English auction: An auction in which a single item is auctioned off to the highest bidder, with the sale ending at a specified time.

eXtensible Markup Language (XML): A language that describes the content of Web pages and other documents in such a way that their contents can be easily transported from one application to another.

Graphics Interchange Format (GIF): A type of image compression used to display line art, simple drawings, and illustrations on the Web.

Guest book: A feature that enables visitors to a Web site to enter comments in a Web page form and then submit them to the site, where they are posted on a page so everyone can read them.

Hypertext Markup Language (HTML): The set of markup instructions used to create Web pages.

Interstitial: A type of Web page ad that appears while a requested page is downloading.

IP address: A series of four numbers separated by dots, such as 206.211.117.12, that identify a server or computer on the Internet. For Web servers, IP addesses are often expressed as domain names, such as Microsoft.com, because names are easier to remember than numbers.

JavaScript: A scripting language designed to add functionality to Web pages.

Joint Photographic Experts Group (JPEG): An image compression method used to present complex images, such as photographs, on the Web.

Key: A long series of encoded numerals and letters (for instance, 40 data bits or 128 data bits) used to encrypt information transmitted over the Internet.

Keywords: *a)* Special words that you add to the HTML code for your Web pages so search engines can find them more easily, or *b)* Words or phrases entered in search boxes to find files that contain those words or phrases.

Live database: A connection to a database that passes a browser's request for information from a Web server to a database server, where the information is gathered dynamically from a database and sent back to the Web server, which then sends it to the browser.

Load testing: Tests that evaluate how well a Web site can handle simultaneous multiple requests.

Lurking: A way of "eavesdropping" on newsgroup discussions by reading messages without posting any responses or posting any messages to originate a discussion.

Mailing list: A group discussion forum in which participants communicate by means of e-mail messages.

Message board: A Web page that publishes messages submitted by visitors. Other visitors can read them and respond with their own comments, thus creating a virtual discussion.

Network Access Point (NAP): A point of connection to the Internet backbone, a high-speed part of the Internet that is maintained by some of the major telecommunications companies.

Orphan pages: Pages that aren't linked to anything else on a Web site.

Plug-ins: Applications designed to work within a browser window to give the browser added functionality.

Portable Network Graphics (PNG): An image compression format developed as a replacement for GIF and that has higher compression and improved color quality compared to GIF.

Public key encryption: A form of Internet security that involves the exchange of public and private keys.

Quick Win auction: An auction in which the seller sets a threshold price for an item. If a bidder matches the threshold price, the sale closes immediately and that bidder is declared the winner.

Redundant Array of Inexpensive Disks (RAID): A powerful computer that contains many disks that store your data so multiple computers can access them simultaneously.

Secure Sockets Layer (SSL): A Web security standard that involves public key encryption and digital certificates and is built into major Web servers and browsers.

Site map: A visual representation of a Web site's structure.

Template: A Web page designed by a professional that contains placeholder content that you replace with your own headings, text, and images.

Thread: A series of responses and counter-responses in a discussion group organized by topic.

Usage Analysis Reports: A feature new to FrontPage 2002 that gives you information about the visits your site receives.

Usenet: A set of 30,000 different forums called newsgroups. Usenet's newsgroups give individuals with similar interests the chance to "converse" by typing messages to one another.

Web-based catalog: A set of pages that presents sales items so customers can learn about them to make purchases.

Web components: Software built into FrontPage, accessed from its **Insert** menu, that allows you to easily add functionality to your site, such as hit counters, marquees, and search forms, without requiring complex programming.

Web host: A company that rents space on a Web server to individuals and businesses in order for them to publish files that are accessed with a Web browser

Web server: A computer that makes images, text files, and other files available on the Internet.

eXtensible Markup Language (XML): A language that describes the content of Web pages and other documents in such a way that their contents can be easily transported from one application to another.

Index

About the Author

The writings of Greg Holden, founder and president of a small business called Stylus Media, take many forms. He prepares documentation for companies and creates online courses. He writes columns and articles for both print and electronic publications. His previous books include *Windows 98 Registry Little Black Book (Coriolis)* and *Starting an Online Business for Dummies (Hungry Minds)*. He took a short break from computer related material to write *Literary Chicago: A Book Lover's Guide to the Windy City,* which was recently published by Lake Claremont Press. He also has published a number of his short stories and poems. Among the publications he produces are the prodigious output of his bright, funny, and very creative daughters, Zosia and Lucy Holden. They are currently collaborating on a play based on the story of Queen Elizabeth. To find out more, visit his personal and business Web site at www.gregholden.com, or send e-mail to greg@gregholden.com.

Work smarter
as you experience
Office XP
inside out!

You know your way around the Office suite. Now dig into Microsoft Office XP applications and *really* put your PC to work! These supremely organized references pack hundreds of timesaving solutions, troubleshooting tips and tricks, and handy workarounds in concise, fast-answer format. All of this comprehensive information goes deep into the nooks and crannies of each Office application and accessory. Discover the best and fastest ways to perform everyday tasks, and challenge yourself to new levels of Office mastery with INSIDE OUT titles!

- **MICROSOFT® OFFICE XP INSIDE OUT**
- **MICROSOFT WORD VERSION 2002 INSIDE OUT**
- **MICROSOFT EXCEL VERSION 2002 INSIDE OUT**
- **MICROSOFT OUTLOOK® VERSION 2002 INSIDE OUT**
- **MICROSOFT ACCESS VERSION 2002 INSIDE OUT**
- **MICROSOFT FRONTPAGE® VERSION 2002 INSIDE OUT**
- **MICROSOFT VISIO® VERSION 2002 INSIDE OUT**

Microsoft®
mspress.microsoft.com

Target your
solution *and fix it*
yourself—*fast!*

When you're stuck with a computer problem, you need answers right now. *Troubleshooting* books can help. They'll guide you to the source of the problem and show you how to solve it right away. Use easy diagnostic flowcharts to identify problems. Get ready solutions with clear, step-by-step instructions. Go to quick-access charts with *Top 20 Problems* and *Prevention Tips*. Find even more solutions with handy *Tips* and *Quick Fixes*. Walk through the remedy with plenty of screen shots to keep you on track. Find what you need fast with the extensive, easy-reference index. And keep trouble at bay with the Troubleshooting Web site—updated every month with new FREE problem-solving information. Get the answers you need to get back to business fast with *Troubleshooting* books.

Self-paced
training
that works
as hard as you do!

Information-packed STEP BY STEP courses are the most effective way to teach yourself how to complete tasks with Microsoft® Office XP. Numbered steps and scenario-based lessons with practice files on CD-ROM make it easy to find your way while learning tasks and procedures. Work through every lesson or choose your own starting point—with STEP BY STEP modular design and straightforward writing style, *you* drive the instruction. And the books are constructed with lay-flat binding so you can follow the text with both hands at the keyboard. Select STEP BY STEP titles also provide complete, cost-effective preparation for the Microsoft Office User Specialist (MOUS) credential. It's an excellent way for you or your organization to take a giant step toward workplace productivity.

- **Microsoft Office XP Step by Step**
  ISBN 0-7356-1294-3

- **Microsoft Word Version 2002 Step by Step**
  ISBN 0-7356-1295-1

- **Microsoft Excel Version 2002 Step by Step**
  ISBN 0-7356-1296-X

- **Microsoft PowerPoint® Version 2002 Step by Step**
  ISBN 0-7356-1297-8

- **Microsoft Outlook® Version 2002 Step by Step**
  ISBN 0-7356-1298-6

- **Microsoft FrontPage® Version 2002 Step by Step**
  ISBN 0-7356-1300-1

- **Microsoft Access Version 2002 Step by Step**
  ISBN 0-7356-1299-4

- **Microsoft Project Version 2002 Step by Step**
  ISBN 0-7356-1301-X

- **Microsoft Visio® Version 2002 Step by Step**
  ISBN 0-7356-1302-8

mspress.microsoft.com

Get a **Free**
e-mail newsletter, updates,
special offers, links to related books,
and more when you

register on line!

Register your Microsoft Press® title on our Web site and you'll get a FREE subscription to our e-mail newsletter, *Microsoft Press Book Connections.* You'll find out about newly released and upcoming books and learning tools, online events, software downloads, special offers and coupons for Microsoft Press customers, and information about major Microsoft® product releases. You can also read useful additional information about all the titles we publish, such as detailed book descriptions, tables of contents and indexes, sample chapters, links to related books and book series, author biographies, and reviews by other customers.

Registration is easy. Just visit this Web page and fill in your information:

http://mspress.microsoft.com/register

Microsoft

- -

Proof of Purchase

Use this page as proof of purchase if participating in a promotion or rebate offer on this title. Proof of purchase must be used in conjunction with other proof(s) of payment such as your dated sales receipt—see offer details.

E-Commerce Essentials with Microsoft® FrontPage®
Version 2002
0-7356-1371-0

CUSTOMER NAME

Microsoft Press, PO Box 97017, Redmond, WA 98073-9830